The Letters of Paul,
Fifth Edition

The Letters of Paul, Fifth Edition

Conversations in Context

CALVIN J. ROETZEL

WESTMINSTER
JOHN KNOX PRESS
LOUISVILLE • KENTUCKY

© 2009 Calvin J. Roetzel

Fifth edition
Published by Westminster John Knox Press
Louisville, Kentucky

11 12 13 14 15 16 17 18—10 9 8 7 6 5 4 3 2

Scripture quotations from the New Revised Standard Version of the Bible are copyright © 1989 by the Division of Christian Education of the National Council of the Churches of Christ in the U.S.A. and are used by permission.

Scripture quotations marked RSV are from the Revised Standard Version of the Bible, copyright © 1946, 1952, 1971, 1973, Apocrypha copyright © 1957, 1977, by the Division of Christian Education of the National Council of the Churches of Christ in the U.S.A. and are used by permission.

Scripture quotations marked NEB are taken from the New English Bible, © The Delegates of the Oxford University Press and The Syndics of the Cambridge University Press, 1961, 1970. Used by permission.

Book design by Sharon Adams
Cover design by Mark Abrams
Cover art: The Arrival of Saint Paul at Neapolis. *Byzantine Mosaic. Scala / Art Resource, NY*

Library of Congress Cataloging-in-Publication Data

Roetzel, Calvin J.
   The letters of Paul : conversations in context / Calvin J. Roetzel.—5th ed.
      p. cm.
   Includes bibliographical references (p.   ) and index.
   ISBN 978-0-664-23392-1 (alk. paper)
   1. Bible. N.T. Epistles of Paul—Textbooks.   I. Title.
   BS2650.55.R64   2009
   227'.06—dc22

                                             2009008879

PRINTED IN THE UNITED STATES OF AMERICA

∞ The paper used in this publication meets the minimum requirements
of the American National Standard for Information Sciences—Permanence
of Paper for Printed Library Materials, ANSI Z39.48-1992.

Westminster John Knox Press advocates the responsible use of our natural resources.
The text paper of this book is made from 30% postconsumer waste.

In Memory of My Parents
οἱ πτωχοὶ τῶν ἁγίων

Contents

Preface to the Fifth Edition

I originally wrote this book for my students who were largely clueless about how to read letters almost two thousand years old. Since the first edition, teachers, laity, seminarians, pastors, and even one prison inmate have joined the readers' circle and offered suggestions for improving the book. I have read them all and am grateful for their assistance. While the former revisions addressed gaps and urgent issues left hanging or in need of explication, this edition is the product of a line-by-line and word-by-word close reading of the earlier edition. I have tried to smooth out lumpy phrasing; I have revised my treatment of the prolonged Corinthian correspondence; I have noted how my mind has changed or remained the same since the first edition; and, while duly noting the brilliance of Paul's theologizing, I now believe his theologizing was tempered by his doubts, physical limits, tortured dealings with rebellious and suspicious house churches, prison experiences, lingering pain from the unrequited love of his children/converts, personal regrets for his angry outbursts, and deep anxiety about the welfare of the churches.

For those readers coming to Paul's letters for the first time, I hope to heighten an awareness of ways Paul's theology emerged in and through conflict, and to alert the reader to the brilliance, complexity, and radicality of the theological improvization of this preeminent apostle. I am unapologetically asking more from first-time readers attempting to decipher the record of Paul's protracted and oft-times bitter struggles with his churches. For those who persevere, however, I suggest that there is the promise of rich treasure in this thicket of exchanges. One may find here a radicalized revision of the signifiers of apostleship, a redefinition of the nature of power and weakness, an eschatological vision of reconciliation so grand that it almost takes the breath away, and the excitement generated by an unfinished eschatology.

9

In addition to the great host of teachers, students, friends, and laity named above, I must also thank the editors, past and present, of Westminster John Knox Press who have supported the revisions of this book. Special thanks go to Jon Berquist, the executive editor for biblical studies at Westminster John Knox Press, for his assistance and support. I am also grateful to Lee and Louise Sundet, whose "work of faith, labor of love, and steadfastness of hope" grasp Paul's essence in important ways. I must also thank the Department of Classical and Near Eastern Studies at the University of Minnesota for its generous staff support with the revision; and thanks to Daniel Braden, associate managing editor, for his patience, diligence, and exquisite good judgment. Most especially, I am grateful to Kate Gallagher of CNES for the assistance she gave to a computer Neanderthal like me.

Calvin J. Roetzel, roetz002@umn.edu
Sundet Professor of New Testament
and Christian Studies,
University of Minnesota

Preface to the First Edition

This book was conceived in my work with undergraduates. Many of them were trying to read the letters of Paul for the first time and were frankly bewildered. The meaning of these documents was hardly obvious to them, and the identity of Paul's conversation partners was obscure if not hidden altogether. So I wrote this book to assist people like them—those who are systematically reading Paul's letters for the first time as well as those returning to Paul for a fresh look. The book is meant to be read in a few days before turning to the letters themselves, and its purpose is to sensitize the student to the background of Paul and his readers as well as to the dynamic nature of the letters themselves. It is my hope that the modern reader will come to know the letters less as repositories of static truth than as lively and sometimes turbulent exchanges over the nature of the gospel.

The book also aims to sharpen the reader's historical imagination in order that he or she can begin the task of interpreting the letters. Any beginning reader will no doubt change his or her interpretations many times (just as I have changed my own); but intelligent reading of the letters will necessitate some kind of interpretation, and I have tried to clear the ground with this book so that the reader may begin. I have attempted to warn the reader against certain pitfalls, throw light on some issues involved in the letters, clarify the backdrop against which Paul's mission unfolds, and show the structure and function of the letter itself in the ancient world.

Necessarily there is much here that will be commonplace to the seasoned biblical critic, and my debt to the fraternity of biblical scholars is obvious. I acknowledge it with gratitude. My intent has been to make the fruits of the labors of these dedicated and able Pauline scholars available to the nonspecialist and to help those who are discovering (or rediscovering) Paul to appreciate the need for still further interpretation.

Although space prohibits my naming all the persons who had a hand in this effort, special mention must be made of Professor Lloyd Gaston, who read various stages of the manuscript and offered encouragement, as well as valuable suggestions; Mrs. Carolyn Carlson, my secretary, whose diligent and patient labors helped in innumerable ways; and the members of my Paul seminars at Macalester College (St. Paul, Minnesota) and White Bear Lake Presbyterian Church, who made many useful comments on the content and style of the work. Without the help of these and others I am certain this book would never have been finished.

Easter 1974
Cookson, Oklahoma

Introduction

Contrary Impressions

Few who know him are neutral about Paul. Some love him; others hate him. And so it has always been. Within his own churches he was worshiped by some and maligned by others, called courageous and scoffed at as a coward, viewed as true and dismissed as an impostor. In some quarters he was a persona non grata; in others warmly welcomed. In the second century, Polycarp revered him as "blessed and glorious"; a Jewish Christian sect later rebuffed him as the devil incarnate. To this day Paul continues to provoke and excite, to challenge and antagonize.

A female student, for example, feels insulted by Paul's views of women. She is offended by the popular legend that calls Paul's "thorn in the flesh" a woman, and she is disgusted by the command in 1 Timothy 2:12 that no woman is "to teach or to have authority over men." Rather, as it says there, they are to be silent and submissive, earning their salvation by bearing children if they continue in "faith and love and holiness" (2:11–15). How revolting, she says, that Paul should advise male believers, "It is well for a man not to touch a woman" (l Cor. 7:1), or that he should think it shameful for women to speak in church gatherings. Instead, he advises them to bring their queries to their husbands in private (l Cor. 14:35). Why, she asks, should girls grow up thinking there is something dirty or inferior about being female? Why doesn't Paul command the women not to touch a man? Why must he assume that subordination of women to men is an essential part of the divine order (l Cor. 11:3)? In order to realize her full humanity, must a woman feel she is defying the Creator? Are Christianity and full humanity for women mutually exclusive?

Another student of Paul, however, argues that Paul was not a male chauvinist but a feminist. Paul, in his view, has suffered the double misfortune of being misunderstood and having a bad press. At the risk of sounding defensive, he asks, "What has 1 Timothy to do with the views of Paul?" On this issue scholars are in near-total agreement Paul did not write 1 Timothy (or 2 Timothy or Titus). In the popular mind, however, the viewpoint expressed in 1 Timothy continues to color the interpretation of the genuinely Pauline letters. Such a passage as 1 Corinthians 14:33b–36 is not, it has correctly been noted, Paul's work. It was added later by another hand to make Paul's view conform to that expressed in 1 Timothy. Scholars point out that the verses clearly interrupt Paul's discussion of prophecy. Moreover, the imposition of silence on women in church in this passage flatly contradicts 1 Corinthians 11:5ff. There Paul takes for granted the active, verbal participation of women in the service. Even 1 Corinthians 7:1 ("It is well for a man not to touch a woman") has its positive side. Paul prefers celibacy not because women are "dirty" or because sex is evil but because he feels that the special urgency of the times requires emergency measures. With the end in sight, he feels Christians should brace themselves for traumatic suffering. In the face of the impending distress (7:26), normal domestic concerns must be suspended.

However, what is overlooked in this chapter is the evenhanded way Paul addresses men and women. Concerning marriage Paul says, "Each man should have his own wife and each woman her own husband" (7:2). Concerning sexual intercourse Paul says, "The husband should give to his wife her conjugal rights, and likewise the wife to her husband" (7:3). Concerning sexual abstinence Paul addresses the husband and wife together. Concerning divorce Paul says, "The wife should not separate from her husband . . . and . . . the husband should not divorce his wife" (7:10–11). Concerning mixed marriages Paul says, "If any brother has a wife who is an unbeliever, and she consents to live with him, he should not divorce her. And if any woman has a husband who is an unbeliever, and he consents to live with her, she should not divorce him" (7:12–13). So, throughout the passage, Paul argues for mutual responsibility and the equality of man and woman.

The same impartial treatment is given in 1 Corinthians 11. Verse 3 is usually translated "the head of a woman is her husband." It should read, however, "the source of a woman is her husband." Paul is obviously recalling Genesis 2, where woman is made from a rib taken from man's side. Later, Paul notes that God makes woman the source of man (through giving birth) and thus underscores the interdependence of man and woman (1 Cor. 11:12).

Galatians 3:28, however, best expresses Paul's view: "There is no longer Jew or Greek, there is no longer slave or free, there is no longer male and female; for all of you are one in Christ Jesus." Paul felt that "in Christ" believers already shared in God's new community of the end time. In this new age all barriers that divide the human family are removed, and all obstacles to fulfillment are torn down. Although Paul nowhere attacks prevailing customs that assign women inferior roles in society, he obviously believes they are full partners "in Christ." When one treats women as full and equal citizens in the kingdom of God, it is difficult to hold disparaging views of them.

In response to this, the female student may still harbor doubts. Can she be sure that 1 Corinthians 14:33b–36 was inserted later? Does it really help to say men and women are equal "in Christ" if old patterns of discrimination persist? And in spite of the short exercise in biblical interpretation, she does not like the tone of 1 Corinthians 11:7 where Paul says man is the glory of God but woman is the glory of man. Finally, even if 1 Timothy is not Pauline, it is still in the New Testament and she finds the view of woman expressed in that book unacceptable.

Even in these days of renewed interest in religious studies, many students have a cordial dislike for Paul. In their view, whereas the teachings of Jesus are clear, simple, and basic, Paul's writings are abstract, abstruse, and complex. Where Jesus speaks of a childlike trust in the father God, Paul constructs a complicated system of belief. The death of a sparrow brings a groan from the God of Jesus (Luke 12:6); the God Paul knows cares nothing for animals (1 Cor. 9:9–10). Jesus is warm where Paul is harsh; Jesus is patient where Paul is impatient. Jesus is an unassuming, unpretentious—even unlettered—Galilean peasant with a gift of prophetic insight and empathy for the poor and social misfits. Paul the learned rabbi, on the other hand, is seen as a kind of bully, forcing his dogma on others and merciless in his attacks on opponents. In the view of Paul's critics, this apostle to the Gentiles deflected Christianity away from the path, style of life, and teachings of its founder.

Where some see Paul as a corrupter of the religion of Jesus, others see him as the greatest theologian of all time. They point to his brilliant and incisive interpretation of the gospel for the Hellenistic world. It was Paul who took a message that was Hebraic in concept and idiom and adapted it to a non-Jewish setting without dilution or compromise. It was Paul who faced the hard questions—about the gospel versus Jewish law, the church versus society, Christians versus this world—that had to be answered if the Christian gospel were to remain intact.

Moreover, Paul was a daring and imaginative apostle. As the great pioneer of the Gentile mission, he crisscrossed Asia Minor and plunged into Europe. Tireless in his mission and undeterred by hardship or persecution, Paul pressed on. And he died with his boots on, still longing to go to Spain, the western horizon of the known world.

Where some portray him as a dogmatic grouch, others point to the strains of tenderness in his letters. He tried to be as "gentle as a nurse" with the Thessalonians. He seemed overwhelmed that a brother in Christ, Epaphroditus, would risk his life to serve him. He thought of his converts as his children, and he rejoiced at the restoration of a disciplined member of the congregation. His pastoral concerns surface time and again. Unquestionably, his gentle admonition can give way to harsh polemic. But was this because Paul was dogmatic and inflexible, or because he felt the essential character of the gospel was being compromised?

Some accuse Paul of male chauvinism, and some think he diverted Christianity from its pure source in the simple religion of Jesus. Many Jews accuse Paul of being the father of anti-Semitism in the West. It was he, they claim, who uprooted the Hebraic heritage from Palestine and turned it into a rival of the synagogue. It was he who lashed out in frustration and anger when the Jews resisted his gospel. It was he who warned that acceptance of circumcision meant damnation. And it was he who, as an apostate from Judaism, misrepresented the Hebrew religion. Jews find it difficult to understand why Paul the rabbi would call observance of the law dark and joyless. Had he never read Psalm 19, which speaks of the law "reviving the soul" and "rejoicing the heart"? Was he ignorant, they ask, of the traditions of the rabbis, which speak of the "joy of the commandments"? In their view the acceptance of Paul means the rejection of Judaism. And all too often it has been a short step from the repudiation of Judaism to the persecution of Jews.

Some Protestants would wince at the suggestion that their theology is anti-Semitic. Nevertheless, many, perhaps most, would feel that Christianity according to Paul is the exact opposite of Judaism. They would question whether all Jews find delight in the law. At least the story of Richard Rubenstein would seem to suggest otherwise.

Rubenstein grew up as a secular Jew and started keeping the law in his late teens. He tells of wanting a "cosmic Lawgiver" who would provide order through discipline. But later Rubenstein carne to despise this Lawgiver. His hatred of this exacting Judge ran so deep he wanted to murder him. Then while mourning the death of his son, he suddenly realized that the law could never give him what he desperately wanted, a triumph over mortality. Finally, while going through psychoanalysis, he discovered a kindred spirit in Paul. The release from the law that Paul found in Christ, Rubenstein found through his psychoanalytical experience. Paul's unshacklement from a troubled conscience in bondage to the law perfectly described, Rubenstein felt, his own release from deep personal anguish . Thus he came to know Paul as a "spiritual brother."[1]

According to the usual Protestant view, Paul, like Rubenstein, found the law oppressive. Through Christ Paul learned that salvation has an "in spite of" quality. That is, God loves the individual not because of anything he or she does but in spite of his or her inability to become worthy of love. God simply accepts each person as he or she is. It was Paul's emphasis on this "grace" that was distinctive.

Others get the impression that though Paul differs with Judaism he does not break with it. They note that frequently the traditional juxtapositions of Paul and Judaism have been weak. They observe that Judaism also speaks of salvation by grace. They note that the neat dichotomy between faith and works is not really a judgment against Judaism, for Jewish religion did not make that distinction. Last, and most significant, they find no evidence that Paul ever felt oppressed by the law. Instead, Paul is viewed as a faithful Jew who came to believe that the Messiah had come. This belief did not separate him from Judaism but confirmed his place in it. Thus they feel that Paul did not reject his Jewish heritage but reinterpreted it in light of his experience of Christ. So which was Paul: a Semite turned anti-Semitic, a Christian who rejected his Judaism, or a Jewish Christian who saw his life in Christ as a fulfillment, not a rejection, of Judaism?

The impressions registered here are only a small sample of the opinions about Paul one could assemble. Most readers will bring some notion about Paul to their reading of the letters. Even seasoned biblical critics hardly come to the epistles with a blank tablet. But the honest critic is always testing preliminary impressions against the evidence and correcting them if necessary. The aim of this study is to help the novice read the letters in light of their social and cultural background. Through such a reading perhaps new data will be brought to light that may require the alteration or even surrender of our first impressions. My hope is that such a change will bring our views of Paul into closer conformity with the reality of the man himself.

1

Paul and His World

Most of us can empathize with Polycarp, who complained that neither he nor anyone like him was "able to follow the wisdom of the blessed and glorious Paul" (*Letter to the Philippians* 3.2). Many parts of the letters are "hard to understand" (2 Pet. 3:16). Nevertheless, more information about Paul and the world of his addressees should make comprehension less difficult. Ultimately, Paul's letters are understandable only in the light of his genius and the gospel he preached. However, Paul's religious and cultural context does help to illumine the writings. It may not explain them entirely, but it does shed light. In the discussion below we shall look at some of the ways Paul's milieu, both Hellenistic and Jewish, influenced his message, and on the other side, how the *Sitz im Leben*, or real life setting, of his readers affected their response. This convenient division is made to aid discussion, even though, as we soon shall see, there was no unhellenized Judaism in the first century and no part of the Hellenistic world totally isolated from the Jewish experience. So what we separate for purposes of discussion was not in fact separated in the first century.

PAUL'S HELLENISTIC HABITAT

As the Acts of the Apostles suggests, Paul probably grew up in Tarsus, an important commercial, administrative, and cultural center on the southeast coast of Asia Minor (9:11; 21:39; 22:3). As the provincial capital of Cilicia, Tarsus rivaled Alexandria and Athens in importance. There it was that Paul learned his first language, Greek. There he became familiar with the Septuagint (LXX), the Greek translation of the Hebrew scriptures. There he was most likely taught to read, write, and imitate Greek literary and rhetorical forms. There he received his latinized Greek name, *Paulos* rather than the Hebrew, *Shaul,* which appears nowhere in his letters (but see Acts 13:9). There he acquired an understanding of Hellenistic culture—its anthropology, its political and religious institutions, its cosmology, its sports, and its ecumenical tendencies. There he became acquainted with Greco-Roman rhetoric and mastered the fine art of writing a Hellenistic letter. This rich, cosmopolitan tradition transmitted to Paul through his ancestral religion lingered to shape his messianist thinking in highly original ways. The nucleus of that Jewish tradition was found in the scriptures so important to Diaspora Jews—that is, Jews at home in the Greco-Roman world outside Palestine. An awareness of the role of the Septuagint in Paul's religious outlook is crucial for understanding the letters.

The Septuagint as Paul's Bible

Just as for Helen Keller the discovery and use of language was magical, so also Paul's identity was profoundly influenced by the popular Greek of his day. Language, we know, is no mere passive mirror of the world or a mute tool to be discarded after world construction is done. Rather, language shapes our understanding of reality itself—our understanding of God, Christ, history, the church, and even our very own self. Just as children learn their colors through the promptings of parents, teachers, siblings, and friends, so also religious understanding came to Paul through the language of his native religion.

Much of the language shaping Paul's identity and outlook came from the Greek translation of the Hebrew scriptures that we call the Septuagint. Within a Jewish community steeped in that language, Paul gained his understanding of life and death, fate and freedom, sin and piety, isolation and reconciliation, and inclusion and exclusion.

As an important feature of Paul's Diaspora Judaism, the Septuagint was the Bible not just of the elite scholars but of the common people. While retaining some of its Hebrew flavor, the Septuagint, composed in the ordinary Greek of the day,[1] was fully intelligible even to the illiterate person who heard it read or cited in synagogue settings. Not only was Paul a "Septuagint-Jew," as Adolf Deissmann called him nearly a century ago, but the same was also the case for most synagogue Jews in Tarsus.[2]

Popular legends sprang up supporting its claim to authenticity. According to one fanciful tale, for instance, seventy-two Hebrew scribes from Jerusalem fluent in Greek translated the entire Torah, or first five books of the Hebrew Bible, in seventy-two days. Translated for the library of Pharaoh Ptolemy II Philadelphus (284–247 BCE), the independent renditions of these scholars, according to later legend, agreed in every single detail.[3] (Because of this combination of seventies, we call the book the Septuagint, or LXX, the Roman numeral for seventy.) In reality, the Septuagint was not translated in a little over two months from the Hebrew text but evolved slowly over more than two centuries, and its faithfulness to its Hebrew predecessor varies greatly from book to book.

Once available, however, the text was soon surrounded by a vast body of commentary written to interpret it for Jewish Diaspora communities. In his multivolume works, Philo of Alexandria, a first-century Jew, concerns himself almost exclusively with the interpretation of the Septuagint for his generation. The commentary in the romantic tale of Joseph's marriage to the beautiful Egyptian woman Aseneth had special relevance for Diaspora Jews, who sometimes also fell in love with and married non-Jews.[4] Aristobolus, writing in the second century BCE, attempted to explain anthropomorphic references to God in the Bible to make them more acceptable to the sophisticated, educated Jews of his day.[5] These works, and others besides, all underscored the authority of the Septuagint as God's preeminent vehicle of revelation.

More than a text generating interpretation, however, the Septuagint itself *was* an interpretation. From different periods, from many hands, and scribed in the vernacular Greek of the day, the Septuagint concerned itself with the preservation and interpretation of the "Old Testament" in a Greek appropriate to a new time that also remained true to the spirit of the *Ur-text*. Inevitably certain Greek ideas crept into the translation in at least three important areas.

First, the view of God in the Septuagint reflects a Hellenistic bias. Especially noteworthy is the disappearance of the personal names for God. The Septuagint may render the proper nouns *Yahweh* and *Elohim* with the generic *theos* (god). *El Shaddai*, a common Hebrew proper name *yahweh sebaoth* for God, is most often rendered in Greek with the abstract "Almighty" (*pantokratōr*) or "All-Powerful."

A trend toward abstraction surfaces in Exodus 3:1–4, Elohim's ambiguous response to Moses' clever attempt to worm the secret, powerful divine name from the divine agent. Using a play on words, Elohim slyly answers the impertinent Moses with "'I AM WHO I AM. . . .' Thus you shall say to the Israelites, 'I AM has sent me to you.'" In order for the play on words to work, a knowledge of the Hebrew verb "to be," from which the word *Yahweh* is formed, is required. Such a wordplay, however, is missing entirely from the Septuagint. The Septuagint has instead, "I am The Being. . . . say to the children, 'The Being (*ho ōn*) has sent me.'" Consequently, Yahweh is depicted as the Self-Existent One, the Absolute, or the cosmic, divine being of the Greek philosophers.

A comparable level of abstraction is achieved when the Hebrew God Most High, or *El Elyon*, becomes "the supreme deity" in the Septuagint. Likewise, *Adonai*, whose name implies a cultic relationship between deity and worshiper, becomes "sovereign Lord" (*kyrios*) in the Septuagint.

The Hebrew word *Elohim*, which was used for the one revealed to Abraham, Isaac, and Jacob and the one who gave the law to Moses, is known in Greek as "God" (*theos*) or, following the Hebrew plural form, "gods." Thus for the Hebrew of Exodus 22:28, "You shall not revile *Elohim*," the Greek has, "You shall not revile the gods." This small change had major implications for the practice of a Hebrew religion that traditionally centered on the one God to the exclusion of all others. The literal rendering of the plural "gods" made the septuagintal commandment encourage tolerance of different forms of religious piety, that is, of the "gods." While tolerance of all religious traditions was encouraged, subscription to them was still forbidden.

While Paul's rigorous monotheism would have resisted the Greek spirit of tolerance embedded in the septuagintal translation of Exodus 22:28, he was decisively shaped by the ecumenical tendencies at the heart of Hellenism. Moreover, Paul's churches in the Hellenistic orbit, more open to that spirit than he (e.g., 1 Cor. 10:7ff.), in some cases dictated the issues under consideration in the letters. In the tendency toward abstraction both Paul and his readers came under the influence of the Septuagint, and in one specific case, Paul's understanding of the term "Lord" (*kyrios*) was informed by his Greek Bible.

Second, we see in the Septuagint an understanding of law that Paul shared. One of the most prominent features of postexilic Jewish religion (i.e., after 537 BCE) was the emphasis on Torah. The root of the word *torah* in its verbal form means "to direct" or "to instruct." It may refer to a teacher's instruction, Yahweh's direction, prophetic appeal to the "word of Yahweh," or the instruction derived from the rich and varied story of God's dealing with Israel. In the Greek translation, the word *torah* almost always appears as the Greek *nomos* (law), a translation that lacks the nuances of both languages. Usually *nomos* refers to a code that governs community life or an individual's or community's conduct. In some cases, however, the Greek *nomos* can refer to a cosmic principle like gravity or even mortality. In this latter sense especially, the Septuagint departed from the Hebrew understanding of *torah* and drew near to the Greek understanding of "natural law." While Paul was aware of the nuance *torah* carried, he used *nomos* in Romans 8:2 to refer to being "set free from the law of sin and death," an echo of Genesis 3:1–3, which predicted that death would follow disobedience of the divine command, an obvious etiological legend about the genesis of death. Moreover, Paul nowhere equated, as this passage would seem to, *torah* with sin and death. Similarly in Romans 7:23, where Paul spoke of the "law of my mind," and in 3:27, where he referred to the "law of works" as opposed to the "law of faith," the most accurate translation for "law" would be "principle."

Third, the perception of "faith" in the Septuagint is also significant for understanding Paul's thought. The word for "faith" in Greek (*pistis*) translates the Hebrew noun *'emet*, whose basic meaning is firmness, stability, or reliability. When the Hebrews wanted to speak of faith in someone or something deemed reliable, they always preferred a verb form. We see, therefore, that the Hebrews made precise distinctions between reliability (or faithfulness) and faith or belief in that which is reliable. The Septuagint made no such distinction, and the Greek word for "faith" (*pistis*) was ambiguous enough to allow for both meanings. While this point may seem trivial, it does have relevance for understanding Romans 1:17. In this pivotal passage, which Luther deemed the most important passage in the Bible, Paul quoted from a version of Habakkuk 2:4, but it is uncertain whether he cited the Greek or the Hebrew. The Hebrew of Habakkuk 2:4 is clear and can be translated, "the righteous live by their faith." Perhaps following a slightly different manuscript, the Septuagint has, "the righteous shall live by my [i.e., God's] faithfulness." Paul rendered the passage without the pronoun "my" and took "faith" to refer to individual belief; thus the "one who is righteous will live by faith." Did Paul use a variant of the word *pistis* to mean "belief in" God's work in Christ or to refer to the importance of fidelity to God's covenant or faithful obedience to God's will? Or did he refer to God's fidelity? Scholars have debated this issue without producing a consensus.[6] In using the Greek text Paul may be purposely using a term that is sufficiently ambiguous to suggest multiple meanings. In any case, the point is that the passage is notoriously difficult at least in part because of the ambiguity of the language Paul used, and that ambiguity is only possible if Paul was using the Septuagint.

In this sample of passages we can see how the Hellenistic spirit influenced the translation of the Hebrew scriptures into Greek and how Paul shared the outlook of the Septuagint at some points. While it is true that this intrusion of the Hellenistic spirit did not compromise the fundamental character of the Hebrew religion, it would be inaccurate to say that no change in viewpoint or shift of emphasis occurred. In the comparison below we observe some of those alterations.

Comparison of Translations
of Hebrew and Greek Texts
(* = author's translation, italics= emphasis added)

Translation of Hebrew Texts	Translation of Septuagint*
Who has known the Spirit of the Lord . . . (Isa. 40:13)*	Who has comprehended the mind of the Lord . . . (cf. 1 Cor. 2:16)
He bore the sin of many, and made intercession for the transgressors. (Isa. 53:12)	[He] bore away the sins of many, and on account of their lawlessness was he handed over. (cf. Rom. 4:25)

The rabble among them had a strong craving. (Num. 11:4)	And the people who were among them had an eager desire . . . (cf. 1 Cor. 10:6)
The righteous shall live by their faith. (Hab. 2:4)	"The righteous shall live by my [i.e., God's] faithfulness . . ." (cf. Rom. 1:17)
"By you all the families of the earth shall bless themselves." (Gen. 12:3 RSV)	"In you shall all the peoples of the earth be blessed." (cf. Gal. 3:8)
Moses went up to God. (Exod. 19:3)	Moses ascended to *the mount of* God
And they [Moses and the elders] saw the God of Israel. (Exod. 24:10)	And they saw *the place on which* the God Israel *stood.*
[Isaiah said to Ahaz,] "Look, the young woman is with child and shall bear a son, and shall name him Immanuel." (Isa. 7:14)	Behold, a *virgin* shall conceive and bear a son, and shall call his name Immanuel." (cf. Gal. 4:4)
Elohim said to Moses, "I AM WHO I AM." (Exod. 3:14)	And the God spoke to Moses saying, "I am The Being."
"You shall not make light of Elohim." (Exod. 22:28)	"You shall not speak evil of the gods."

While no comprehensive treatment of septuagintal tendencies and their theological significance is readily available, scholars recognize that certain septuagintal viewpoints influenced Paul's religious outlook. Heard in the home, memorized in the school, read and discussed in the synagogue, the Septuagint was in Paul's blood surely as much as the KJV was in the blood of Milton. Lodged in his soul, the language of the English Bible came to the fore in his discussion of the great issues of sin and justification, law and liberty, election and exclusion, life and death. The language of the Septuagint molded Paul's understanding of faith, legitimated his mission to the Gentiles, and defined his eschatology. This relationship to the Septuagint was dynamic. Its language defined his world and then curved back onto it to illumine and inform Paul's gospel as an apostle of Christ.

Paul's Nonbiblical Hellenistic Language

While the Septuagint was central to Paul's theology, much of his language and important religious expressions came from the wider Hellenistic culture.

The word for "conscience" (*syneidēsis*), for example, commonly appeared in the writings of the Stoic philosophers but is missing entirely from Jewish scriptures. Even allowing that the "thing" may exist when the "word" does not, "conscience," as used by Paul, resembles its Hellenistic parent even when sharing a family likeness with its Jewish forebear. Used by Paul to refer to the inner tribunal of the self, the apostle appropriated the word to defend himself against the charge of insincerity (1 Cor. 4:2), and he called on the conscience of the Corinthians to acknowledge the integrity of his apostleship (2 Cor. 5:11). In the first reference Paul allowed that conscience was culturally conditioned, and thus partially flawed, for he argued that even though no charge was brought against him by his conscience, he was not therefore necessarily innocent. For he recognized that he would ultimately have to stand before the divine tribunal ("I am not aware of anything against myself, but I am not thereby acquitted. It is the Lord who judges me," 1 Cor. 4:4). Elsewhere, however, he spoke of the important function of the conscience for the Gentile unbeliever (Rom. 2:15) as well as the "weak" (1 Cor. 8:7, 10, 12). So Paul's understanding embraced both concepts—conscience that served as an inner critical voice that Paul recognized as culturally shaped, and conscience as an awareness of ultimate accountability to the one God. The two stand in tension in Paul's thought even though both play important roles.

Elsewhere Paul drew on the tradition of the Hellenistic church that predated him. But even if Paul appropriated these traditions from others they were no less his own, for in adopting and using the traditions of others, Paul shared the views expressed even if he did not author them. In the closing admonition of his letter to the Philippians, for example, Paul cited a tradition packed with language from his Hellenistic milieu. There he said, "Whatever is true [*alēthē*], whatever is honorable [*semna*], whatever is just [*dikaia*], whatever is pure [*hagna*], whatever is pleasing [*prosphilē*], whatever is commendable [*euphēma*], if there is any excellence [*aretē*] and if there is anything worthy of praise [*epainos*], think about these things" (Phil. 4:8). A survey reveals ways this passage mirrored a world quite apart from that of the Hebrew parent. For example, *alēthēs*, the true, truthful, or honest, and *semnos*, that which is august, sacred, or worthy of honor, are hardly intelligible apart from their Hellenistic provenance. Anything revealing a higher order, including such diverse things as the majesty of the king's throne, gorgeous dress, eloquent speech, beautiful music, or graceful motion, share the same world. *Hagnos*, much used in Hellenistic circles to refer to the sanctuary, and *prosphilēs*, lovely, pleasing, or agreeable, likewise are of Hellenistic parentage. *Euphēmos*, auspicious, praiseworthy, attractive, or appealing, and *aretē*, a prominent word in Greek philosophy and literature referring to excellence of achievement or mastery of a field, may refer to valor, special merit, honor, good fortune, success, or fame, and likewise is of a Hellenistic geneology. *Epainos*, recognition, approval, or praise, similarly shares the Hellenistic world of the words above.

The alert reader will recognize the nonbiblical character of other materials in the Pauline epistles. Scholars recognize, for instance, that the virtue and vice lists that dotted Hellenistic collections share the world of Paul's letters. Galatians 5:19–23 calls on a catalog of "works of the flesh"—"fornication, impurity, licentiousness, idolatry, sorcery, enmities, strife, jealousy, anger, quarrels, dissensions, factions, envy, drunkenness, carousing, and things like these," to admonish readers to display the "fruit of the Spirit"—"love, joy, peace, patience, kindness, generosity, faithfulness, gentleness, and self-control."[7] While such lists probably came to Paul through Hellenistic Judaism, their deep roots were in Greek philosophy. Except for "love," the virtue list contains nothing that would look strange in conventional Greek ethical writings. The way Paul thought these virtues to be Spirit-driven and thus eschatological was probably his own doing. His use of such lists further demonstrates how fully he inhabited the Hellenistic world and how free he felt to appropriate its idiom in daring ways.

Paul also made copious use of metaphors from the Greek milieu. While not literally true, the metaphor aimed to provoke thought, and to engage the hearer in conversation. If one should say, "Sam Jackson is a horse," or "Stephanie Grant is a gazelle," the hearer will know that these statements are not literally true even though at some level they are true. Thus the hearer is invited to become a partner in an exercise of imagination in which some hidden truth cloaked in the metaphor is explored.

So also Paul's letters invoke images from sport, politics, nature, and religion. In 1 Corinthians 9:24–27, for example, Paul refers to track and boxing. Whereas track stars compete for the honor of wearing a fading laurel wreath, he noted, believers run to win an imperishable spiritual wreath. Boxers aim to defeat the opposition in a slugfest, but Paul pummels his own body into submission to Christ (see also Phil. 3:12–15). Since the message of neither of these statements resides in its literal meaning, the metaphor offers readers an optic through which they may view their world and their place in it afresh. Similarly, when Paul bestowed citizenship in heaven's colony (*politeuma*) on Philippian converts (3:20), he invited them to ponder the fateful difference between this world and another. He admonished fractious Corinthians, whose divisive charismatic puffery subverted the assembly's welfare, to ponder their membership in the "body of Christ" (1 Cor. 12:27). With ironic humor Paul invited them to reflect on a conversation between the ear and the eye. How silly for the ear to say, "Because I am not an eye, I do not belong to the body" (12:16). Designed to puncture inflated pretensions, these metaphors aim to move believers from a self-absorbed, individualistic, arrogant spirituality into a concern for others and for the welfare of the whole body. Similarly, the metaphorical expression "gentle . . . like a nurse" (1 Thess. 2:7) sought to assure a persecuted cell of converts of Paul's tender care for them.[8] All of these metaphors spring from a Greek context and rely on the readers' familiarity with that world to understand Paul's admonition. Please note how skillfully Paul exploited metaphor to serve his mission, to educate the church, and to teach believers the implications of the gospel.

Paul's play with metaphor often signaled a crucial turn or a struggle with a seemingly insoluable problem. In Romans 9:30–33 and 11:11, for example, he sketched a scenario in which Israel, while running a race, comically (or tragically) tripped on a rock placed on the track by God, only to be beaten to the finish by Gentiles who were not even competing. After its introduction in 9:30–33, this farcical construction ferments for more than a chapter before resurfacing in 11:11: "So I ask, have they [the Israelites] stumbled so as to fall?"[9] "By no means!" Paul emphatically retorts. Now we see a curious implication of Paul's metaphor. Unlike other races in which winners require losers (and losers in the Hellenistic world suffered lifelong shame), this race has only winners. Jews who ran the Torah race and Gentiles who did not will both be victorious. When we come to discuss Romans 9–11 and Paul's response to the question, "Now in turning to the Gentiles, has God reneged on promises made to Israel?" we shall see how this metaphor worked to develop and explain Paul's own thinking. In a flash, the metaphor seems to provide a way out of Paul's own dilemma. Mixed with this language drawn from his Hellenistic environment are also metaphorical expressions that are unmistakably Jewish in origin. He called the church "God's temple" (1 Cor. 3:16–17), referred to the Philippian believers as "the circumcision" (Phil. 3:3),[10] and invited the Romans to present their bodies as a "living sacrifice, holy and acceptable to God" (Rom. 12:1).

Inasmuch as Paul's background contained a dynamic blend of Jewish and Hellenistic elements, it is no surprise to find a mix of those elements in his language. This complex and dynamic stew may account for Paul's success in preaching his Jewish gospel in the Hellenistic world. Sensitivity to the history and interplay of those metaphors drawn from Hellenistic and Jewish backgrounds and their function in the letters will give interesting clues to exchanges between Paul and his churches.

Methods of Argumentation

Since Rudolf Bultmann noted Paul's use of the diatribe in the early twentieth century, scholars have recognized Paul's debt to the Stoics.[11] The diatribe originated as a means of argument from the third century BCE onward, and the Cynics refined it to a fine art. Later adopted and adapted by the Stoics, the diatribe came into broad popular use in Jewish circles. A form of argumentation that placed questions on the lips of a hypothetical objector, then offered a response, the diatribe was ideally suited for Paul's response to opponents. For example, Paul sprinkled Romans liberally with such questions as: "Should we continue in sin in order that grace may abound?" (6:1); "What then should we say? That the law is sin?" (7:7); "Is there injustice on God's part?" (9:14). Although the question was hypothetical, its roots were in real-life experience. Particularly in Romans Paul used the diatribe to introduce his discussion of some of the most damaging charges against his gospel of justification by grace for Gentiles, namely, that it encouraged immorality, that it implied that a good gift of God—the law—was evil, and that in choosing the Gentiles God had reneged on promises to Israel.[12]

Critics have shown that Paul used methods of oral argument from Hellenistic rhetoric to persuade his audience. The expense of learning and developing these rhetorical skills either in schools of rhetoric or from private tutors was prohibitive for all except the most privileged. Designed to equip persons for service in law or politics, rhetoric also took literary form in the apologetic letter. Hans Dieter Betz, for example, argues that Paul's letter to the Galatian churches followed this pattern, and he offers an outline of the letter drawn from rhetorical speech.[13] Recognizing its popularity in Roman circles, Betz employs mostly the Latin terms:

    I.   Epistolary prescript (1:1–5)
   II. *Exordium*, or statement of the cause of the letter (l:6–11)
  III. *Narratio*, or autobiographical support for the cause (1:12–2:14)
  IV. *Propositio*, or points of agreement and disagreement (2:15–21)
   V. *Probatio*, or evidential arguments from scripture, experience, Torah, Christian tradition, friendship, and allegory (3:1–4:31)
  VI. *Exhortatio*, or warnings and recommendations (5:1–6:10)
 VII. *Conclusio*, or attack on the opposition (6:11–18).

Although Betz's work provides a fresh look at Galatians, scholars have expressed reservations about the degree of Paul's reliance on classical rhetoric.[14] For example, Paul did not enjoy the privilege prerequisite to such an education, and classical rhetoric as practiced by Cicero was primarily an oral vehicle. Some scholars have doubted that Paul and others adapted classical oral strategies of persuasion to letter writing. Others have objected that while a consideration of strategy may be important, the truth of Paul's gospel, not his political acumen as a persuader, was invariably his primary concern.

While questions about rhetorical criticism will continue to be raised, and confusion will continue, the serious student of Paul cannot dismiss the concerns of rhetorical criticism: "Its interest in the arrangement of an argument and persuasion throws light on the foreground of the text. Such a focus on the politics of persuasion draws attention to the foreground rather than exclusively on the background of the text and rightfully brings the reader into the text's context."[15]

As we shall see, Paul's method of scripture interpretation owed much to his Pharisaism. However, in Galatians 4:21–5:1, with its allegory of Sarah and Hagar, we have an example of a popular Hellenistic method of text interpretation. Allegory is the veiled presentation of meaning, usually in the form of a story, where each part of the story stands for a deeper truth. Unlike metaphor, allegory is self-enclosed, carrying its own explanation and leaving less room for the creative role of the listener (see Mark 4:14–20).

First used by the Greeks responding to the unseemly and even immoral actions of the gods of the classical myths, allegory was employed by the Stoics to rationalize those actions by seeking in them a deeper meaning. An instance of this use of allegory appears in the explanation of the adulterous relationship between Aphrodite and Ares. Aphrodite invites Ares, "Come and lie down, my darling, and be happy! Hephaistos [my husband] is no longer here but gone" (Homer, *Odyssey* 292–93). But their tryst ends abruptly when the suspicious husband, Hephaistos, returns and finds them out, snaring them in his net. Using an allegorical approach, the Greek philosopher Heraclitus found in this text not just a bawdy affair but the harmonious relationship between love and conflict (*Homeric Questions* 69). Allegory thus became the key that unlocked the treasure of texts dealing with gods at war, deceit, and treachery.

While instances of allegory appear in the Old Testament and the Qumran texts, and apocalyptic allegory is present in Jewish pseudepigraphical writings, it was the literature of Diaspora Judaism that exploited the allegorical method to the fullest. One of the most skillful in this use was a first-century Jewish philosopher and interpreter, Philo of Alexandria. Like the Greeks, Philo believed that the literal meaning of a text was only its surface and most superficial meaning, and that the literal text pointed beyond itself to a deeper reality. Philo expressed contempt for unimaginative literalists, calling them "slow-witted" (*On Flight and Finding* 179), "obstinate," and "rigid" (*On Dreams* 2.301), and noted that it is silly to think God actually planted a garden of "soulless" plants. The reference to God's planting a garden in Genesis 2:8, Philo argued, was not to literal trees and herbs, but to divine plants that have virtue, insight, and wisdom to distinguish between the ugly and the beautiful (*On the Creation* 154). Similarly, since no botanist knows of a "tree of life" (Gen. 2:9), Philo suggested that image was to "reverence toward God . . . by means of which the soul attains to immortality" (*On the Creation* 154). When we discuss Paul's use of allegory (e.g., the story of Sarah and Hagar in Gal. 4:21–5:1), Philo's use of allegorical interpretation will be instructive.

Although Paul never knew Philo, he grew up in a Diaspora setting (probably Tarsus) that in some ways resembled that of Philo, and for that reason a consideration of Philo's writings is useful.

Hellenistic Religion and Philosophy

In the Hellenistic world the line between religion and philosophy blurred. The philosopher's search for wisdom was often informed by religious piety, and even when philosophers were self-consciously atheistic, as were some Sophists in the fifth century BCE, they vigorously engaged religious issues. Even the Epicureans from the third century BCE did not, as some suggest, deny the existence of the gods. They asserted instead that it was useless to solicit their aid in prayer or to propitiate them with sacrifice, for they were either indifferent to human concerns or chose not to intervene in them. Conversely, major religious figures of the day like Apollonius of Tyana and Philo of Alexandria worked in the current philosophical idiom. We are being faithful to the spirit of the time, therefore, when we link religion and philosophy in this treatment. Both were vital parts of Paul's world and that of his churches.

Any suggestion that Paul's hearers had no religious practice before baptism is, of course, erroneous. Although Gentiles made up a great, if not the greater, part of Paul's congregations,[16] some, perhaps most, had at least a nodding acquaintance with Jewish traditions, institutions, philosophy, and scriptures. As "God-fearers" sympathetic or even partial to Judaism but not yet converts, some of Paul's hearers might have been more receptive to Paul's Jewish gospel. Others, however, worshiped the popular deities of the Greco-Roman world. Aware of their participation in the rites of Hellenistic religions, Paul reminded his converts that they had "turned to God from idols" (1 Thess. 1:9), and he warned them about the danger of a lingering reverence for the powerful religious symbols associated with their "pagan"[17] devotion. He urged the Corinthians to "flee from the worship of idols" (1 Cor. 10:14), and warned that idolaters (i.e., converts who clung to old religious rites) would not inherit the kingdom of God (Gal. 5:20). But sometimes the divide between life in the new age and the previous existence was indistinct, moving Paul to forbid participation in the local cults even while permitting the consumption of meat offered to idols. (In the entire New Testament such behavior is endorsed only in 1 Cor. 8:1–13 and 10:14–22.) Paul's mission, therefore, did not pour his gospel into a religious vacuum but contended with other religions for the truth of and loyalty to his gospel in a highly pluralistic setting. Sparked off by the conquests of Alexander in the third century BCE that opened up the whole eastern Mediterranean to a dynamic exchange of ideas, the older religions jockeyed with the new for converts.[18] But all were affected by a disenchantment that characterized the age.

The causes of this first-century malaise go back to the third century BCE, a period of severe economic depression, civil war, infanticide, and depopulation, the decline of the city-state, and a serious weakening of the judicial system that worsened the suffering. Infanticide of female infants was common, whereas sons were spared, for it was assumed that from a family with two sons one would die in a war leaving only one to maintain the family legacy. The decline of social institutions and the rise of religious doubt virtually destroyed the old religions. To be sure, certain primitive forms of religion remained. But even though people still stood in awe of the power and mystery of certain primal forces, devotion to the old gods—Zeus, Aphrodite, Apollo, and others—was on the wane.

With the collapse of traditional religion, Hellenistic piety assumed many new forms. In some cases the old corporate theology gave way to a type of individualistic piety fixed on some particular god or even foreign deity. In other cases belief in an impersonal, divine force present in the world (e.g., in Stoicism) replaced the venerable tradition. In still other instances many felt no kinship with any divine principle that gave the cosmos any semblance of order. The feeling was pervasive that the world was controlled by an oppressive, blind, impersonal, cosmic force called *heimarmenē*. Ruled by a dark necessity that was a stranger to love, many felt like reeds at the mercy of a mindless wind. This shift in mood and darkness of spirit cast menacing shadows over the Hellenistic landscape, and the great dream of one world free of barbarism and corruption soured. Any hope that any political power could deliver the good life evaporated. As Helmut Koester notes,

> In Athens, the city in which the most magnificent cultic buildings were erected, the visible presence of splendid temples did little but create the impression that this city was only a museum of classical greatness. The more the old traditions received support and were subsidized by the government, the more the cultic activities of the temples were estranged from the religious consciousness of the majority of the population.[19]

This eclipse of the old had far-reaching implications. For example, in place of the earlier Greek fascination with the body and appreciation for beauty and order in the universe, there appeared a devaluation of the world and the body. The Greek word for "athlete" (*askētēs*) came to mean "ascetic."[20] Gilbert Murray once characterized this period:

> This sense of failure, this progressive loss of hope in the world, in sober calculation, and in organized human effort, threw the later Greek back upon his own soul, upon the pursuit of personal holiness, upon emotions, mysteries and revelations, upon the comparative

neglect of this transitory and imperfect world for the sake of some dream-world far off, which shall subsist without sin or corruption, the same yesterday, today and forever.[21]

Even granting this decline of traditional religions, their wasting away hardly left a landscape barren of religious expression. Fertility cults remained viable in the rural areas, the mystery religions enjoyed a resurgence in the cities, the healing cult of Asclepius became increasingly popular, and religious movements from the East grew in favor in the cosmopolitan West. Because of the urban character of Paul's mission, the last three are of special interest to us here.

The Mystery Religions

Perhaps because of their success in guarding their secrets, we know little about the mystery religions in first-century Greece.[22] What we do know harmonizes well with the spirit of the time. Although participation in the mysteries was most often corporate, the central concern of the mysteries was for salvation through direct identification with the deity or a surrogate of the deity. This knowledge was less intellectual than mystical, less rational than relational. Through the prescribed rites the participants received more than a vision—they experienced solidarity with the god. Preparation included elaborate cleansing rites (lustrations or baptisms), and in some of the mysteries sexual union in a cultic setting offered ecstatic union. Through ritual mergers with the deity, initiates experienced a state of blessedness: the terror of history was overcome, release from the corruption of this world was achieved, and immortality became a present reality.

The Eleusinian Mystery. The dying and rising god or goddess at the center of the mystery cult normally had his or her first home in agriculture, with its vital interest in the turning of the seasons. In that context the deity's life and death had practical issue for the renewal of crops. Eventually, however, under the influence of the mystery religions, the ancient fertility rites changed focus from the renewal of crops to the renewal of life after death.[23] In the words of Firmicus Maximus, we see how the fate of the god became the fate of the initiate:

> Take courage, ye initiates! As the god was saved,
> So too for us comes salvation from suffering.[24]

Most typical of this pattern was the Eleusinian Mystery, based on a myth in which Hades-Pluto kidnaps Kore-Persephone, the beautiful young goddess of fertility, carrying her off to the underworld to rape her. In her absence Demeter, her mother, mourns, the earth languishes, and the grain wilts. Demeter's desperate search for her daughter meets success only after her persistent appeal persuades Zeus to intervene and rescue the people from starvation and death. As a result, Kore-Persephone spends eight months of every year on earth and four months in the underworld. (The four months were the hot, dry summer months when the grain lay dormant.) Though little is known of the rituals marking these seasonal passages, surely rites of mourning and celebration existed. But evidence from the Roman period proves that the Eleusinian Mysteries had a reach far beyond their immediate agricultural home. Cicero, one of the most important Roman jurists and philosophers of the Roman period, was an Eleusinian initiate and spoke of the power of the mystery to enable believers to "live with joy . . . and die with a better hope."[25] A number of emperors accepted initiation into the cult (Augustus, Hadrian, Marcus Aurelius, and others), but the expense of the initiation discouraged participation by the poor and slaves. The attention given in the mystery to ties with the dead heightened its appeal. Yet there was no community of Eleusinian initiates, and the mystery's highly individualistic character separated it radically from the early Christian community.

The Isis-Osiris Mystery. One of the most popular mysteries of the first century was the Isis-Osiris (or Serapis) cult, a transplant from Egypt that flourished in the cities ringing the Mediterranean. Isis was ritually recalled as an Egyptian goddess, the consort of Osiris, who was murdered by his brother Seth and departed to become lord of the netherworld. Though linked to the realm of the dead, Osiris held the secret to the powers of life and fructification. He brought the benevolent Nile floods that caused the Delta to bloom. He caused the wine to ferment, the bread to rise, and the crops to yield their fruit. Osiris's green face, still evident in tomb drawings from the second century Egypt BCE, symbolized his intimate association with verdant nature's abundance.

Although the history of the Osiris myth informing the first-century mystery is complex, the basic outline of the sacred story is known. Two brothers were born of the sun god Ra, Seth, the older, jealous, rival sibling, murdered Osiris, dismembered him, and heaved the mutilated carcass fragments into the Nile. Stricken with grief, Isis, Osiris's consort, scoured the land in search of her lover. Eventually, she located the fragments of his body, reassembled them, breathed life into the reassembled corpse, and consummated her love. From this sexual union issued Horus, Osiris's heir to the throne and the pharaoh of Upper and Lower Egypt. Later interred by Anubis, the jackal-headed god of the dead, Osiris returned to the netherworld to become lord of the Nile, causing it to flood annually, and thus joining issue with the soil to assure abundant harvests. Meanwhile, Horus, his son, ruled the land from a throne shaped like the lap of his mother Isis.

Depicted often as a black or Apis bull, a powerful symbol of fecundity, Osiris became the guarantor of life after death and the god with whom

Egyptian women and men identified as they faced their own mortality.[26] Through their participation in this myth, they expressed their hope to some-day join the great god Osiris and thus be absorbed in the great rhythm of the universe.[27] Osiris's name when combined with Apis, the name of the beauti-ful, virile black bull in which he was manifest, produced Serapis (from Osiris and Apis), the Greek version of the Egyptian cult that became highly popular well into the Roman period. In the translation into the Greek experience by Alexander's successors, the Ptolemies, however, it was Isis, not Osiris, who became the dominant figure. So this primal myth, so deeply rooted in Egypt's fertile cultural landscape, promised victory over mortality to its initiates and became influential with the masses in the great urban centers of the Greco-Roman world. To establish its importance it is unnecessary to see parallels, as does Koester.[28] Nevertheless, Paul's account of dying and rising with Christ (Rom. 6:3–5) and the rite of participation in the Isis initiation may have reso-nated with many in Paul's congregations who were aware of the cult and may have even been attracted to its wondrous vision of Isis:

> . . . the mother of the universe,
> The mistress of all the elements,
> The first offspring of time,
> The highest of the deities,
> The queen of the dead.[29]

Verbal descriptions of Mary betray the influence of the Isis myth decades after Paul's death, and thus reveal the continuing appeal of this mystery reli-gion. But most would have recognized the profound differences between Paul's gospel and the message of Isis. Whereas the Isis cult promised a tri-umph over death in the present, the triumph over the power of death for Paul remained a future prospect. And, of course, although both begin with the story of a tragic murder (Jesus and Osiris), Paul's gospel had a historical dimension that the Isis-Osiris myth lacked and a radical monotheism that would have been totally alien to the Isis-Osiris mystery.

The Dionysiac Mystery. No sketch of the mysteries would be adequate with-out some reference to Dionysus, the most popular Greek mystery of the Hel-lenistic age. Although a venerable god of distant antiquity, Dionysus's land of origin is disputed.[30] However that dispute turns out, all recognize that Dio-nysus was revered in Greece before the sixth century BCE and still appealed to many into the first.

Dionysus's myth of origin recalled that he was conceived in a tryst between the god Zeus and the mortal Semele, the daughter of Cadmus, the king of Thebes. His birth, like his conception, stood outside the order of nature. Jeal-ous of Semele's success with Zeus, Hera tricked Semele into begging Zeus to reveal his full splendor to her. After initially resisting, Zeus reluctantly agreed, but in the theophany Semele was struck down, consumed by a bolt of lightning. Dionysus, the foetus, was rescued from the dying Semele (birth one) and carried to full term by Zeus in his thigh (euphemism for abdomen?), from whence he eventually emerged (birth two). Devotees, identifying with Dionysus, spoke of themselves as "born again" or recipients of a "second birth." Once grown, Dionysus descended to Hades to rescue his mother, Semele, and return her to Mount Olympus to live with the gods. In addition to presiding over a cult of rebirth, Dionysus was best known as the bringer of wine, and his victory over death was symbolized by a green ivy headband, a symbol of immortality.

Vase paintings from the sixth and fifth centuries BCE depict maenads, or female worshipers, in wild, ecstatic, nocturnal, and highly erotic dances. Under the power of Dionysus they broke free of onerous work at looms and shuttles. Other sources describe the feast of *sparagmos* in which women in fits of ecstasy tore flesh from living animals and devoured it raw in a reckless act of abandon and divine possession. Since Dionysus was present in both the wine and wild animals, to eat the sacred flesh and drink the sacred wine was the mythical basis for their enthusiasm (literally having "god within"). And given the prominence of both the bloody sacrifice and wine from the crushed grape, the symbolic association of blood and wine as living sacrifice was natural. Whether the church's association of blood and wine in the Eucharist was influenced by the Dionysiac mysteries is uncertain. What is certain, however, is that the command to drink the wine as Jesus' blood, so repulsive to Jews, would have sounded entirely natural to Paul's hearers familiar with the Dionysiac mystery.

Men also worshiped Dionysus, though usually segregated from women. In their stag parties they drank copious amounts of the wine symbolically containing the spirit of the god. Apparently only in the spring festival did women and men join together in one joyous act of celebration. But whether segregated or integrated, men and women throughout Greece, the islands, and onto the coast of Asia Minor hailed Dionysus in intoxication and dance as the "'Raw-Eater,' 'Man-smasher,' 'Great Hunter,' 'Steer,' 'Roarer,' 'the-one-with-the-black-goatskin,' 'Erect,' 'Tree-like,' 'Flowerer,' 'Liberator.'"[31] These metaphors associated with Dionysus reveal some of the complexity and irreconcilable polarity of this god. He stood for blood and gore as well as rescue and salvation. His dark side touched on bloodshed and pollution, his light side on liberation and freedom. His savagery and destructiveness linked him with death; his rescue of his mother from Hades established him as the giver of life. His association with life and death, light and darkness, the world above and the world below, and the wild and the tamed inevitably tied him to contradictions endemic to human experience.

From the third century BCE to the first, however, the gravity and complexity of the earlier Dionysus gave way to a vision of the god much more in tune with Hellenistic ideals. Now more a symbol of the sophisticated, refined lifestyle of the Hellenistic period and an advocate of the ecumenical vision of the one civilized world, Dionysus was increasingly used by rulers to reinforce political agendas. Nevertheless, Dionysus did not lose touch with the common lot of humanity. His gospel promised strength to endure life's trials and offered rescue from death in the world to come. His association with wine, dance, and drama remained unshakable, and his powers remained sufficiently broad to be implored by emperor and slave alike. His tolerance for excess made it easy for his followers to identify with him.[32] His affirmation of the physical legitimated the sensual element in the human experience and offered release from the mundane. Caroline Houser aptly summarizes the basis of Dionysus's appeal: Dionysus, she notes, "is a realist who knows the dark and frightening side of nature as well as the light and joyful side. He promises transcendence or metamorphosis, not annihilation."[33]

In sum, one might say that the primary emphasis of the Dionysiac mystery was on the struggle between life and death. The emphasis on the life-giving power of the phallus must be seen against an awareness of death as the one great absolute. As early as the fifth century BCE the mystery was concerned with the terror and bliss of the afterlife. This emphasis on funereal elements continued well into the Roman period. Yet the Roman version of the worship of Bacchus (for Dionysus) differed in the way it exaggerated certain elements in the Greek version. Devotees of Bacchus, for example, were much more direct in their pursuit of erotic pleasure, and the Roman maenads, or female devotees, much more provocative than their Greek counterparts. Although Paul's warnings against drunkenness and lust may not have been specifically aimed at the devotees of Dionysus, surely the context required such warnings, for Paul would have been acutely aware of the hold of this mystery on some of his followers.

The Healing Cult of Asclepius

No ancient was a stranger to illness, and that human extremity often prompted an appeal to the gods for help. In the Hellenistic world that request most frequently was lifted up to Asclepius, the god of healing. Son of the god Apollo and the mortal Coronis, according to one account, Asclepius was born at Epidaurus, which later became the location of an impressive sanctuary in his honor. According to the myth, Asclepius died as a mortal but returned to earth as a god to live and serve humanity as the compassionate god of healing. Devoted primarily but not exclusively to the poor and disadvantaged, Asclepius was known as the kind, compassionate god. Seeking relief from sickness at any one of more than three hundred sanctuaries dedicated to him at Epidaurus, Athens, Corinth, Pergamum, the island of Cos, and other places, the masses came. There were 160 rooms for guests at Epidaurus alone. As precursors of modern holistic medicine, these centers ministered to the mind and spirit as well as the body. Like that at Epidaurus, for example, these centers included libraries, gymnasia, theaters, baths, clinics for physicians, and a holy place (*abaton*) where the ill slept, hoping for a healing encounter with the merciful god Asclepius. For example, we are told that at Epidaurus, Ambrosia, a young girl who was blind in one eye, was visited by Asclepius as she slept in the *abaton.* "The god appeared before her, telling her that she would be cured and that she had to dedicate a pig made of silver as a token of her gratitude. Having said this he cut out the bad eye and immersed it in medicine. She awoke at dawn, cured."[34]

Although no such centers of healing existed in Jewish or early Jesus circles, as the Gospels show there was a profound interest in the powers of charismatic healers. One difference, however, was that the emphasis on healing in the Asclepius cult was individualistic, whereas the corporate dimension of Jewish and Christian healing stories is unmistakable. Although Paul's addressees, like all people of the time, and he himself suffered the usual number of illnesses and physical handicaps, except for 2 Corinthians 12:7–12 the letters themselves record no single healing he performed (cf. Gal. 3:5). He did note that he was able to perform mighty works (Gal. 3:5) and that he suffered from various afflictions, but he more strongly emphasized God's strength made manifest in his weakness (2 Cor. 12:9) in contrast to those who display their miracle-working powers as proof of the truth of their gospel. Yet healing cults were very much part of the environment in which Paul proclaimed his gospel and may have influenced his hearers more than we know.

Stoicism

The personal agony and social upheaval of the third century BCE provided the ingredients for the formation of Stoicism. With the shaking of the foundations that came with the collapse of Alexander's empire, questions of theodicy were raised in the sharpest possible way. Social upheaval, civil war, famine, corruption, infanticide, and tyranny prompted the question: If the gods care about the plight of humanity, why do they fail to redress the wrongs inflicted by this hostile world? If providence favors justice and fairness, then why is life so unfair?

The Stoics answered by affirming rather than denying a divine presence in the world. "God" for the Stoics was less a divine personality who actively engaged in human affairs than a divine principle (*logos* or divine reason) that pervaded and governed the universe. As Edwyn Bevan noted, for the Stoic "the whole universe was only one Substance, one *Physis*, in various states" and "that one Substance was Reason, [and] was God."[35] The Stoics held that like humans, the world had a soul that directed its affairs, and existence was deemed fundamentally rational. Even natural disasters such as floods, earthquakes, or famine advanced the divine purpose in ways beyond human comprehension; perhaps they controlled population or served hidden purposes. In this spirit, Chrysippus once remarked that even the lowly bedbug was an instrument of the divine reason, because it kept people from sleeping too much or too long. The humble pig, likewise, mirrored this divine reason, for its "soul of salt" allowed its flesh to be preserved for eating, and its tendency to fatness made its meat delicious and nourishing. Chrysippus had the rather optimistic view that if the world could have been better arranged, the divine reason would have made it so. In the third century BCE, the famous Stoic Cleanthes well articulated this vision in his hymn to Zeus:

> For nought is done on earth apart from thee,
> Nor in the earth nor in the sea,
> But skill to make the crooked straight is thine,
> To turn disorder to a fair design
> Ungracious things are gracious in thy sight
> For ill and good thy power doth so combine.[36]

Once a person understood the universe to be fundamentally rational, he or she could accept whatever happened with equanimity (or *apatheia*). *Apatheia* was no mere resignation (as its English cognate, *apathy*, suggests) but a source of strength based on the conviction that a divine will controlled and directed all things. *Apatheia*, therefore, was the gateway to true freedom, for the truly disinterested person was untrammeled by the cares of the world. In the Stoic view, a kind of self-sufficiency or spiritual autonomy characterized the life of the truly liberated person. Though Stoicism was pantheistic (i.e., the universe was infused with divine soul), it was no mystery religion. Its emphasis on the inner life and personal initiative, however, did give it a highly individualistic character. Its stress on personal detachment and the orderliness of the cosmos undermined any interest in history. Since the world moved in ways predetermined by cosmic reason, it minimized the importance of either a past or a future. As Bultmann once said, "The Stoic believes that it is possible to escape from his involvement in time. By detaching himself from the world he detaches himself from time. The essential part of man is the Logos, and the Logos is timeless."[37]

Paul's early years were probably spent in Tarsus, a center of Stoic teaching. Certainly his letters show signs of Stoic influence. Both his use of the diatribe to argue his case in Romans and his creative appropriation of the allegorical method of scripture interpretation owe something to the Stoics.

His tendency to view believers as citizens of heaven (Phil. 3:20) rather than of the city (or city-state, *polis*) strongly resembles a Stoic vision. Possibly even the inclusivism of Paul's vision of an eschatological *oikoumenē* that embraced the whole inhabited world may owe something to a Stoic cosmopolitanism (Rom. 10:18).

At other points, however, Paul's worldview differed markedly from that of his Stoic contemporaries. His gospel's emphasis on history, rooted in a historical event, based on a historical person, and the anticipation of a fulfillment in a historical (real) future all separated Paul from his Stoic peers.

Unlike the Stoic view of freedom as spiritual autonomy, freedom for Paul meant liberation from hostile, cosmic powers (e.g., King Death, or Satanic Sin) for service to Christ. The Stoic was confident that individuals could win freedom through their own dedication; Paul took freedom to be an eschatological gift of God. And whereas the Stoic's concern centered on freedom, and thus on the individual, Paul's emphasis was communal, and thus implied a positive interaction of persons in a common bond. We see, therefore, that while Paul used the Stoic idiom, he normally subordinated it to his gospel and in the process transformed it. But what was true of Paul was not always true for his converts, who were often inclined to familiar and even natural compromises that sometimes led to sharp exchanges between them and the apostle.

Cynic Philosophy

Strictly speaking, the Cynics were not philosophers but advocates of a lifestyle and a method of teaching. They were called philosophers by their contemporaries, nevertheless, and because of their influence they deserve our attention. The word "Cynic" comes from the Greek for dog (*kyon*), an epithet hung on these culture critics of their time. The Cynics traced their lineage back to Diogenes of Sinope (fourth century BCE), and their presence in the urban centers of Paul's day was significant. Claiming to live by nature (*physis*) and thus being fundamentally countercultural, they expressed their contempt for the well-dressed by wearing rags, for the well-groomed by their unkempt appearance, for the wealthy by begging, and for the politically powerful by their contempt for those in power. As keen observers of nature, they modeled their lives by its rules. Living as naturally and comfortably as possible, they, like animals, defecated in public places and had sexual intercourse wherever they felt the urge. Like other creatures, they sought to reduce life to its barest simplicity. So impressed was Diogenes, for example, by a child's drinking from cupped hands that he discarded his cup, saying, "A child has beaten me in the plainness of living."[38] Greatly elevating boldness of speech, they appropriated for themselves a freedom of speech that was usually reserved for citizens in the assembly. For instance, so overawed was he by Diogenes's example that Alexander the Great reputedly told the philosopher, "Ask me any boon you like."[39] To which Diogenes allegedly replied, "Stand out of my light." Paul, like the Cynics, speaks of having the boldness "in our God to declare to you the gospel of God in spite of great opposition" (1 Thess. 2:2). Although they were not atheistic, Cynics might have found religious language discomfiting,[40] for they usually viewed such language as an expression of popular religion, which they sharply criticized as a superstitious endorsement of the status quo.

Understandably, many found Cynic behavior—their ragged, dirty clothing, their smelly hair, their matted, unkempt beards, and their surly manner—to be revolting. Writing in the middle of the first century, Seneca scoffed at their behavior and at their "repellent attire, unkempt hair, slovenly beard, open scorn of silver dishes, a couch on the bare earth and . . . other perverted forms of self-display."[41] In spite of popular disdain for them, Cynics, nevertheless, did at points influence New Testament writings. Paul's use of the diatribe came at least indirectly from Cynics and Stoics. Some of his language (e.g., "boldness of speech") shows some debt to the Cynic philosophers. The lists of hardships that he notes in 2 Corinthians 11:23–29 closely follows a Cynic pattern. Paul's own understanding of the radical character of his wandering mission may have owed something to the Cynic practice. Yet, at other points, Paul emphatically distanced himself from wandering popular preachers whom many deemed hucksters preying on simple souls. Paul's letters reveal little inclination to engage in a radical critique of society. Why should they? He was convinced that the form of this world was passing away and would soon be replaced by a new creation. And Paul, much more than any Cynic preacher, saw the necessity of religious institutions and the importance of corporate support for the life of radical obedience to God (e.g., the offering for the church in Jerusalem).

So in being aware of this vibrant conceptual context in which Paul preached, we must also exercise caution, for conceptual parallels may not mean or suggest agreement. It is important to see that Paul based his critique of the world and his readers on the gospel he preached, which was significantly different from the Cynic philosophy and ethos.

Neo-Pythagoreanism

Because of its ability to synthesize diverse traditions, Pythagoreanism enjoyed a widespread revival in the first century BCE. With the venerated name of Pythagoras to legitimate their teachings, the Neo-Pythagoreans forged a union of philosophy and religious piety that had genuine popular appeal. Far from being just an exercise in speculation, this philosophy concerned itself with cultivating a sensitivity to the divine element within. The axiom that "like seeks like" was primary to both Pythagorean (sixth century BCE) and

Neo-Pythagorean thought (first century BCE). This meant that humans, being divine, constantly seek to return home to a cosmic, divine source, like the movie character E.T. surveying the heavens and muttering, "home"; the aim of life was to strip off the body to allow the spirit to rejoin the divine. Naturally this loyalty to one's higher nature required repudiation of the flesh, because it is by flesh, they believed, that the spirit was tethered to this world. This emphasis on liberation from the body often led to a repression or a sublimation of sex (i.e., body), and to a life of poverty free from earth's trappings. Sometimes a vow of silence was taken to stifle traffic with this world and afford fuller contemplation of the world of spirit.

Since the soul was divine, and the divine eternal, Neo-Pythagoreans firmly believed the soul was immortal, and this led to belief in transmigration. Soul was not the exclusive property of human life: the divine element went beyond the human family to include animals, and formed the basis of the Neo-Pythagorean conviction that the divine ether was present in animals, and this led them to ban the eating of meat and to forbid the wearing of clothes made from animal pelts or wool.

A strong mystical current ran through Neo-Pythagoreanism. Like the god-intoxicated worshipers of the mysteries, they called themselves *entheoi* (those with god within) or even *ekstatikoi* (those possessed or beside themselves with the spirit). This enthusiasm (literally, infusion with god) often manifested itself in miraculous works. In some circles miracles were thought to reveal the divine within of the one performing them. In this view, charismatic male figures, or "god-men," performed divine or miraculous deeds as authenticating signs.

For some Neo-Pythagoreans, numbers held a significance beyond their signification as abstract ciphers. Apparently this reverence for numbers sprang from the conviction that harmony was the essence of divine nature. The precise rhythm of the cosmos as well as the delicate and perfect balance between odds and evens, between the one and the many, and between finity and infinity, suggested a divine principle holding opposites like good and evil, light and darkness, male and female, and so on in a divine harmony that embraced the whole universe. And between the one and the many they saw a fundamental reality that manifested itself in the division between male and female, light and darkness, good and evil, and so on. Although their interest in astrology and numbers did prompt the Neo-Pythagoreans to an accurate reading of the movements of the heavenly bodies, their aim was not scientific but religious. The heavenly spheres, they held, were more than the expression of a divine order—they were also its source. The astral bodies were in some sense divine, and the will of the gods could be learned from their movements.

Knowing that divine will was important because those bodies were thought to fix the destiny of the world. The goal of knowledge was to penetrate to the very heart of the cosmos and to find truth "as something at once beatific and comforting." This philosophy "presents the human being as cradled in a universal harmony."[42] The saving quality of this knowledge was especially precious in the first century BCE because of the loss of inner security that had come with the decline of social structures, and the loss of faith. Neo-Pythagoreans found comfort in their belief that there was some connection between the "fixed glare of alien power and necessity"[43] in the stars and the destiny of the world.

In the view of some, Neo-Pythagoreanism was a degenerate philosophy. The movement did address itself, however, to a major concern of the time. Increasingly, many felt ruled by powers they could not pretend to comprehend or understand. Life seemed capricious and unfair; the only certainty was uncertainty. The elder Pliny articulated a widespread feeling in the cities when he said,

> We are so much at the mercy of chance
> that Chance herself, by whom God is
> proved uncertain, takes the place of God. [44]

Added to this sense of helplessness before powerful forces was a growing suspicion that the powers were careless. Many felt as though they were mere playthings of Fate (*Moira*), Chance (*Tychē*), or Necessity (*Anankē*). Life, they believed, was determined by forces that were fundamentally blind to and heedless of moral distinctions. Although Neo-Pythagoreanism did not elevate reason, it did offer an alternative to surrendering to Fate. It promised desperate men and women a way out of this world. By touching the divine within, believers could anticipate liberation of the divine spark from its fleshly prison and a reunion of it with the source of all being and truth. Freed from the tyranny of capricious, irrational powers, life assumed meaning and purpose that made it tolerable.

The character of first-century Neo-Pythagorean thought is perhaps best exhibited in the life of Apollonius of Tyana. Although his highly romanticized biography was not commissioned until 216 CE (over a century after his death),[45] the piety reflected in it conforms rather well to Apollonius's actual first-century outlook noted by historians. Renouncing wine, meat, and marriage, Apollonius wandered about barefoot, clad only in "landwool" (linen), which did not rob animals of their clothing. Through gifts to the poor he rid himself of the burden of wealth, and through a vow of silence that reputedly lasted for five years he screened out this world to concentrate on the divine. His travels carried him as far east as India, as far south as Egypt, and as far west as Rome. He conferred with the sages in Nepal, preached and performed miracles through Asia Minor and Greece, visited naked sages on the upper Nile, and advised public officials in Rome.

His preaching emphasized a strong link between salvation and self-knowledge. Inasmuch as knowing the self meant an existential or deep religious knowing of the divine within the self, he claimed self-knowledge to be synonymous with becoming divine. Consequently, to know oneself is to know all things, since the gods know everything. Moreover, the truly good person is divine, that is, one whose actions reflect what one essentially is. These divine acts reach beyond high moral concerns to include miraculous deeds. In the biographical account, for example, Apollonius not only denounced Roman tyranny, repudiated gladiatorial combat, exhorted the common people to improve their morals, and admonished all to be responsible citizens; he also predicted a plague, raised a dead girl, healed a boy bitten by a mad dog, exorcised demons, and quelled riots. There is little cause for wonder that when Nero asked Apollonius at his trial, "Why do people call you god?" he reputedly answered: "Every man believed to be good is honored with the title god."[46] Persecuted under Nero for his "meddlesome business," he was apparently martyred under Domitian near the end of the first century. One tradition, however, speaks of an end befitting an immortal: his mysterious disappearance and ascension before his execution.

Although the biography of Apollonius is late, his activity as a wonder-worker, wise man, lawgiver, and patron of the mysteries is in tune with the spirit of the age. Whereas the literary portrait of Apollonius broadly stroked by Philostratus reflects some later concerns, the basic outline of his sketch closely resembles the portrait of first-century Neo-Pythagorean philosophy presented by others.[47] Given the spiritual hunger of the fatalism felt by many of the period and given the hopeful emphases of Neo-Pythagoreanism, its success among rich and poor, privileged and slave, literate and illiterate, is hardly surprising. And considering its broad popular appeal, the likelihood is great that it influenced some of Paul's hearers, perhaps rather significantly.

Gnosticism

Gnosticism (Greek *gnōsis*, "knowledge") was important in the experience of the early church. Although the background of Gnosticism is extraordinarily complex, it is likely that the spirit of the Hellenistic age played some role in its genesis and formation. It is unlikely, however, that Gnosticism was merely an acute hellenization of early Christianity, as Harnack claimed generations ago; it surely was at home and flourished in a deeply disenchanted age.

Whether Gnosticism antedated Christianity is much disputed, but gnostic materials with sources that go back to the second century CE were discovered at Nag Hammadi in Egypt in 1945. Now published, these materials assist in sketching the contours of thought in this movement.[48] The polemical description of Gnosticism by the church fathers in the late second century CE was formerly discounted, but read in light of the Nag Hammadi codices that description is not the caricature some thought it to be. Since our earliest secure historical evidence for Gnosticism is the second century, it is not always applicable to Paul, but certain features of the second-century version anticipated the first.

While the presence of the divine *logos* in the natural world allowed the Stoic to view the environment positively, the devoted gnostic viewed the world as incurably evil. If the creation is evil, then it followed that its creator also must be evil. Thus the god of this evil world became an anti-god or demonic figure. This radical dualism between the god above and the god below, between matter and spirit, between light and darkness, between knowledge and ignorance, formed the core of gnostic thought.

The denigration of matter profoundly influenced gnostic anthropology. The product of an evil being, imprisoned in a demonic world, unconscious of the divine within, humans wander aimlessly in perpetual stupor. Were it not for the great high god who takes pity and sends a redeemer to remind them of their true origin and destiny, all would be hopelessly lost. But once awakened from the ignorance of one's divine origin, gnostics experienced salvation fully here and now. Liberated from the bodily prison, the "spiritual" person realized absolute freedom, a freedom that embraced both stringent asceticism and voluptuary license. In the repudiation of the flesh (asceticism), gnostics exhibited their freedom *over* the body. In their indulgence, gnostics demonstrated their freedom *from* the body, in that what is done in the body does not affect the real self. Moreover, since the fallen god, Yahweh, gave the laws, lawbreaking became a signifier of freedom from the clutches of that god.

The Corinthian correspondence opens a window onto a community with some of these tendencies. But those links are hardly iron clad, for it is anachronistic to argue for a second-century movement in the first. It is likely, however, that pre-gnostic emphases on wisdom (*gnosis*), libertinism, devaluation of the creation, a realized eschatology or spiritual elitism, and even an ascription of evil to the god of this world (2 Cor. 4:4) were shared by some of Paul's converts. Those early gnostic tendencies received fuller development a century later in certain Egyptian and Syrian churches. Certain Pauline texts like 1 Corinthians 15:50—"flesh and blood cannot inherit the kingdom of God"—when taken out of context could be made to support gnostic Christianity.[49]

Summary

Each of the movements described above is in some ways peculiarly its own but in other ways fully representative of the spirit of its age. Apart from these movements, what had previously been central to Hellenism continued, namely, an openness to other cultures and an openness to the surprises that came from engagement with other religious views. Although such cross-fertilization could be and often was fruitful, the risk was great that the new gods and foreign ways would radically alter or even supplant traditional religious views.

One other motif survived—a sense of community or *sympatheia*[50] with the divine. By the first century the heroic period of Hellenism had faded, but if the traditional gods of classical Greece had lost their power to save, they had also lost their enervating characteristics. Most still felt related to a divine principle or divine element that bound all together, and erased artificial distinctions between man and woman, barbarian and Greek, slave and free. Moreover, it was the godly ether shared by the animals that linked them with humanity through *sympatheia*.

A significant development in the Hellenistic period, however, was the emerging split between the celestial and terrestrial worlds that revealed a terrifying rupture between flesh and spirit, between the world below and the world above. Whether this dualism was homegrown or imported is unclear. What is clear, however, is that it found conditions favorable for growth in Hellenistic soil. Even if many of Paul's readers had never read or heard any of the philosophers, they would have been influenced by the spirit of the age. Once we realize that Paul's gospel ran counter to this Zeitgeist, we can begin to locate the points at which Paul's readers would have found it difficult to understand or accept his message without emendation. Undoubtedly, Paul's gospel was a source of joy and hope to many, but the acceptance of his kerygma did not change cherished ideas overnight. Only reluctantly did Paul's converts surrender their view that matter was evil, that salvation was an individual not a corporate experience, that history was circular, or that God could be apprehended directly without the need of historical media like scripture or apostles (1 Cor. 4:1–5). Over these and other habits of being, Paul and his converts often clashed. Once these points of friction are spotted we can better read the letters as real conversations over real concerns.

In the discussion above we have seen important elements of the social, cultural, and spiritual environment inhabited by Paul and his churches. Their Greek Bible inevitably contained Hellenistic idioms. The mythology embedded in that language shaped their understanding of the human condition and of the Christian gospel. For that reason, in their dynamic interaction with a rich, Hellenistic cultural legacy Paul's letters offered flashes of insight that generated new symbols, inspired new visions of the present and the future, destabilized patterns of religiosity that were taken for granted, and infused existing structures with ferment and even protest. This dynamic interaction was profoundly influenced by Paul's Hellenistic Jewish home environment of his formative years. To that consideration we now turn.

PAUL'S JEWISH ENVIRONMENT

Paul's letters contain an amalgam of Jewish and Hellenistic influences. That he spent his formative years in a bustling, cosmopolitan trade center with an energetic Stoic school, that his first language was Greek, that his Bible was the Septuagint—these seem clear. It is hardly surprising, therefore, that traces of that Hellenistic influence are recognizable in his letters. But was that Hellenistic influence dominant? John Knox was so firmly convinced of the dominance of that Hellenism on Paul's thought that he wondered if Paul ever did study in Jerusalem under the great Rabbi Gamaliel II as Acts claims (22:3).[51] But given the pervasive reach of Hellenistic culture and that there was no unhellenized Judaism in the first century, there is no need to know (if ever we could know) whether Hellenism or Judaism dominated Paul's thought. Given the reach of Hellenistic culture in Paul's day even into Jerusalem, the dichotomy is false. What is clear, however, is that Paul skillfully appropriated literary forms and devices, expressions, methods of rhetorical argumentation, and concepts whose genealogy was Hellenistic. The special language and outlook of his Greek Bible, the creeds, hymns, and language of the Hellenistic church and/or the Diaspora synagogue, as well as a host of influences from the culture at large, all informed Paul's thought to a significant degree. Yet, in spite of his openness to the Hellenistic world, Paul was proud of and loyal to his Israelite heritage, and that heritage shaped his identity in crucial ways. Paul's letters show that he vigorously claimed a location in that heritage.

Paul the Pharisee

In Philippians 3:5–6 Paul refers to himself as "circumcised on the eighth day, of the people Israel, of the tribe of Benjamin, a Hebrew born of Hebrews; as to the law, a Pharisee; . . . as to righteousness under the law, blameless." Acts also attests to Paul's Pharisaism. Going beyond what Paul himself reported in his letters, Luke's Acts suggests that Paul remained a loyal Pharisee until his death. Given the unflattering picture of the Pharisees in the Gospels, Luke's positive assessment of Paul's Pharisaism may surprise many.[52] But the harsh polemic against the Pharisees in Matthew reflects the struggle between church and synagogue in a later period and should not be read as an objective description of the Pharisees of Jesus' time. Much work has been done in recent years on the nature of first-century Pharisaism, and a brief consideration of some of that work will help us better understand Paul.

Even though the portrait of the Pharisees painted by the Gospel writers distorts historical reality, much that is historically reliable can be gleaned from the Gospels. From them we learn about the Pharisaic emphasis on ritualistic purity. Careful to eat the right kind of foods, to purify (not merely wash) vessels used in food preparation, and to exclude the unclean (such as tax collectors and prostitutes) from table fellowship, the Pharisees obviously treated all of life as a ritual. Unlike the priests, who took the laws in Leviticus relating to sacrifice, eating temple food, and cultic preparation to apply only to the temple itself and its worship, for the Pharisees the "setting for law observance was the field and the kitchen, the bed and the street."[53] Taking quite literally the command in Exodus 19:6 to be a "kingdom of priests," the Pharisees attempted to act as if all of life was a temple service.

This preoccupation with ritual purity noted in the Gospels was an important though single dimension of Pharisaism. Other aspects of this movement occur in the writings of Josephus, a first-century Jewish author. In his history of the Jewish War (66–70 CE), Josephus says: "The Pharisees, who are considered the most accurate interpreters of the laws, . . . hold the position of the leading sect, attribute everything to fate and to God; they hold that to act rightly or otherwise rests, indeed, for the most part with men, but that in each action Fate cooperates. Every soul, they maintain, is imperishable, but the soul of the good alone passes into another body, while the souls of the wicked suffer eternal punishment."[54]

This "leading sect," we are here told, affirmed a classic paradox—belief in divine predestination (Fate) and the demand for responsible human behavior. Moreover, the value of every soul was linked with the belief in the resurrection of the righteous, which is to occur at the grand, final assize when God will vindicate the pious and punish the wicked. Here Josephus notes the Pharisees' accurate interpretation of the law; elsewhere he admires their simple lifestyle, their repudiation of luxury, and the "respect and deference" that they show to their elders and their teachings. They, unlike the Essenes, live among the townfolk and are intensely involved in the workaday world.[55] In the respect they pay to the traditions of the elders and in their acceptance of the concept of the resurrection, whose origin was probably as late as 165 BCE, Pharisaism displayed an openness to innovation that was remarkable.

While Jacob Neusner argues that the Pharisaism of Paul's day was concerned primarily with ritualistic purity and, therefore, was apolitical, Ellis

Rivkin objects that first-century Pharisaism was revolutionary and concerned with issues ranging far beyond ritual cleanness.[56] As scholars devoted to the study of both the oral and the written law, the Pharisees gradually replaced the priestly class as authoritative interpreters of the law and gained sufficient power to impose their rulings on the society at large. As the dominant political and religious force in Israel, the Pharisees were in a position not only to interpret but also to promulgate law. According to Rivkin, the Pauline letters and the Gospels corroborate this understanding of Pharisaism. Paul speaks of his Pharisaic past when he was "far more zealous . . . for the traditions of my ancestors" (Gal. 1:14). The Gospels disparage the Pharisees as those who "sit on Moses' seat" in positions of authority (Matt. 23:2), and recognize the deference shown them in the marketplace and the honor they enjoy in the synagogue, while Acts notes the special authority they have to persecute Christians (Acts 9:1–2).

While Rivkin's critique of Neusner is telling, his thesis suffers from its narrow dependence on Josephus and from its reading of Gospel texts written after the destruction of Jerusalem as if their portrait of the Pharisees applied equally to the prewar period (i.e., before 66 CE). Although flawed in this regard, it is entirely possible that Rivkin's work will require some expansion of Neusner's rather narrow definition of Pharisaism to include concerns that go considerably beyond ritualistic purity. In such a case, Paul's harassment of messianists may have been motivated if not authorized by his Pharisaism. But can we go further? Did Paul continue in the way of the Pharisees after his apostolic call? Luke tells us that he did. In Acts 25:8 Luke has Paul say in his own defense, "I have in no way committed an offense *against the law of the Jews*, or against the temple, or against the emperor" (italics added). In his speech before Agrippa, Paul says, "I have belonged to the strictest sect of our religion and lived as a Pharisee" (Acts 26:5).

Certainly, Paul's letters do bear traces of a Pharisaic inclination. His view that the resurrection of the just comes at the end of the age, his concept of predestination linked with an emphasis on human responsibility, his liberal estimate of what was scriptural, his involvement in the workaday world, his spiritualization of sacrificial language (cf. Rom. 12:1–2), and his method of scriptural exegesis all seem to reflect his Pharisaism. But there is evidence on the other side as well. His free association with Gentiles, his casual attitude toward the laws of purity, the role the Messiah played in his thought, and his interpretation of the law all divide him from the Pharisaism we later see. Certainly by the strictest interpretation Paul compromised his Pharisaic tradition, but to say that he rejected it outright is going too far. It is more accurate to say that the letters offer a fresh and sometimes radical appraisal of those traditions in light of his conviction that the crucified Jesus was the Messiah whose resurrection set in motion the final eschatological breakthrough.

Paul's Jewish Methods of Scripture Interpretation

The apostle's ties to his Jewish heritage are also evident in his methods of scripture interpretation. First, his scriptures were exclusively and emphatically Jewish. As we noted above, Greek ideas did intrude through the Greek translation of the scriptures, but the story of the Jewish people told in the scriptures is fundamentally a Jewish story about God's election and the responsibilities that went with the gracious offer of a covenant. In the full light of that grand narrative that Paul inhabited, he crafted his gospel. His various methods of interpretation aimed to show how Messiah Jesus, crucified and risen, fulfilled the hopes and expectations of that script. Many of those methods Paul probably learned from his Jewish teachers. His use of midrash, his appeal to Jewish legend, his use of scripture to interpret scripture, his collection of random texts clustered around a common theme, his reading of the prophets as seers, his reasoning from the lesser to the greater, and his attempt to draw analogies through link words are all methods of exegesis that Paul shared with the learned interpreters of his day.

One important method of scripture interpretation used by the rabbis was midrash, an exegesis that sought to find in a text its inner significance, to discover principles or laws for living, or to reveal the authentic or true. Note Paul's use of midrash in 1 Corinthians 10. Drawing on Israel's wilderness experience he found instruction for a church in which some viewed the sacraments as a magical guarantee of salvation. Paul cautioned against such overconfidence, reminding his readers that their life as a sacramental community was prefigured in Israel's wilderness wandering. Israel too ate sacred food (manna) and Israel also drank the supernatural drink (water from the rock). Yet Paul warned that Israel's status as a sacramental community in no way exempted them from accountability. Their murmuring brought death, and their idolatry brought the fall of more than twenty thousand in a single day. Thus Paul drew a lesson from the biblical account of Israel's wilderness experience for a wayward church that took salvation (and God) for granted.

Other images Paul used came from legend related to biblical traditions but not specifically mentioned in his scriptures. In Galatians 3:19 he spoke of the role the angels played in the giving of the law. In 1 Corinthians 10:4 he referred to the moving rock in the wilderness, and in 1 Corinthians 11:10 he noted a command given to women to cover their heads in the service of worship "because of the angels." At the very least Paul's willingness to cite these legendary materials that go beyond the biblical story shows how broad his understanding of the sacred tradition was.

In 2 Corinthians 3:6–17 Paul used one text to interpret another. First he contrasted the covenant made with Moses with that forecast by Jeremiah:

"The letter kills, but the Spirit gives life" (3:6). Then he told the old, familiar story of the giving of the law to Moses "chiseled in letters on stone tablets" (2 Cor. 3:7). Because the brilliant splendor of that event was reflected by the face of Moses, he veiled his face to shield the people from the blinding light. Paul suggested in allegorical fashion that like Moses' face, the true meaning of the Torah, which was veiled up to now, has been revealed. The glory associated with the giving of the law, as great as it was, was surpassed as sun to moon by that of the Christ event. Paul then concluded with a quotation from Isaiah that he believed forged a link between this glory of Christ and the outpouring of the Spirit to come at the end time: "Now the Lord is the Spirit, and where the Spirit of the Lord is, there is freedom" (2 Cor. 3:17).

Another instance of the interpretation of one passage by another may be seen in Galatians 3. While discussing the promise given to Abraham, Paul quoted Genesis 12:3: "In you shall all the peoples of the earth be blessed" (LXX). In another version of the same account the expression "in you" he changed to "in your seed [or offspring]" (Gen. 22:18). After concluding that the phrase "in your seed" referred to the statement "in you," Paul made a rather dramatic interpretive leap. Reading "seed" as singular, he took this key word to refer not to Abraham's many descendants but to one descendant (or "seed"), that is, to Christ. Thus Paul interpreted Genesis 12:3 by way of Genesis 22:18 to mean, "All the Gentiles shall be blessed in you [Christ]" (Gal. 3:8).

While such exegesis may strike the modern reader as highly arbitrary or even historically false, Joachim Jeremias was correct when he wrote that Paul here used a method of scripture interpretation commonly utilized by the rabbis.[57] Such methods, however arbitrary they may appear to moderns, linked the messianic movement that Paul knew with Israel's story in a dynamic and highly imaginative way.

Paul's collection of random texts around a common theme echoes a method of exegesis commonly used in Jewish circles. In Romans 3:10b–18, for example, are six quotations threaded together like beads on a string. Held together by a theme that Paul wanted to emphasize, these citations from assorted biblical texts address a common topic—the universality of human sin. The cumulative effect of such clustering was to underscore a central point of the first three chapters of Romans, namely, to establish beyond excuse or special pleading the need of all people, Jew and Gentile alike, for the righteous work of God in Christ.

In another instance, Paul read the prophets as if they were forecasters of the eschatological future of the apostle's present. Paul either alluded to or quoted the prophets more than forty times,[58] and Paul understood almost all of those references to refer to his present and near future. The prophets, he believed, predicted the dawning eschatological age (Rom. 1:2; 3:21; 16:26, etc.). They foresaw the rejection of Jesus by most of the Jews and the inclusion of the Gentiles now taking place (Rom. 3:29; 9:25–26; 10:20; 15:12). They anticipated the laying of the new cornerstone in Israel in the person of Jesus (Rom. 9:33) and they saw the covenant Paul believed was being established in his own day (2 Cor. 3:14–18). They spoke of the present manifestation of God's righteousness (Rom. 3:21), and their rejection foreshadowed the death of Jesus (1 Thess. 2:15). This use of the prophets by Paul reveals his preoccupation with the "end time," and this preoccupation colored the way he read all ancient texts. In this respect also his method of exegesis was shared by other Jewish exegetes. The Qumran texts contain the same tendency to read the prophets as seers whose predictions focus on the "day of the Lord." The Qumran sectarians believed that the secrets (Hebrew *razim*) of scripture heretofore unknown were revealed to their leader, the Teacher of Righteousness, and after his death to the members of the community. Selected members of the community studied those texts literally day and night to learn their secrets and like Paul to read themselves into the text. While Paul's focus was different from this form of inspired exegesis, his basic conviction that scripture contained eschatological secrets about the present was the same.

With the benefit of historical criticism we know that the prophets spoke to their own time and their predictions had a limited horizon. Yet to say that Paul and the sectarians of the Dead Sea community were simply mistaken is to impose unfairly our canons of historical-critical interpretation on them. More important than whether they misread scripture is how the sacred texts functioned for them. For Paul the scriptures did more than rehearse a sacred story of a venerable past. They also anticipated a future. This reading of the scriptures of old not only embraced the writer's future, it also established and rehearsed a dynamic relationship between the storied past and the community's present. In this dynamic vision the past provided the key that unlocked the future, and the future provided the optic for viewing the past. Thus the ancient texts were never about a dead past, but about a past always pregnant with meaning for the future. The scriptures served as a powerful force to legitimate the proclamation of the early church and to anchor the gospel in the history of Israel. By attending to the ways the scriptures came to life for Paul and how they functioned in the letters, we should gain a clearer idea not only of how the apostle's argument unfolded but also of how the past remained alive for him.

Jeremias (and Otto Michel before him) found evidence in the letters that the apostle followed the rabbis in other ways.[59] The first rule of Hillel involved the reasoning from the lesser to the greater. Similarly, in Romans 5:15 and 17 Paul tried to show how one person's act can affect human destiny. First, he offered Adam as a negative example. Just as many were partners with Adam in disobedience and died, so also, Paul argued, many may participate in the obedience of the one man Jesus and live. But the comparison, Paul continued, was inapt in that the grace experienced "in Christ" was more efficacious than the power of sin experienced "in Adam." The development of Paul's argument thus moved from the lesser (Adam) to the greater (Christ), and in so doing followed a pattern of argument already practiced by the famous rabbi, Hillel.

The second rule of Hillel followed by Paul, Jeremias tried to show, involved drawing analogies through catchwords. In Romans 4:1–12, where this method is employed, Paul opened with a quotation from Genesis that "Abraham believed [trusted] God, and it was *reckoned* [counted] to him as righteousness" (v. 3, italics added). That Abraham received the promise through grace rather than through works was corroborated, Paul held, by Psalm 32:2, where the psalmist understood forgiveness of sin to mean that "the Lord will not reckon [count] his sin" (AT [author translation]). Finally, we are told that just as righteousness was reckoned (counted) to Abraham because of faith rather than works, so also Gentiles who believe in God because of Christ's faithfulness will be reckoned (counted) as righteous (4:22–23). We see here how Paul used the word "reckon" to link the faith of Abraham ultimately with the inclusion of the Gentiles in the eschatological community. Although the content Paul gave this argument from the lesser to the greater reflected his commitment to Messiah Jesus, the method he used in making his point belongs to the rabbis.

Paul and Jewish Apocalypticism

While recognizing that Paul's views on eschatology completely suffuse his interpretation of scripture, let us pause for a moment to note the relationship of Paul's eschatological outlook to Jewish apocalyptic traditions.[60] Such terms as "wrath" (*orgē*), the "day" (*hēmera*), "death" (*thanatos*)," "righteousness" (*dikaiosynē*), "judgment" (*krisis*), and the distinction between the two ages (*aiōn*) are hardly intelligible apart from their Jewish milieu. And the similarity between Paul and Jewish apocalypticism goes far beyond the colorful terminology they share. Both are dominated by an eager longing for and an earnest expectation of the end time. In both burns the intensity that comes from living on the boundary between two worlds—one dying and the other being born. Both share the link with Israel's past, and both hope for the *imminent* fruition of God's promises. Although Paul's understanding of Jesus as beginning God's future age differs from the ideas in Jewish apocalypticism, the two share a conviction that their generation was to be the last. This heightened awareness of the impending divine denouement influenced everything Paul said to the churches. Everything he enjoined concerning marriage

(1 Cor. 7:26), regarding settling disputes in the church (Rom. 14:10–12), for celebrating the Eucharist (1 Cor. 11:32), as well as concerning the urgency informing his own sense of mission is hardly intelligible apart from Paul's conviction that his was the last generation of humankind.

No discovery has more revolutionized biblical studies than the 1947 find of the Qumran scrolls by Muhammad ed-Dib, a bedouin boy searching for a lost sheep. Stored in jars and hidden in caves on the northwest corner of the Dead Sea in anticipation of the arrival of a Roman legion on the march (c. 68 CE), now after more than 1,800 years the scrolls have emerged to reveal much about the life and religion of an intense apocalyptic sect that had withdrawn from priestly service at the temple in Jerusalem. Convinced that the ruler Jonathan the Maccabee of the Hasmonean ruling family had polluted the temple by taking over the high-priestly office, these rebellious priests abandoned this holy place to follow the injunction of Isaiah 40:3: "In the wilderness prepare the way of the LORD."

Archaeological excavations have shown the Qumran site to be an impressive establishment. Built around a system of reservoirs and canals catching and delivering water for daily needs and ritual bathing, these facilities included a large assembly hall, a scriptorium for transcribing sacred texts, a kitchen, bakery, pantry, watchtower, a kiln for baking pottery, and even a laundry and stable. Scholars judge that at its peak the site may have supported approximately two hundred members. These impressive facilities supported a community that was chiefly (though not exclusively) celibate for almost two hundred years, all the while living in feverish expectancy of God's final visitation.

The apocalyptic tone of their writings is unmistakable, and though there is no evidence for a direct link between the Qumran community and New Testament writings, indirect influence is evident. Like the Qumran community, Paul himself divides humanity into two camps—the children of light and the children of darkness (1 Thess. 5:4). Like the Qumran community, his conviction that his was the last generation of humankind was unshakable. Like the Qumran community, he associated God's righteousness with the redemption of the elect. Like the Qumran community, he discouraged (though he did not forbid) marriage in anticipation of the final eschatological crisis (1 Cor. 7:26, 32–35). Like the Qumran community, he insisted on purity in the community in anticipation of the final judgment (1 Thess. 3:13; 4:7–8). And like the Qumraners, Paul believed the raging cosmic conflict between God and "the ruler of this world" was replicated in microcosm in the life of every believer, and by God's grace the believer could be victorious.

Though abundant precedent exists in Jewish circles for apocalyptic tendencies resembling those of Paul, differences existed as well. Paul and the early church held that in Jesus' death and resurrection the end time had already begun. Whereas the Qumran community retreated to the wilderness to prepare for the end, Paul encouraged no such separation. The priestly community at Qumran expected God to inaugurate a purified cult in Jerusalem, but Paul harbored no such expectation. The members of the Qumran community had fantasies about fighting in God's final battle for control of the world, but no such hope was voiced in the Pauline letters. We see, therefore, that Paul's apocalypticism hardly originated with him or even the church before him but was deeply rooted in the Jewish experience. Yet in important ways his life "in Christ" reshaped the Jewish and Christian apocalyptic myth that he inherited.

In all the ways noted above—his views of the resurrection and predestination, his liberal assessment of what was scriptural, his uses of traditional methods of scriptural interpretation, and his extensive use of imagery from Jewish apocalyptic thought—the Hebrew tradition informed Paul's thought. Hans Joachim Schoeps quite properly stated that Paul's argument is obscure if not altogether incomprehensible apart from its relationship to Old Testament traditions.[61] To this we might add the use of that tradition made by the Jewish interpreters of Paul's day.

In the discussion above we have seen that Paul was deeply influenced by both the Hellenistic and Jewish traditions of his day. Yet this combination of Hellenistic and Jewish elements hardly originated with Paul. It came at least partly prepackaged in the Jewish tradition he knew and the Christian tradition he came to know. In the Asia Minor of Paul's youth the Jews had already accommodated themselves to their Greek environment. Philo notes how they attended the theater, took part in sports, gave their children Greek or Latin names, intermarried with Gentiles, and decorated their tombs with Greek art. This accommodation, however, was an uneasy one fraught with surprise and fear of the loss of identity.

The Jews of the Asia Minor of Paul's youth were well integrated into the community. They were good citizens up to a point. But at that point, where they believed the claims of Gentile society eclipsed those of Torah, community solidarity was reaffirmed, a solidarity firmly rooted in the great scriptures and traditions of Israel. Judging by the archaeological evidence, even Palestinian Judaism had been hellenized to a degree. E. R. Goodenough drew attention to numerous Greek inscriptions found in Jerusalem itself.[62] A Greek word, "Sanhedrin" (*synedrion*), designated the most significant judging body in Palestine, and astonishingly a few Greek manuscripts were found among the scrolls from the Qumran sect. We see, therefore, to quote the revered W. D. Davies, that "the traditional convenient dichotomy between Judaism and Hellenism was largely false. In the fusions of the first century the boundaries between these are now seen to have been very fluid."[63] That hardly means, however, that they were nonexistent.

Using different information, Martin Hengel came to substantially the same conclusion in his well-documented study.[64] Therefore, to attempt to understand Paul exclusively in light of his Hellenistic or his Jewish background is to misunderstand him. For example, Philippians 2:6–11, a pre-Pauline Christian hymn that Paul edits to serve his epistolary interests, offers a smooth blending of these worlds. Whether the background of the hymn is basically Jewish or Hellenistic has been hotly debated. The issue is made more complex by the presence of both Jewish and Hellenistic elements in the hymn. The opening line of the hymn transports the reader into the heavenly realm, the primary abode of Jesus, who, humbling himself, takes the part of a "slave" in human form and descends to earth. Obedient unto death, he is exalted to assume the place he once occupied with God and now will receive the praises of all humankind. The hymn ends with a paean of praise: "At the name of Jesus every knee should bend . . . and every tongue should confess that Jesus Christ is Lord." Scholars have taught us that this closing doxology is an echo of Isaiah 45:23: "To me every knee shall bow, every tongue shall swear." In this echo of Isaiah and probably also in the allusion to the role of the "slave" assumed by Jesus, we have vestiges of the Hebrew scriptural tradition. But in the references to the world above as Jesus' first habitation and the world below as the locus of his ministry, as well as in the descent-ascent motif (i.e., Jesus' coming down to death and ascending to his former home), and in the cosmic lordship bestowed on the glorified Christ to whom all powers "in heaven and on earth and under the earth" (2:10) will do obeisance, we see evidence of Hellenistic influence. We see, therefore, that the riddle of the hymn's background finds its solution in neither the Jewish tradition nor the Hellenistic milieu alone. What we see in this pre-Pauline hymn is a synthesis of Jewish and Hellenistic elements. Traces of a Jewish heritage remain, but these have coalesced with a Hellenistic cosmology (or view of the world) and Jewish soteriology (or understanding of salvation).[65]

Some have claimed to see Hellenistic influence as dominant in Paul's messianism. Others are just as firmly convinced of the overriding importance of Judaism in Paul's thinking. But there is no need to know, if ever we could know, whether either exclusively dominated Paul's thought. What is clear is that he employs certain literary forms and devices, expressions, methods of argumentation, and concepts that come from a Hellenistic tradition. The special language and outlook of his Greek Bible, the creeds, hymns, and language of the Hellenistic church, and/or the synagogue of Diaspora Judaism, as well as a host of influences from the culture at large, all informed Paul's thought to a significant degree. In spite of his openness to the Hellenistic world, Paul's Jewish heritage was a dominant feature of his religious world. Though Paul revalued his Pharisaism, he did not abandon it altogether. His scriptures were

Jewish, and his methods of interpretation were shaped by his Jewish experience. His apocalypticism is understandable only in light of the Jewish apocalyptic thinking of the day. His understandings of history, election, death and resurrection, and the divine vindication of the martyrs are deeply rooted in the sacred story of Israel. So to understand Paul as solely either Jew or Hellenist is to misunderstand him. He was both at once, and his ability to move freely in both worlds ideally equipped him to take a gospel that was fundamentally Jewish and translate it into understandable language for the non-Jew.

But the burden of this translation did not rest on Paul's shoulders alone. Given the presence of Jews in all the major cities of the Mediterranean world (Acts 15:21), we must assume Gentiles learned about Judaism from direct contact with individual Jews and synagogue congregations. Salo Baron's estimate that every tenth Roman was a Jew and that twenty percent of the population of the empire east of Italy was Jewish sounds incredibly high;[66] nevertheless, it is widely granted that the Jewish minority exercised an influence on the Hellenistic world out of all proportion to its size. Paul, for example, can assume that his predominantly Gentile congregations knew about Jewish scripture. It is unlikely that this familiarity with scripture was grounded in Paul's preaching alone. The archaeological evidence suggests that every major city in the Mediterranean world had at least one synagogue. We know of nine synagogues in Rome, and the largest building in first-century Sardis was the synagogue. A post-Pauline synagogue in Corinth was strategically located near the heart of the city. The number, size, and location of these buildings show that the Jewish presence could not be ignored. Moreover, although many Gentile "Godfearers" (sebomenoi) did not convert to Judaism, they attended the synagogue and were strongly attracted. It was not unheard of for such a person to abstain from eating pork, to observe the Sabbath, to study Torah, and to have a son circumcised, while still holding back from full conversion.

Through active but not necessarily organized proselytizing, Jews influenced, if they did not convert, their Gentile neighbors. Baron could be right that Jews wandered from city to city, contending for the loyalty of their hearers, and Matthew seems to allude to this practice in his condemnation of Pharisees who "cross sea and land to make a single convert" (23:15). And considering the vast commerce of the Mediterranean, recognition of the Torah was undoubtedly spread by Jewish merchants.

Alexandria, with a combined population, was "almost as much a city of the Jews as of the Greeks."[67] Philo, a contemporary of Paul, suggests that the knowledge of the law by "one half of the human race" annoyed the other half. Although Philo's statement applies only to Alexandria, it is notable nonetheless, for it shows that the flow of influence from the Hellenistic to the Jewish world was not all one way.

As important as the Hellenistic world and Jewish tradition were in shaping Paul's thinking, the most formative item in Paul's experience was his meeting with the risen Lord (1 Cor. 9:1; 15:8). Scholars have frequently called this Paul's conversion, but over a generation ago Johannes Munck argued that by Paul's own description that meeting resembled less a conversion from the revivalist period than an Old Testament prophetic call. Like Jeremiah of old, Paul said that God "set me apart before I was born" (Gal. 1:15) and described himself as "called . . . , set apart for the gospel of God, which he promised beforehand through his prophets" (Rom. 1:1–2).[68] That Paul viewed himself as a latter-day Jeremiah is unlikely. But it is almost certain that Paul regarded his critical turn as a call, like Jeremiah's or Isaiah's, and not just a psychological change. In the view of some scholars the Acts account of Paul's Damascus road encounter (Acts 9:1–30; 22:3–21; 26:4–20) does denote a sudden conversion experience. Increasingly, however, others caution us against making the views expressed in Acts normative for understanding Paul.[69] Whereas the term "conversion" suggests a radical break with the past, Paul's Damascus experience produced no such repudiation. Although he did turn from persecuting the church to nurturing it, he consistently linked the church (or its gospel) with God's promises to Israel (e.g., Rom. 9:4–5). His conviction that the Messiah had come distinguished Paul from the Jewish majority, but it did not divorce him from his Jewish tradition.

Paul's relationship to Christ was central but it was not exhaustive. Any emphasis on his relationship to Christ that excludes consideration of his Hellenistic and Jewish habitat, or any stress on the habitat to the exclusion of his gospel, distorts our view of Paul and the gospel he preached. It is important, therefore, while reading the letters to remember that Paul was many things at once—a Hebrew of the Hebrews, a Pharisee, a member of the tribe of Benjamin, a Hellenistic Jew, an apostle of Christ, and a missionary to the Gentiles. Though these aspects of his life did not all hold equal place in Paul's theology, each of them contributed something. Alertness to the way these forces work on Paul should give us a fuller appreciation of the range, complexity, richness, and subtlety of his epistles.

2

The Anatomy of the Letters

The earliest writings of the New Testament are the seven undisputed letters of Paul, and no letters have more profoundly influenced Western history than these. These letters offer a window through which we can view at a great distance the conflicted personality of Paul—Paul the sickly, weak apostle and Paul the proud and assertive emissary of Christ, Paul the gentle one and Paul the blustery, threatening presence—and a troubled young church struggling to understand itself as God's elect of the last days even while it was still prone to old habits.

Even a casual glance at these letters reveals that they are real letters dealing with life-or-death matters and not mere abstract dogmatic treatises. Even though in Paul's time there was no postal service available to the public, and even though writing materials were expensive and the delivery of messages uncertain, the Hellenistic period of Paul and his readers was quintessentially the period of the letter. Handbooks on letter writing were circulated, and a whole class of professional scribes sprang up to serve the government bureaucracy, to assist wealthy patrons in need of their reading and writing skills, and to read and write letters for the illiterate. In this period, as during the colonial period in the United States, receiving a letter from families separated by an ocean was a major event. By thus substituting presence for absence the letter bridged the yawning gulf between recipient and sender; it provided a vehicle for instruction and exhortation, for praise and blame; it offered a means of consolation and encouragement, and an instrument for self-defense. It is hardly an accident, therefore, that twenty-one of the twenty-seven books of the New Testament are letters or letter facsimiles. Though letters are common to us, or perhaps becoming uncommon in the computer age, their meaning is often not transparent.

In this chapter we shall examine the anatomy of the letter for intimations the letter structure offers of Paul's intent. Because the letter structure was such an important part of the ancient letter, a comparison of the key elements of the Hellenistic letter with those in Paul's letter to Philemon may be illuminating (see table). So although the anatomy of the Pauline letter may be unfamiliar to us, we are sensitive to the nuances that the structure of letters may carry. Once the letter-writing conventions that Paul used are understood, the alert reader will also find clues to Paul's intent in his creative use of those conventions as well. The discussion below will treat both the form and the function of the main elements in the Pauline letter. Our purpose is to show the working of the separate parts, not to offer an exhaustive discussion of each member. Before turning to our survey of the separate elements of the letter, let us display a typical Greek papyrus letter. From such a model the basic skeleton of the letter will become clear, and we shall better understand how Paul duplicates letter-writing patterns of his own time as well as how he altered them. Sensitivity to the way Paul adopted and altered that structure is valuable for our attempt to understand the letters.

All conversations have a structure. A "Hi" and a "See you later" bracket an exchange between friends. A "Hello" and a "Goodbye" frame a telephone conversation. A "Dear Jane" and a "Yours sincerely" mark the boundaries of a personal letter; even e-mail exchanges often contain some convention of meeting and parting. These conventions, which we take for granted, provide a framework for conversation and serve as doorways through which a graceful entry to or smooth exit from the conversational circle is possible. And however habitual this litany of meeting and parting may be, it is a vital part of sharing another's presence.

All conversations do have a structure, but not all structured conversations are letters. A telegram, an announcement, and a letter all come in envelopes and all are instruments of communication between separated persons, yet the difference between them is instantly apparent to even the most casual reader. It is the structure as well as the content that identifies the letter as a letter. It begins, continues, and ends in a predictable way. We were all taught early that the sender's return address, date, greeting, body, and conclusion form the skeleton of a personal letter and that all letters have this same structure, more or less. But the skeleton of the letter receives the flesh and blood that make it unique through the information shared and concerns expressed by the writer. Thus letters, like people, share a common frame, and yet each is distinct.

Paul's letters, like our own, have a structure. Fortunately, the discovery of thousands of Greek papyrus letters from ancient times has helped us define more precisely the shape of the letter in Paul's day. Study of those papyri has identified the parts of the ancient letter, as well as the function of each part.[1]

We now know that the use of the letter-writing conventions of his time was just as natural (or even unconscious) for Paul as for us. But his use of those conventions was hardly mechanical, for Paul, like writers today, altered the traditional epistolary forms to suit his own purposes. And it is the alterations he made that tell us most about Paul's self-understanding, his intentions, and his theology.

However complex such an analysis may sound, each reader will recall how carefully he or she pondered the structure of an important letter. The letter from a boyfriend, for example, may begin "Dear Sue," which in and of itself may seem insignificant. But suppose the previous letter began "Dearest." Then the form of the greeting may raise a host of questions: "Is he worried and distracted?" "Is he losing interest?" "Is there another?" "Is he taking me for granted?" And on and on Sue goes, combing the letter looking for clues in the structure of the letter to the writer's deep and true intent. So although the anatomy of the Pauline letter may be unfamiliar, we are sensitive to the nuances that the structure encodes. Once the letter-writing conventions of Paul are understood, clues to his intent and creative use of those conventions will become more apparent.

The discussion below will treat both the form and the function of the main elements in the Pauline letters. Our purpose is to show the working of the separate parts, not to offer an exhaustive treatment of each member. Before turning to our survey of the separate elements of the letter, let us display a typical Greek papyrus letter. From such a model the basic skeleton of the letter will become clear, and we shall better understand how Paul duplicates letter-writing patterns of his own time as well as how he alters them.

Irenaeus to Apollinarius his dearest brother	SALUTATION
many greetings. I pray continually for your	PRAYER
health, and I myself am well. I wish you to	
know that I reached land on the sixth of the	
month Epeiph and we unloaded our cargo	BODY
on the eighteenth of the same month. I went	
up to Rome on the twenty-fifth of the same	
month and the place welcomed us as the	
god willed, and we are daily expecting our	
discharge, it so being that up till today	
nobody in the corn fleet has been released.	
Many salutations to your wife and to	CONCLUSION
Serenus and to all who love	(Greetings, final wish,
you, each by name. Goodbye. Mesore 9[2]	date)

A comparison of the key elements in this letter with those in Paul's shortest letter, Philemon (RSV) may be illuminating (see table, p. 62).

	Papyrus Letter	Pauline Letter
I. *Salutation*		
A. Sender	Irenaeus	Paul, a prisoner for Christ Jesus, and Timothy our brother,
B. Recipient	to Apollonarius his dearest brother	To Philemon our beloved fellow worker and Apphia our sister and Archippus our fellow soldier, and the church in your house:
C. Greeting	many greetings	Grace to you and peace from God our Father and the Lord Jesus Christ.
II. *Thanksgiving* (Prayer)	I pray continually for your health and I myself am well	I thank my God always when I remember you in my prayers
III. *Body*	[Information about his arrival on the grain boat from Egypt]	[Discussion of his return of Onesimus the slave]
IV. *Closing commands*	[absent here but present elsewhere]	receive him. . . . charge my account. . . . Refresh my heart in Christ. . . . Prepare a guest room for me. . . .
V. *Conclusion*		
A. Peace Wish	[absent]	[absent here but present elsewhere]
B. Greetings	Many salutations to your wife and to Serenus and to all who love you, each by name.	Epaphras, my fellow prisoner in Christ Jesus, sends greetings to you, and so do Mark, Aristarchus, Demas, and Luke, my fellow workers.
C. Kiss	[absent]	[absent but present elsewhere]
D. Close	Goodbye.	The grace of the Lord Jesus Christ be with your spirit.

Although we can draw no firm conclusions from a comparison of only two letters, the parallels are obvious. Other comparisons would yield similar results. It is evident, however, that Paul's relationship to Christ dictated some change of emphasis. The sender is described as a "prisoner for Christ Jesus," and the close goes beyond "Goodbye" to place both Paul's addressees and himself in the presence of "Jesus Christ." Other similarities and differences will become obvious in our discussion below of the anatomy of the Pauline letter. We shall now take each of the parts in order of appearance.

THE SALUTATION

The salutation is one of the most stable elements in the ancient letter. The form is rather precise. Unlike our modern letter, the salutation includes the names of both sender and recipient, as well as a greeting. In spite of the highly stereo-typed nature of the letter opening, it remained pliable in the hands of Paul. In Philemon, Romans, and Galatians we will see how Paul molds the salutation to his purposes in the letter as a whole. In Philemon Paul addressed the master of Onesimus, a runaway slave who had sought refuge with Paul. Through Paul, who was in prison at the time, Onesimus was converted (v. 10), thus setting the stage for the letter. In his letter Paul reminded Philemon that his apostolic mission gave him (Paul) a prior claim on Onesimus. Moreover, while he was in prison he needed the slave's assistance. Nevertheless, Paul reported that he was returning Onesimus with the request that he be treated "like a brother." It is interesting that as early as the salutation Paul identifies himself as "a pris-oner for Christ Jesus." Thus the condition central to Paul's plea for leniency to Onesimus (the condition of bondage) surfaces in the opening line of the letter.

In Romans we see Paul's most original adaptation of the conventional let-ter opening. Writing to a church that he had neither founded nor visited, Paul was eager to establish the "orthodoxy"[3] of his gospel and the legitimacy of his claim to be an apostle. In some quarters Paul was looked upon as a theological maverick, an imposter, and an interloper (if not a troublemaker) in the apos-tolic circle. It is quite likely that Paul's awareness of his notoriety inspired the baroque formulation in Romans 1:1–7. The salutation found there includes both a summary of Paul's gospel and a definition of his apostolic mission.

The message that he proclaimed, Paul wrote, was no dangerous innovation but derived from the promises that God made "through his prophets in the holy scriptures" (Rom. 1:2). Drawing on traditional formulations, Paul sum-marized his gospel for all to judge. He wrote of Jesus' descent from David, God's designation of Jesus as "Son of God" through the resurrection, and his own appointment as apostle to the Gentiles by the risen Christ (1:3–6). We see, therefore, how as early as the salutation Paul defended his apostleship by relating it back to God and thus establishing his right to be heard. By insert-ing this traditional material into the salutation he hoped to refute the slan-derous rumors that he was a dangerous innovator and an apostle of discord unworthy of their trust. By showing the integral place of his mission in God's plan of history, Paul put forward a strong claim for the support of the Roman church for his mission to Spain.

The salutation in Galatians, likewise, shows how brilliantly Paul bent ste-reotypical conventions to his use, and thus offered a clue to the purpose of his letters. In 1:1 Paul referred to himself as "an apostle sent neither by human commission nor from human authorities, but through Jesus Christ and God the Father, who raised him from the dead."

With the formalities of the letter opening out of the way, Paul plunged into the body of the letter. What had been hinted at in the salutation (and in the expression of astonishment that displaced the thanksgiving) now received careful and prolonged treatment. In Galatians 1:10 Paul began a vigorous defense of his apostleship that stretches through chapter 2. He lashed out at those who sought to discredit his apostleship and who were trying to discredit his gospel. By asserting that his gospel was "not of human origin" (an assertion that would make no sense were he not so charged) and that he did not "receive it from a human source" (1:11–12), Paul sought to establish his independence of the Jerusalem circle and to defend the authenticity of his message. It is possible, if not likely, that the young Galatian church saw in Peter, James, John, and others a direct link to Jesus that Paul could not claim. Paul had received his gospel secondhand from human agents, with the result that the Jerusalem gospel and practice offered a powerful rejoinder to Paul's claim to legitimacy. So even in the salutation, Paul tried to establish the integrity of his apostolic credentials and the authority of his gospel. Once again we see him altering a highly stereotyped form to address the specific needs of his readers.

THE THANKSGIVING

More than any other secondary work, Paul Schubert's epochal *Form and Function of the Pauline Thanksgivings*[4] stimulated an interest in the form and function of the various parts in the Pauline letters. Although Schubert's thesis has been refined, his basic hypothesis is still intact: the thanksgiving is a formal element of most Pauline letters, and it terminates the letter opening, signals the basic intent of the letter, and may serve as an outline of the major topics to be considered in the body of the letter.[5] Coming immediately after the salutation, the thanksgiving appears in all of Paul's letters except Galatians, where an expression of astonishment appears instead (Gal. 1:6). In each case Paul brings into view the situation of the recipients.

In 1 Corinthians 1:4–9, for example, Paul linked references to the charismatic speech and knowledge of the Corinthian converts to an allusion to the future "day of our Lord Jesus Christ." A study of 1 Corinthians will show that Paul here signaled to the reader the basic concern of the letter. Scholars have long noted that the Corinthian preoccupation with "wisdom" (1:18–4:21) and charismatic speech (chaps. 12–14) sprang from a religious enthusiasm that claimed salvation in this world. Paul's reference in the thanksgiving to the future "day of our Lord Jesus," therefore, may indicate his resolve to adjust the eschatological perspective of his Corinthian converts. For Paul's emphasis on a future "day of the Lord" should qualify the religious puffery of those who claimed a salvific immediacy already in the here and now.

The thanksgiving in 2 Corinthians 1:3–7 functions like that in 1 Corinthians 1:4–9 in that it offers a preview of one major emphasis that appears in the body of the letter.[6] Paul alluded to the abundance of his sufferings through which he participated in the sufferings of Christ. He then invited his addressees to share also in "our sufferings" so that they might also share in "our comfort." Against those who sought to validate their claims with visions, mighty works, prodigies of the Spirit, charismatic eloquence, and exegetical superiority, Paul exalted his imprisonments, beatings, shipwrecks, and other afflictions not as signs of weakness but as signifiers of divine power (2 Cor. 11:20–12:10). What his adversaries took to be the "stench of death" raised by these signs of physical vulnerability and apostolic mendacity, Paul instead interpreted as the "aroma of Christ" (2 Cor. 2:14–17). In 2 Corinthians 6:3–10 Paul again defined his suffering, persecution, and poverty as an optic through which the power of God was manifested. As a participant in the sufferings of Christ, he found legitimacy for a ministry under attack (see 7:5–12). In 2 Corinthians, therefore, the thanksgiving offered a sober reflection on a troubled relationship between Paul and his converts and serves as a window onto the broad landscape treated in this anthology of letter fragments.

An additional word is necessary. James M. Robinson has shown that in his thanksgivings Paul is not mechanically following a fixed epistolary form.[7] Rather, the apostle grafted onto this traditional epistolary form materials from a liturgical tradition. Thus he has created a hybrid form in the thanksgiving in 2 Corinthians 1:3 that sounds a liturgical note: "Blessed be the God and Father of our Lord Jesus Christ." We should be aware that Paul did not slavishly follow a precut pattern but created his own. Moreover, we should not assume that this was a conscious, manipulative exercise on Paul's part, anymore than our own use and modification of the letter-writing conventions of today for e-mail are crassly self-conscious. As hinted at in the previous paragraph this thanksgiving reflected on the recent troubled relationship with the Corinthians, rather than predicating the themes to emerge in the broader collection. If Robinson's treatment were corrected to account for the place it holds on the heels of the angry Pauline "letter of tears" immediately preceding (2 Cor. 10:1–13:10), then it would have accounted for the softer touch of this "thanksgiving" (see discussion below).

THE BODY OF THE LETTER

After passing through the thanksgiving, the reader enters a vast and varied conversational world. The landscape is as broad as Paul's theological understanding and as diverse as the needs of the churches. But in spite of the range and variety in the body of the letters, there is a pattern that reoccurs throughout. A request or disclosure formula (e.g., "I beseech you. . . ." and "I would not have you ignorant . . .") often signals crossing the threshold into the body. The letter ending is usually marked by an announcement of Paul's travel plans and a contemplated visit by the apostle.[8]

Galatians alone lacks any reference to Paul's travel plans. Robert Funk's explanation of this omission is attractive. In Galatians 4:12–20 Funk saw a substitute for the usual reference to an upcoming apostolic visit. There Paul reflected on his previous visit and wished that he could return again (but of course he could not). In the view of Funk: "This is a travelogue in a situation where travel . . . is out of the question, i.e., in a situation where Paul cannot add the promise of an oral word to the written word, he recalls the previous oral word and wishes he might renew it."[9] The function of this travelogue was to reinforce the written word with the promise of an apostolic visit.

Others have noted an autobiographical section, or a report by Paul on his activity, near the beginning of the body in most letters. In Galatians he speaks of his relationship to the Jerusalem church (1:10–2:21). In 2 Corinthians he reports on the hardships he has suffered (1:8–2:13). In Philippians he speaks of his imprisonment (1:12–26), and in 1 Corinthians he recalls his ministry among his addressees (1:10–17). In each case this autobiographical note is fully integrated into his theological argument. The report on his situation is made to impinge directly on the situation of his readers. By reciting the demands made on him as an apostle of Christ, Paul warned his hearers that like demands may be made of them.

We see, therefore, that although the topography of the body of the letter is necessarily less predictable than that of the thanksgiving, there are guideposts to lead the reader through it. Since the body embraces the full range and richness of Paul's theological outlook, we should expect it to offer difficulties, but we should be prepared also for pleasant surprises. Functionally, therefore, the body and thanksgiving of the letter complement each other. As Funk well said: "The thanksgiving looks back . . . on the effects of grace already experienced . . . the body . . . [looks ahead and] calls the readers again into the presence of Christ, that the word of the cross may take effect anew."[10]

PARAENESIS (ETHICAL INSTRUCTION AND EXHORTATION)

At least three different types of ethical instruction appear in Paul's letters. First, there is the cluster of unrelated moral maxims, strung together like beads on a string. Often there is little to hold them together except their similarity of form, or perhaps a catchword carried over from one to another. A good example of this type of material appears in Romans 12:9–13:

> Let love be genuine; hate what is evil, hold fast to what is good; love one another with mutual affection; outdo one another in showing honor. Do not lag in zeal, be ardent in spirit, serve the Lord. Rejoice in hope, be patient in suffering, persevere in prayer. Contribute to the needs of the saints; extend hospitality to strangers.

In this short paragraph thirteen different injunctions are given and at least twelve different topics are mentioned, no one of which has much to do with any other. We shall continue this discussion in the next chapter, but it is necessary here to say that Paul was probably dependent on tradition for this type of material.[11]

Second, scattered throughout Paul's letters we find lists of virtues and vices in which both Jewish and Hellenistic traditions merge.[12] These lists, like those of the injunctions above, contain items that have only the most casual relationship to each other. In Galatians 5:19–23, for example, we find such a catalog:

> Now the works of the flesh are obvious: fornication, impurity, licentiousness, idolatry, sorcery, enmities, strife, jealousy, anger, quarrels, dissensions, factions, envy, drunkenness, carousing, and things like these. . . .
> By contrast, the fruit of the Spirit is love, joy, peace, patience, kindness, generosity, faithfulness, gentleness, and self-control.

The third type of paraenetic material is a prolonged exhortation or homily on a particular topic.[13] Strongly reminiscent of an oral situation, these materials are highly personal and supportive (e.g., "I became your father," 1 Cor. 4:15). Pastoral in tone, such exhortations appear frequently throughout Paul's letters. The bulk of 1 Corinthians (chaps. 5–15) probably belongs to this type of material. Paul there deals one by one with problems brought to him in an oral report by Chloe's people and by a letter from the church.

First Thessalonians 4:13–18 and 5:1–11 will illustrate this paraenetic style. Both sections treat topics of concern to Paul's readers—the resurrection of the dead and the unpredictable suddenness of the end. And both close with an exhortation ("Therefore encourage one another with these words," 4:18; and "Therefore encourage one another and build up each other," 5:11).

For our purposes it is important to distinguish individual paraenetic units from sections of paraenetic material. Individual units (including types 1 and 2) appear haphazardly throughout all of the letters. But the paraenetic section knits together the body of the letter and stretches to the conclusion

(Galatians, Romans, 1 Thessalonians, and possibly 1 Corinthians and Philippians). Although some of this instruction or exhortation has little specific relevance for any particular church, Paul often tailors general ethical traditions to fit particular needs. General admonitions to refrain from vengeful acts, to do good to outsiders, to obey the leaders, and to build up the church occur with some regularity in the epistles. But these act not as a rule book for solving every problem; rather, they are focal instances of how the gospel is to take effect. Many sources inform this material, and by no means does Paul proclaim it as original; but his weaving of it shows a master's hand at turning general moral saws to specific and concrete account.

CONCLUSION OF THE LETTER

Unlike the opening of the letter, the conclusion has received scant attention. Increasingly, however, scholars have discovered clues in it important to the letter's agenda.[14] Analysis of the conclusion has isolated its various parts with some precision, and in the light of such analysis we can see the particular use of Paul's endings.

Like the letter opening, the conclusion is a stable element in the epistolary structure. We usually find there a peace wish, greetings, and a benediction (or grace). Occasionally, we see an apostolic pronouncement. And generally, all of this is preceded by a battery of last-minute instructions. Bridging the gap between the instruction cluster and the conclusion is the peace wish. Once Paul crosses this threshold with his readers, he has committed himself to parting, and he soon brings the conversation to a close.

The peace wish, of course, did not originate with Paul. The shalom (peace) greeting of the Semitic letter was probably familiar. Used both in meeting and parting, the word "peace" expressed a desire for the total well-being (bodily health as well as inner peace) of the person. Reminiscent of the coveted "blessing" of the Hebrew scriptures, the shalom greeting often went beyond the simple exchange of amenities to a joint affirmation of faith. This peace wish occupied the ultimate position in the conclusion of the Semitic letter. In this regard it corresponded to the "goodbye" (errōso) of the Greek letter to the final wish for the well-being of the recipient (e.g., "you will do me a favor by taking care of your bodily health"). The peace wish for Paul, however, occupies a penultimate position in the conclusion.

In the letter opening Paul usually greets his converts with a grace, putting both parties in the presence of God (e.g., "Grace to you and peace from God our Father and the Lord Jesus Christ"). In the conclusion, greetings are sandwiched between the peace wish and the grace, and thus the closing peace wish echoes the opening greeting and brings us full circle: (opening) grace and peace; (closing) peace and grace. Before parting, however, Paul once again places himself and his hearers in the presence of God, and the note of the peace wish extends God's presence beyond this meeting point of the present letter and the future divine saving presence ("live in peace; and the God of love and peace *will be with you*," 2 Cor. 13:11, italics added). So although the peace wish is part of the letter's conclusion, Paul's mind opens out onto awesome possibilities ahead.

For Paul, however, the peace wish was more than a priestly benediction. It also gathered unto itself the major concerns of the letter. In 1 Thessalonians, for example, Paul addressed a demoralized and distressed church. Some members had died before the expected return (*parousia*) of Christ; others fixed on the imminent end had fallen into sloth (4:9–11). So the peace wish of 1 Thessalonians reiterates Paul's major concerns. By declaring that God will preserve the believer's "spirit and soul and body" blameless at the end, it affirmed a future that some had come to doubt and others mistakenly already claimed in the present. Thus Paul bent a stereotypical form to his own theological ends.

Occasionally a prayer request ("Beloved, pray for us," 1 Thess. 5:25) stands adjacent to the peace wish. Although it has no exact parallel in the papyrus letters, it may have its counterpart in the assurance of remembrance in the letter opening and in the closing request to keep the writer in mind. The Hellenistic letter often opened with the assurance "I pray for your health" and concluded by asking, in turn, for the recipient's prayerful thoughts. One writer, for example, complaining that he is having difficulty navigating the river past the Antaeopolite nome, requested prayers on his behalf: "Remember the night-festival of Isis at the Serapeum."[15] Likewise, at the beginning of 1 Thessalonians Paul includes the addressees in his prayers (1:2), and before closing he asks his addressees to include him in theirs (5:25; see also Rom. 1:9 and 15:30). By such usage, Paul models a vital reciprocity of life in the family of God. In the opening announcement of his prayer for them and in the closing request for their prayer, he demonstrates a corporate rhythm of giving and receiving. Paul and his readers share a world.

Following the peace wish and prayer request, the impending separation between Paul and his readers becomes more and more prominent.[16] The closing greeting from Paul and his coworkers and the command to greet one another signal the imminent end of the epistolary meeting. Even where it is not explicitly stated, one may assume that this greeting will be conveyed by the kiss. Some view this kiss as a prelude to the celebration of the Eucharist. Although Paul's letters were read to the gathered church, and might introduce a celebration of the holy meal, there is little internal evidence to support the view that such was the normal procedure. Rather than a liturgical gesture,[17] the kiss functioned as a greeting, which Paul harnessed to serve his epistolary interests. Through the command "greet one another with a holy kiss" Paul reaffirmed the relationship created by Christ between himself and his spiritual family, and also between the members of the congregation themselves (1 Thess. 5:26).[18]

The benediction, "the grace of our Lord Jesus Christ be with you," is the most stable of the concluding elements. Appearing in every complete letter, this closing formula varies little. Here again Paul has accommodated an epistolary convention to his Christian perspective (e.g., "The grace *of the Lord Jesus* be with you," 1 Cor. 16:23, italics added). Occasionally, however, a solemn warning or sober adjuration precedes the benediction. The tone of 1 Corinthians 16:22 is especially threatening: "Let anyone be accursed [*anathema*] who has no love for the Lord." In the other letters similar adjurations appear in the same position (1 Thess. 5:27 and Gal. 6:17). It is improbable that the Corinthian admonition is a eucharistic formula that aims to exclude unworthy or unbaptized persons from the Lord's Table. More likely the Corinthian command is a decisive reminder of the central exhortation of the letter. The warning includes those who curse Jesus (1 Cor. 12:3), those who hurt a brother through arrogant use of their charisma, and those who profane the body of Christ. In this pronouncement Paul addresses the total epistolary situation in which the loveless behavior of some believers threatens to destroy the church.

Galatians 6:17 contains another apostolic warning: "Let no one make trouble for me; for I carry the marks of Jesus on my body." It is possible that Paul intended to draw an unfavorable comparison between the "good showing in the flesh" (i.e., circumcision) of his addressees and the "marks" of Jesus (scars) that have been inflicted on his body by beatings, shipwreck, and other causes. Paul apparently understands his own suffering as a replication of Jesus'; consequently, to trouble the apostle, the Lord's representative, is to injure the Lord himself. These adjurations grate against modern sensibilities. They sound mean and vindictive. Yet they are understandable in terms of Paul's sense of his mission. Thus Paul set himself in the tradition of the prophets of old commissioned to speak the word of Yahweh for judgment and healing.

Sometimes, of course, the line blurred between the apostle's words and those of God. Believing himself appointed as an apostle of the risen Christ, Paul re-presented Christ to his hearers for judgment and healing; and thus, in his view, the words he spoke carried authority of the one who sent him. Evidently Paul viewed the letter as an instrument of his apostleship. Thus it assumed an official quality beyond the usual correspondence between friends. The letter, serving as an extension of Paul's apostolic presence, placed the community in the Lord's presence, with everything such status promised and demanded. So although Paul's letters are highly personal and at times deeply moving, we fail to appreciate their scope and power if we ignore their apostolic character. And that character set Paul's letters apart from the papyrus model. Paul's letters are suffused with a strong theological emphasis quite unlike that of the papyrus letters. Moreover, the papyrus letters concern themselves primarily with daily concerns whereas the Pauline letters are informed by a strong ideological tendency. These differences led Klaus Berger, a noted German New Testament scholar, to assert that the letters of Cynic philosophers resemble the Pauline letters.[19] In the way they exhorted students to avoid any pleasure that fostered injustice, in the way they promoted asceticism, or provided a philosophical justification for begging, Berger saw a family resemblance to the Pauline letters.[20]

The Cynic letters to which Berger appeals, however, have little in common with Paul's letters. Almost all of them are pseudonymous, some of them written over a century after the death of the author to whom they are attributed. The letters themselves are more like diatribes or treatises on a given topic than an intimate conversation between two separated parties. And where the formulaic letter closing in Paul's letters is developed to reflect Paul's religious relationship with his addressees, the closing of the Cynic letters is often missing altogether, or contains only a few words. It is more likely that Paul's style is influenced not only by the form of the stereotypical papyrus letter, but also by rhetorical strategies of persuasion, consolation, comfort, admonition, and argumentation that were popular in the Hellenistic world.[21]

While we have fewer than 125 Hebrew and Aramaic letters from this period, that letter tradition also contributed something to Paul's style. The peace wish, for example ("Grace to you and peace . . .") that appears in all of Paul's letters (1 Thess. 1:1; Gal. 1:3; 1 Cor. 1:3; 2 Cor. 1:2; Phil. 1:2; and Phlm. 3) had deep roots in a venerable Hebraic tradition. As early as the sixth century BCE, for example, a letter etched on a piece of broken pottery at Lachish in Israel opens with a peace wish: "Thy servant Hoshaiah hath sent to inform my lord Yaosh: May Yahweh cause my lord to hear tidings of peace [shalom]."[22]

We see, therefore, that Paul was influenced by a rich and varied letter-writing heritage. Through the skillful use of his pen and by bending these traditions to serve his ends, Paul so skillfully and creatively used the epistolary tradition so as to have had an enormous impact on the emerging identity of the early church. But Paul's letter-writing skill was aided by the growing importance of the letter in the Hellenistic age. Like immigrants who share their letters from home with the whole community, so also in the first century receiving a letter was a community event. All people—rich and poor, underclass and privileged, patrons and slaves, men and women—experienced the reception of a letter as an exciting event that most often was shared with family, friends, and wider circles. Because they were so precious, because they put them in the presence of the absent ones, because they found in them encouragement, consolation, and instruction, one can easily understand why they were often treasured and kept. So even though the theological depth and practical guidance of Paul's letters played a major role in their collection, preservation, and inclusion in the New Testament canon, the importance of the letters qua letters also made a contribution.

To summarize, we have noted the importance of reading Paul's letters as letters, and we have seen how Paul constrains to his own use the epistolary conventions of his time. We have noticed that Paul's message informs and even transforms his medium. Although the letter was for Paul the most effective means of conversation between separated persons, it was more. It was an extension of his apostleship. A reader of the letters who is aware of the subtle interplay between form (medium), content (message), and agent (apostle) may appreciate more fully the subtlety of Paul's gospel and the influence these letters have had on their readers over the centuries.

Paul founded cells of converts across Asia Minor and into Europe. In his absence they struggled to survive, to understand and apply his gospel, to keep the Christ experience alive, to experiment with the freedom gained, to meet life's daily challenges, to face recurring doubts about the sufficiency of Paul's gospel, to test the truth of his apostolic claim, and to assess his fundamental honesty. Paul's letters bridged the temporal distance between him and his converts, placed him in their and them in his presence (Gal. 4:13–14; 1 Thess. 2:1–11; 3:3–4), and recalled their shared experience (Rom. 1:8–9; 1 Cor. 5:1–5; Phil. 1:3–8; 1 Thess. 1:2; 1 Cor. 1:4–6). The letters, however, did more than bridge the distance between separated parties, they also offered a device to exhort and advise (1 Thess. 5:23; 1 Cor. 1:8; Phil. 2:15), to comfort and console (2 Cor. 1:3–7), and to remind converts of what they tended to forget (1 Thess. 2:1–2, 9; 4:1–2, 13; 5:1–2). The letters also offered a vehicle for responding to criticisms so damning that if sustained, they might fatally compromise Paul's mission (Gal. 1–2; 2 Cor. 10:1–13:10, and possibly Phil. 3). Paul prevailed at least in part not only because of his theological brilliance, but also because of his skillful manipulation of epistolary traditions to his use.[23]

3

Traditions behind the Letters

Why do we appeal to tradition? Why do we quote famous people, poets, novelists, orators, and scholars? Why do we appeal to texts, historical precedent, and even to legend and myth? It is not just to enliven our speech, though it does do that. It is not just to overcome the impoverished nature of our vocabulary, though it also does that. It is not just to amuse, though it even does that. Rather it is that the tradition opens up in us a level of insight or understanding that we had not known before. Through the shared experience of the ages, we are delivered from a trivialized view of the human and nonhuman world and enabled to appreciate more fully the heights and depths of the human spirit.

For Paul these heights and depths were known through the historic interaction between God and Israel into which he read the death, resurrection, and expected return of Christ. Through our study of his use and interpretation of those materials we stand to gain a better appreciation of Paul the man, and of his very real letters dealing with great religious and human exigencies.

From the outset a difficulty faces our investigation of the traditions behind the letters. Early in Galatians Paul declares that his message was "not of human origin; for I did not receive it from a human source, nor was I taught it, but I received it through a revelation of Jesus Christ" (Gal. 1:11). Elsewhere, however, Paul drew on church tradition and scripture, cited a primitive Christian kerygma (gospel), repeated liturgical formulas, quoted Christian hymns, prayers, and confessions, and used traditional ethical admonitions. These were all composed by real people—so how could the apostle maintain that his gospel did not come from a mortal being?

The statement above from Galatians does not reveal an inconsistency in Paul's thought so much as it shows the extremity of a problem in the Galatian church. Paul's Galatian enemies had charged that his reliance on the Jerusalem apostolic tradition ("human authority") invalidated his claim to be an apostle of Christ. And this attempt to impugn his apostleship was nothing less than an attempt to discredit his kerygma (the gospel that he preached). His claim to be an apostle of Christ was, to be sure, extraordinarily weak. He had never known the historical Jesus. His gospel to the Gentiles was an outrageous novelty differing dramatically from that preached by the Jerusalem "mother church," unauthorized or at least questioned by the apostle Peter. He had little more than a vision claimed to authenticate his apostleship. But all kinds of folks, good and ill, claimed visions. How, his opponents asked, can an impostor preach an authentic gospel? In his absence, Galatian critics, possibly from Jerusalem, intruded who viewed his kerygma as woefully deficient and in need of correction. They supplemented it with the observance of "days, and months, and seasons, and years" (4:10), with circumcision, and with the worship of "elemental spirits," all practices Paul equated with slavery (4:9).

Paul scorned this Galatian amalgam, calling it "no gospel at all." He condemned their criticism of his gospel as a fundamental distrust of the God who gave it. He placed a dual curse on his gainsayers. In response, while not denying that he used human formulas in his preaching, he argued that his authority for that preaching came directly from Christ (Gal. 1:11), and thus to deny his gospel implied a renunciation of Christ. Once the polemical cast of 1:11–12 is recognized, Paul's claim to be dependent on no person for his kerygma does not contradict his admission elsewhere of dependence on tradition (e.g., 1 Cor. 15:3–4). Moreover, Paul can ascribe to Jesus in person what actually came through the church (1 Cor. 11:23–25). Obviously, he viewed the church as the Lord's community, and thus, to his mind, what came from the church was also from the Lord.

Nevertheless, the identification of traditional elements is valuable for understanding Paul's letters. These traditional materials may reveal his theological emphases, his views of scripture (though not all of his traditional materials are scriptural), and possibly also his own background. Understanding his use of that material, however, is fully as important as recognizing the selections he makes. For in every letter he adapts traditional materials to address problems as diverse as those dealing with sex, taxes, divorce, legal disputes, money, power, basic mutual, human respect, and the common fate of the human and natural environment, and as weighty as those dealing with the marks of a true apostle, the reconciliation of the world, the grand design of God's eschaton, and the theological basis of hope. Tradition for Paul was no "thing in itself" whose meaning was transparent. The past required interpretation and application. For Paul these materials were not inert deposits or fossils from an archaic past, but dynamic realities coming out of a living past, impinging directly on the present, and anticipating the future. In the discussion below we shall list representative traditional materials that shaped Paul's thinking.

THE KERYGMA

It is a surprise to many that Paul did not begin his mission as an apostle of Christ with a prefabricated theological system that he simply imposed on every new context. Paul's theology was an emergent one hammered out in the crucible of conflict and refined by controversy, and there is some evidence that his mind sometimes changed in the heat of these exchanges (for example, see the somewhat more favorable view of law in Romans than in Galatians). That hardly means, however, that there was nothing shared and solid at the core of Paul's gospel.

C. H. Dodd, a great and venerable scholar from Cambridge, taught us that the apostle shared a basic structure of his gospel with the early church. Although the emphasis of Paul's preaching and his interpretation of the kerygma of the early church differed from that of his predecessors, in six core areas, Dodd believed, there was mutual agreement (see Gal. 2:2):

a. The arrival of the messianic age as foretold by the prophets.
b. The inauguration of this new age in the ministry, death, and resurrection of Jesus.
c. The exaltation of Jesus.
d. The presence of the Holy Spirit in the church as a sign of Christ's "power and glory," and as a sign of the end time.
e. The imminent return of Jesus as the consummation of the messianic age.
f. The call to repentance coupled with an offer of forgiveness.[1]

Although these elements appear nowhere altogether in the same place, most of them surface somewhere or other in the Pauline letters. The following list shows where some of those elements are found:

a. Prophecy fulfilled (Rom. 1:2)
b. Messianic age inaugurated in Jesus who was born of the seed of David, died according to the scriptures (Rom. 1:3; Gal. 1:4), was buried (1 Cor. 15:4), was raised (1 Thess. 1:10; Rom. 1:4; 8:34)
c. Who was exalted (Rom. 8:34; Phil. 2:9)
d. The continuing presence of the Spirit of God (Rom. 8:26ff.; 1 Cor. 12)
e. Jesus' expected return (1 Thess. 1:10; Rom. 2:16)
f. Call to repent and welcome the return of Christ (Rom. 10:9).

First Corinthians 15:3–7 is a classic example of primitive tradition that Paul incorporated to address his converts. There seems to have been some

who were so persuaded that they already fully shared in the resurrected life of
the hereafter that they had real questions about the resurrection of the body.
In response Paul offers:

> For I delivered to you . . . what I also received,
> that *Christ died for our sins* in accordance with the scriptures,
> that *he was buried*,
> that *he was raised* on the third day in accordance with the
>   scriptures, and
> that *he appeared* to Cephas, then to the twelve. (italics added)

EUCHARISTIC AND BAPTISMAL FORMULAS

In his hortatory or instructional materials Paul often alludes to traditions that
his addressees were expected to know. The reference in 1 Corinthians 6:11 to
being washed points to baptism. A baptismal tradition also appears in Romans
6:4–5, "Therefore we have been buried [past tense] with him by baptism into
death . . . and if we have been united with him in a death like his, we will certainly be united [future tense] with him in a resurrection like his."

Similarly in 1 Corinthians 11:23–25 Paul directly quotes the eucharistic
liturgy: "I received from the Lord what I also handed on to you, that the Lord
Jesus on the night when he was betrayed took a loaf of bread, and when he had
given thanks, he broke it and said, 'This is my body that is for you. Do this in
remembrance of me.' In the same way he took the cup also, after supper, saying, 'This cup is the new covenant in my blood. Do this, as often as you drink
it, in remembrance of me.'"

THE LANGUAGE OF PRAYER

Paul frequently alludes to prayer and in some places bursts into a spontaneous doxology (e.g., Rom. 7:25: in response to the rhetorical question, "Who
will deliver us from this body of death?" Paul responds, "Thanks be to God
through Jesus Christ our Lord"). Some of his prayers are simply the outpouring of a full heart, but others have a traditional ring (Gal. 1:5; Phil. 4:20). It
is often difficult to distinguish between prayers that Paul creates and those he
cites. It is possible, however, to recognize fragments of traditional prayers in
the epistles. Words such as *amen* (Gal. 6:18; 1 Cor. 14:16; and 2 Cor. 1:20),
maranatha ("Our Lord, come," 1 Cor. 16:22), and *abba* (Gal. 4:6; Rom. 8:15)
all belong to a tradition that predates Paul.

HYMNS

For generations before the time of Jesus, hymns of praise had been rising to God from temple and synagogue. It is natural, therefore, that the early Christian church, deriving from Judaism, should be a singing church. While the early hymns of the church were from the Psalms, the church soon created new songs appropriate to its Christian status. Traces of this early hymnody appear in Paul's letters as well as the rest of the New Testament (e.g., Col. 1:15–20; 1 Tim. 3:16; Eph. 5:14). The rhythm, parallelism, clearly defined strophes, poetic expression, and the absence of Pauline vocabulary or ideas establishes Philippians 2:6–11 as a pre-Pauline Christian hymn. Even in English translation (RSV) its hymnic character is obvious:

Pauline Introduction

Have this mind among yourselves,
which you have in Christ Jesus,

Hymn

I
who, though he was in the form of God,
did not count equality with God
a thing to be grasped,

II
but emptied himself,
taking the form of a servant,
being born in the likeness of men.

III
And being found in human form
he humbled himself
and became obedient unto death.[2]

IV
Therefore God has highly exalted him
and bestowed on him the name
which is above every name. . . .[3]

WORDS OF THE LORD

In 2 Corinthians 5:16 Paul says, "though we once knew Christ from a human point of view, we know him no longer in that way."[4] Some scholars see this statement as evidence that Paul was personally acquainted with Jesus. If Paul did know Jesus during his ministry, however, it is astonishing that he would barely mention the words and deeds of Jesus in the entire letter corpus. For example, if we had to depend on Paul for information about Jesus' life, we would know only the obvious that he was "born of woman" (Gal. 4:4), that he was in David's line (Rom. 1:3), and that he died on a cross (Phil. 2:8; 1 Cor. 1:23). We would not know his mother's name, that he had sisters, that he taught in parables, or that his ministry was centered in Galilee. If Paul is silent about the words and deeds because he assumes they were known to his readers, then it is strange that he quotes Jewish scriptures even when he presupposes that they are familiar to his readers. Moreover, even though Paul often summarizes his own preaching, Jesus' ministry receives little emphasis (1 Cor. 2:1–2).[5] Although Paul expresses little interest in Jesus' ministry or the content of his preaching, he does lay heavy stress on three items: the cross, the resurrection, and Jesus' imminent return. For Paul, these salvific moments were anchored in history, but in his mind they possessed a significance that transcended history. As in the Gospels, the words of Jesus that Paul quoted or to which he alluded assume a transcendent character as sayings of the Lord. The sayings of Jesus occupy little space in Paul's letters, but they add important weight to his ethical teaching.[6]

a. *Quotations from Jesus (italics added)*

(1) 1 Cor. 7:10–11		To the married I give this command—not I but the Lord—that the *wife should not separate from her husband . . . and that the husband should not divorce his wife.* (See Matt. 5:32; 19:9; Mark 10:11–12; Luke 16:18.)
(2) 1 Cor. 9:14		The Lord commanded that *those who proclaim the gospel should get their living by the gospel.* (See Luke 10:7, the laborer deserves his wages.)
(3) 1 Cor. 11:23–24		The Lord Jesus . . . said, *"This is my body that is for you. Do this in remembrance of me."* In the same way he took the cup also, after supper, saying, *"This cup is the new covenant in my blood. Do this, as often as you drink it, in remembrance of me."* (See Matt. 26:26–28; Mark 14:22–24; Luke 22:19–20.)
(4) 1 Thess. 4:16–17		The Lord himself, with a cry of command,[7] with the archangel's call and with the sound of God's trumpet, will descend from heaven, and the dead in Christ will rise first.

(5) 1 Cor. 14:37, which alludes to but does not quote a saying.

b. *Echoes of Sayings*

(1) 1 Cor. 4:12		When reviled, we bless, when persecuted, we endure.

Rom. 12:14	Bless those who persecute you; bless and do not curse them.
Luke 6:28	Bless those who curse you; pray for those who abuse you.
(2) 1 Thess. 5:15	See that none of you repays evil for evil.
Rom. 12:17	Do not repay anyone evil for evil.
Matt. 5:39	Do not resist an evildoer.
(3) Rom. 13:7	Pay to all what is due them—taxes to whom taxes are due.
Matt. 22:15–22	Then the Pharisees [asked,] ". . . Is it lawful to pay taxes to the emperor, or not?" . . . Jesus, aware of their malice, said, " . . . Show me the coin used for the tax. . . . Give . . . to the emperor the things that are the emperor's, and to God the things that are God's."
(4) Rom. 14:13	Let us therefore no longer pass judgment on one another, but resolve instead never to put a stumbling block [*skandalon*] or hindrance in the way of another.
Matt. 7:1	Do not judge, so that you may not be judged.
(5) Rom. 14:14	Nothing is unclean in itself.
Mark 7:18–19	"Do you not see that whatever goes into a person from outside cannot defile, since it enters, not the heart but the stomach, and goes into the sewer?" (Thus he declared all foods clean.)
(6) 1 Thess. 5:2	The day of the Lord will come like a thief in the night.
Luke 12:39–40	If the owner of the house had known at what hour the thief was coming, he would not have let his house be broken into. . . . You also must be ready, for the Son of Man is coming at an unexpected hour. (See Matt. 24:42–43.)
(7) 1 Thess. 5:13	Be at peace among yourselves
Mark 9:50	Be at peace with one another.
(8) 1 Cor. 13:2	If I have faith, so as to remove mountains . . .
Matt. 17:20	If you have faith the size of a mustard seed, you will say to this mountain, "Move . . ." and it will move.

PARAENETIC TRADITION

Over a generation ago, Martin Dibelius noticed the traditional nature of Paul's ethical instructions (paraenesis).[8] We know now that the apostle drew on pre-Pauline or even pre-Christian traditions for his moral exhortation. Characterized by a terse, gnomic style, these materials usually fall near the end of Paul's letters (e.g., Gal. 5:13–6:10; 1 Thess. 4:1–5:22; 2 Cor. 13:11) and possess a certain uniformity in content and vocabulary. Admonitions to do good and to avoid evil, warnings against immorality, exhortations to nonviolence, and encouragement of subjection to leaders, edification of the church, and kindness to outsiders all appear in more than one of Paul's letters. Since these concerns are shared in many early Christian writings (1 Peter, *Ignatius*, Hebrews, *1 Clement*, *Barnabas*, *Hermas*, the *Didache*, and the Pastoral Epistles), it appears that the main contours of Paul's paraenetic materials did not originate with him but were the common property of the early Jesus movement.

Almost unanimously scholars agree that Paul appropriated ethical injunctions, but that he deployed them in a way appropriate to each addressee is hardly in dispute any longer. Until recently most scholars followed Dibelius, who held that the paraenesis had no particular situation in mind. Arguably, to attribute all of the sins enumerated in the vice lists to particular churches would be mistaken.[9] Recently, however, support for Dibelius's view has softened.[10] If Paul gave other traditional materials[11] like the thanksgiving and conclusion immediate application, would he not also mold the paraenetic tradition to each epistolary situation? Victor Paul Furnish has shown how Paul gave specificity even to the more general lists of virtues and vices.[12] For example, the vice list in 2 Corinthians 12:20–21 deals with divisive behavior (bickering, pettiness, arrogance, etc.), antisocial acts like anger, selfishness, slander, gossip, and sexual immorality—all of which characterize Corinthian behavior mentioned elsewhere.[13] Therefore, even the general lists have specific applicability when used by Paul.

In 1 Thessalonians 5:16–18 also, Paul adopted a general paraenetic tradition to a specific situation, and did so to exhort the discouraged to persevere. In his own words Paul encourages and admonishes:

> *pantote* (*always*) do good . . .
> *pantote* (*always*) rejoice,
> *adialeiptos* (*without ceasing*) pray,
> *en panti* (*in everything*) give thanks.[14]

The parallel construction, the adverb and prepositional phrase in the emphatic position, and the repetition of the key emphasis—"always . . . , always . . . without ceasing, . . . in everything"—hammers home Paul's main point: the need for perseverance. This emphasis on the need for persistence in the life of faith is stressed throughout the letter.

In 4:13 we learn that death has invaded this inspired community; blinded by disappointment and discouragement, some wanted to give up. Misguided enthusiasts quit work to await the Lord, only to become a burden on the rest of the church. Both the freeloaders and the disillusioned, the brazen and the timid, receive the same admonition to persevere in the life of faith. For their comfort or discomfort, Paul reminded them that Christ will return to rescue his own, whether living or dead. In the meantime, he admonished them to hold fast to the life of faith and retain hope, for "this is the will of God" (5:18). Over and over again Paul urged the faltering to do "more and more" good (4:1, 10; 5:11).

We see, therefore, how Paul structured traditional paraenetic materials, adding key words at strategic points, to underscore the fundamental point of the letter—the need for steadfast endurance until the end. So even these traditional materials, as general as they seem, have specific and immediate relevance for the Thessalonian church. Although Dibelius correctly maintained that the paraenetic sections were not the property of Paul to the same degree as are the sections of sustained theological argument, it is hardly accurate, as David G. Bradley has done, to call the paraenetic materials a "bag of answers to meet recurring problems and questions common to the members of different early Christian communities."[15]

Types of Paraenetic Tradition

a. *Wisdom Sayings*

Wisdom materials, rooted in everyday experience, need not make explicit theological claims, can move easily across ethnic and class boundaries, and may spring as easily from the lips of the peasant woman as the privileged scribe. Note, for example, Paul's appeal to such materials to instruct, admonish, and correct his addressees.

(1) "You reap whatever you sow" (Gal. 6:7).

(2) "The one who sows sparingly will also reap sparingly, and the one who sows bountifully will also reap bountifully" (2 Cor. 9:6).

(3) "Bad company ruins good morals" (l Cor. 15:33).

(4) "A little yeast leavens the whole batch of dough" (Gal. 5:9).

b. *Vice and Virtue Lists*

As part of the cultural vernacular these lists stood ready to hand when the need arose (see above) for correction or exhortation.

(l) They were filled with every kind of "wickedness, evil, covetousness, malice. Full of envy, murder, strife, deceit, craftiness, they are gossips, slanderers,

God-haters, insolent, haughty, boastful, inventors of evil, rebellious toward parents, foolish, faithless, heartless, ruthless" (Rom. 1:29–31; see also Gal. 5:19–21 ; 1 Cor. 5:10–11; 6:9–10; 2 Cor. 12:20).

(2) "The fruit of the Spirit is love, joy, peace, patience, kindness, generosity, faithfulness, gentleness, and self-control" (Gal. 5:22–23; see also Phil. 4:8, which includes prominent Greek philosophical terms like *prosphilēs*, "lovely"; *euphēmos*, "gracious"; *aretē*, "excellence"; and *epainos*, "praiseworthy").

c. *Imperative Cluster*

"Let love be genuine; hate what is evil, hold fast to what is good; love one another with mutual affection; outdo one another in showing honor. Do not lag in zeal, be ardent in spirit, serve the Lord. Rejoice in hope, be patient in suffering, persevere in prayer. Contribute to the needs of the saints, extend hospitality to strangers" (Rom. 12:9–13).

d. *Developed Exhortation or Topical Moral Essay*

See the sustained admonition concerning the mutual responsibility of the strong and weak in Romans 14:1–15:13; also note 1 Thessalonians 5:1–11.[16]

In the discussion above we saw how Paul drew on early Christian tradition as well as Jewish and even "pagan" sources. Paul freely used the epistolary conventions of his time and frequently tapped a vast reservoir of Christian and non-Christian paraenesis. The alert reader will spot these and other traditional materials in reading the letters. Sometimes Paul will identify the nuggets of tradition with phrases like "I delivered what I also received, that . . . ," or "it is written that . . . ," or "this we declare by the word of the Lord, that. . . ." Elsewhere, however, only a break in the context, an interruption in the stream of thought (e.g., Phil. 2:6–11), or an unusual construction of words or sentences will signal his use of sources. In other cases unusual vocabulary or theological statements that sound uncharacteristic of Paul may arouse suspicion that traditional elements are present. But we must not merely notice that certain materials were appropriated; we also should observe to what specific end. Fully as important as what was used is how it was appropriated in context.

How, the reader should ask, did Paul use traditional elements to address the problems of his readers? How did he bend the traditional elements to serve his theological arguments? Where did his theological outlook require alteration in the understanding of tradition, and what do these alterations reveal about the intent of the letter itself? Although these questions are sometimes unanswerable, they are worth asking nevertheless, for through them may come a heightened awareness of the horizons of Paul's thought. Even our failures to decipher the meaning of these moves by Paul may be instructive in teaching us the limits of our exegesis. But more importantly, these questions about Paul's use of tradition may uncover new dimensions of Paul's theology.

4

The Letters as Conversations

Dealing as they do with such mundane matters as sex, taxes, diet, lawsuits, circumcision, ecstatic speech, and intramural squabbles, Paul's letters bear the unmistakable imprint of this world. Among other things, the concreteness of the letters shows how seriously Paul took his readers, and how painstakingly he tried to interpret his gospel for them. Once we realize how the ferment in the churches prescribed the scope if not the content of Paul's writings, then it may become obvious why Paul's theologizing was inextricably linked to real life situations in the churches.[1] Study of the epistles isolated from their context resembles reading answers at the end of an algebra book without the corresponding problems. Any one of the excellent summaries of Paul's theology would give the reader a grasp of the range and diversity of Paul's thought. This study, however, will focus on the dynamic and sometimes turbulent interaction between the apostle and his converts in the hope that the reader will thereby gain a deeper appreciation of the vigor and ingenuity of Paul's emerging theology.

Since reading Paul's letters resembles overhearing one end of a telephone conversation and trying to imagine what the unheard conversation partner is saying, the voices of Paul's converts and antagonists are difficult to reconfigure. In some ways our task is like that of a detective who, with painfully few clues, must reconstruct what happened at a crime scene. My construction of the sometimes endearing and oft-times angry exchanges between Paul and his addressees could be debated at great length. I hope, however, that even if my interpretation does not point to true north, it may point to that magnetic north that, with proper allowances, may guide the modern reader through the rugged and confusing terrain of the letters.

Chronological Outline of Paul's Ministry and Writing*

Date of crucifixion	ca. 30	
Paul's call ("conversion")	ca. 34	Gal. 1:15, 16
Paul's ministry in Arabia/Nabatea	34–37	Gal. 1:17
Paul's escape from Damascus ruled by an ethnarch, presumably Aretas IV of Nabatea	37/38	2 Cor. 11:32–33
First trip to Jerusalem (two-week stay)	37/38	Gal. 1:18
Mission in Syria and Cilicia (Paul's home province)	38–47	Gal. 1:21
Second trip to Jerusalem, Paul's gentile mission "endorsed"	ca. 47 (between 46 and 48)	Gal. 2:1–10
Edict of Claudius expelling Jews	49	Acts 18:2 and Suetonius
First mission in Europe (Philippi, Thessalonica, and Achaia)	48–52	Acts 15:36–18:17
Ministry in Achaia, including Corinth	fall 50– summer 52	Acts 18:1–3
1 Thessalonians Arraignment before proconsul Gallio:	summer/fall 52	Acts 18:12–17
Paul in Ephesus	fall 52–56	
Lost letter written to Corinth	52	1 Cor. 5:9
1 Corinthians	53	
Letters from Ephesus and Macedonia collected in fragmentary form in 2 Corinthians	54–57	
Galatians	ca. 55	
Imprisonment	late 55 into early 56	2 Cor. 1:8–11
Philippian correspondence from prison, probably in Ephesus Philemon possibly came from this imprisonment	ca. 56	
The "painful letter" to Corinth	56	2 Cor. 10:1–13:10
Reconciling letter to Corinthians from Macedonia	fall 56	2 Cor. 1:1–2:13; 7:5–16
Circular letter to churches in Achaia urging completion of offering	fall 56	2 Cor. 9
Paul winters in Corinth preparing the offering and delegation for delivery to Jerusalem	56–57	
Paul departs with delegation for Jerusalem with offering for the "poor among the saints" and final visit to Jerusalem	spring 57	Rom. 15:25–33
Arrest, imprisonment and transfer to Rome	ca. 57–59	Acts 25:4–28:16
Execution	60–64	Acts of Paul and Thecla 11.1–7

While this construction is hypothetical, most scholars agree that Paul's apostolic activity began in the thirties and ended in the early sixties. And almost all agree that the evidence of the letters is to be preferred over that of Acts. While some scholars would arrange the letters in a different order, most agree that the majority of Paul's letters were written in the fifties, though a few place all of the letters in the forties. Given the complexity of Paul's case, it is amazing that we have the agreement that we do.

*Calvin J. Roetzel, "Paul the Apostle," in *The New Interpreter's Dictionary of the Bible*, vol. 4, ed. Katharine Doob Sakenfeld, 411(Nashville: Abingdon Press, 2009). Used by permission.

THE THESSALONIAN CORRESPONDENCE (c. 51 CE)[2]

Paul's Preaching

After his release from prison in Philippi (l Thess. 2:2), Paul came to Thessalonica with his coworkers, Timothy and Silvanus. While working a trade to earn bread, Paul preached "in power and in the Holy Spirit and with full conviction" (1:5). Converts turned to God from idols to embrace Paul and his gospel (1:5–6, 9–10; 2:2–9; 3:2).

Exactly how, where, and when he preached we simply do not know, but at the center of his gospel stood an emphasis on the death of Jesus, his resurrection by God (1:10; 4:14), and the imminent return of Christ that would consummate the arrival of a new era, the judgment of the wicked, and the collection of the "saints" (2:19; 3:13; 4:15; 5:23). Although Paul nowhere records a sermon for us, his letters contain vestiges of his preaching in statements like: "Now I would remind you, brothers and sisters, of the good news that I proclaimed" (1 Cor. 15:l): "For you know what instructions we gave you through the Lord Jesus" (1 Thess. 4:2), and so on. Problems compelled Paul later to offer different applications of his gospel for each church, but certain elements in the first encounter probably reoccurred with some frequency, for example, the eschatological significance of Jesus' death and resurrection, an emphasis on the urgency of the moment, and an appeal to live a godly and holy life in anticipation of the impending denouement. The summary below is offered as a facsimile of the first phase of an extended conversation between Paul and his converts:

> Yahweh is God of the Israelites, and to the Israelites came God's promises, commandments, kings like David, prophets and Messiah Jesus from the seed of David, and through the great patriarch of the Jews, Abraham, God's promises have been extended to all peoples, so Yahweh is not God of the Jews only, but also of the Gentiles. Now in the last days the promises are being fulfilled in Messiah Jesus, the Righteous One who was crucified by the Romans, but whom God vindicated as the Righteous One by raising him up from the dead. Thus he became the firstfruit of an end time, and will soon bring to completion the triumph of God's righteousness when Jesus will return to judge the world, to vindicate the righteous, and to collect the elect, both Israelites and Gentiles. He will come from heaven with his angels and flaming fire; he will grant mercy and peace to all who believe in him. Those who believe in him and are baptized into the ranks of God's people now are blessed by the Spirit; they taste the joys of the kingdom of God and are freed to struggle and ultimately triumph over the demonic rulers of this world. As Creator, God has favored all peoples through the creation and its sustenance

with rain and good harvest. But instead of the Creator Gentiles have worshiped the creation and self-made idols. But now in this new time God in Jesus has set out to reclaim the world, which was slipping into the control of the great cosmic evil powers—King Sin and Emperor Death—and through him overlooked the error, sin, and ignorance of repentant Gentiles. Turn to God from the worship of idols, and turn to the Creator instead of the creation; enjoy a foretaste of the freedom that will come to all believers one day. Be baptized into Jesus' death and rise up to walk in newness of life in the Spirit. Be alert, watch, live a godly and holy life in preparation for the return of the judge and savior Messiah Jesus.[3]

The Report of Timothy

To avoid the charge that they were religious hucksters peddling gospel for gain, Paul and his companions worked "night and day" to support themselves while evangelizing at Thessalonica. Occasionally their earnings were supplemented by money sent from the house church in Philippi (Phil. 4:16). At first, Paul's own example gave his gospel an authentic ring and it enjoyed good success. But among the Gentiles Paul met resistance and ultimately left Thessalonica, perhaps involuntarily (1 Thess. 1:9–10; 2:15).

During the trek south, however, thoughts of the troubled church in Thessalonica haunted Paul. Concerned about the usual problems facing new converts in a fledgling church, Paul felt an almost irresistible urge to reverse his journey and to return to Thessalonica, but he was hindered, he said, from doing so (2:17–18). Unable to bear it any longer, he dispatched Timothy to remind this circle of Christ of his teaching (3:1–3), to encourage it, and obviously to check on it. Weeks later, Timothy rejoined Paul in Corinth, reporting on problems in the church and lingering doubts about the apostle. Timothy might have carried a letter to supplement the oral report, but only the faintest traces of its contents are decipherable.[4]

In spite of his best efforts, Paul could not escape the charge that his preaching was for personal gain. His sudden departure would have only confirmed the suspicions of some that he, like other wandering preachers and teachers, had breezed into town, covered his greed with false rhetoric, lined his pockets with money from gullible believers, and then abandoned his followers when he came under fire from officials or hostile critics (2:14, if authentic). Because of Paul's success among the God-fearers, certain Jews, convinced that his gospel was antinomian or inimical to Judaism, may also have accused Paul of error and uncleanness (2:3): "error" because his gospel did not come from God, and "uncleanness" because he taught disregard for the laws of Torah and thus encouraged libertinism. But this is sheer speculation. There is not one single quotation of scripture in 1 Thessalonians answering critics; such a lack would have been highly unusual were Paul responding to Jewish opposition (e.g., see Galatians).

Timothy's return after some weeks brought both encouraging and discouraging news. Paul still enjoyed the support of the congregation, but the small cell of believers now suffered brutal persecution. This coercion and intimidation for their new association with Christ and participation in this "sect" (1:4–6; 2:1–2; 3:3–4), when coupled with the premature death of believers, sparked an existential crisis in the community. Some worried that Paul's promise of the imminent return of Christ was false (4:17); the hope of others flagged; some may have despaired of ever again being with loved ones now departed (1:3; 2:19; 4:13; 5:8). Timothy also brought word that the full weight of Paul's injunctions to live a life in readiness for Christ's return had escaped those ignorant of Jewish laws and customs and who were socialized as Gentile males to frequent prostitutes. Moreover, Timothy reported tensions between those so caught up in the spirit and earnest expectation of the imminent end of the age that they had quit work and became a burden to others.[5] Naturally, resentment would flare when others had to care for these idlers (5:14). Except for these concerns, Timothy's report was positive. A great reservoir of goodwill and affection remained for Paul (3:6). Despite the loss of hope in the community, faith and love remained. But the threat of disillusionment was real, and Paul responded with 1 Thessalonians.

Paul's Letter to the Thessalonians

The outline below sketches Paul's response. Instead of the harsh polemic of other letters, this epistle blossoms with assurance and comfort, gentle admonition and conciliation, encouragement and affection. Reflecting Paul's sensitivity to the "pagan" past of his addressees and to their persecution and discouragement, Paul appropriated inclusive election and familial language to construct a surrogate family. The thanksgiving assured them that they were "beloved of God" who had chosen them (1:4). Later he made persecution and election correlates of those in Christ (1:6; 2:12–16; 3:3). And for those rejected by or alienated from extended families, friends, and associates, his language set them in a constructed circle of care. While his warm and inclusive language could hardly erase the loneliness, confusion, and even desperation of being an outcast, it could and did construct a surrogate household to nurture, encourage, remind, support, and console (5:14). Headed by the great patriarch, "God the Father" (1:1), his "beloved" (1:3–4) could share the company of "brothers and sisters" (*adelphoi*, used 8 times for emphasis). Paul underscored his love and care for them. He recalled being "gentle" among them like a wet nurse caring for her children (2:7) and like a father nudging his little ones on (2:11–12). This special relationship through Christ (1:1), he noted, set them apart from those behaving with "lustful passion, like the Gentiles who do not know God" (4:5). And he reassured ruptured families that they could look forward to the imminent return of Christ when they would join with those torn from their embrace by death.

He also admonished the idle to work with their hands; he encouraged the disheartened and gave them new cause for hope (i.e., the dead will precede the living into the eschatological kingdom); he admonished the fainthearted to persevere "more and more"; he urged teachers to use care in teaching; and he gently corrected misunderstanding and admonished all to persevere in the life of faith and love with hope.

Outline of Paul's Letter to the Thessalonians
(1 Thessalonians)

1.	Address and Salutation	1:1
2.	Thanksgiving	1:2–10; 2:13; 3:9–10
3.	Personal Defense	2:1–3:13
	a. Recollection of the mission	2:1–16
	(1) Paul's pastoral work	2:1–12
	(2) Response of the believers	2:13–16
	b. The mission of Timothy	2:17–3:13
	(1) Paul's desired visit	2:17–20
	(2) Sending of Timothy	3:1–5
	(3) Timothy's return and report	3:6–10
	(4) Prayer	3:11–13
4.	Ethical Exhortation and Instruction	4:1–5:28
	a. The ethical demands of the gospel	4:1–12
	(1) Previous instructions	4:1–2
	(2) Sanctification excludes sexual impurity	4:3–8
	(3) Mutual love	4:9–10
	(4) Idleness	4:10–12
	b. Concerning the dead in Christ	4:13–18
	c. Concerning Christ's return	5:1–11
	d. Final paraenesis	5:12–22
	(Random instructions)	
5.	Closing (Peace Wish, Kiss, Apostolic Command, and Benediction)	5:23–28

THE CORINTHIAN CORRESPONDENCE (c. 53–56)[6]

Paul came to Corinth in "fear and in much trembling" (1 Cor. 2:3). Perhaps he was afraid that he would receive the same harsh treatment that had cut short his ministry in Thessalonica and Philippi. What he feared might be a ministry of just a few weeks, however, stretched into a year and a half, and the gospel that first took root in the city enjoyed success in the surrounding countryside as well (2 Cor. 1:1). During his relatively long stay in Corinth, Paul received assistance from Aquila and Prisca, Jewish Christian refugees from Rome who "risked their necks" for him and earned the gratitude of all the Gentile churches (Rom. 16:3–4; see also Acts 18:1–4).

While at Corinth Paul evidently spoke in tongues (l Cor. 14:18) and demonstrated other charismatic gifts ("signs and wonders and mighty works"). In the face of the "impending distress," Paul chose to remain celibate (1 Cor. 7:7, 26). Evidently these examples had a profound effect on the congregation, for Paul later devoted extensive discussion to both marriage and ecstatic speech.

After leaving Corinth, perhaps involuntarily, Paul eventually settled in Ephesus for about three years (c. 52–55). Among others, Timothy, Titus, Aquila, and Prisca worked with him there. Apollos also, an Alexandrian Jew, trailed Paul to Corinth, enjoyed good success for a time, and ultimately joined him in Ephesus. If the account in Acts is historical (8:24–28), the eloqunce of Apollos, his agile, imaginative exegesis, his enthusiasm, his skill in debate, and his resourceful personality endeared him to the Corinthians. It is unnecessary to assume that Apollos caused the problems in Corinth in order to see how it may have aggravated certain enthusiastic tendencies.

While at Ephesus, Paul sent a letter, now lost, addressing certain problems in the Corinthian church (1 Cor. 5:9).[7] We are uncertain what those problems were. Perhaps a rumor of excesses had come to Paul. Or the presence of Apollos may have encouraged forms of enthusiasm that were disruptive to congregational life. Under the power of the Spirit Paul probably uttered ecstatic speech (*glossolalia*) while at Corinth. Since life in the kingdom of God was understood as life in the Spirit, it is hardly surprising that what was once an expression of life in the kingdom became a condition for life in the kingdom. Effect was thus regarded as cause: ecstatic speech was thought to induce salvation, rather than salvation inducing speech.

Angel speech, as it was called (see 1 Cor. 13:1), indicated who was in tune with the divine, or who had "knowledge." Those "in the know" felt so secure in Christ and so sure of their power to prevail over this world that they behaved in ways that Paul would have found foolhardy. Since they felt that idols had no real existence, they freely attended pagan celebrations, participated in pagan cultic meals, and ate meat offered to idols. It is possible, if not likely, that this "knowledge" led some to attempt to live above mere accidental distinctions, like sex, since in Christ they felt they followed Paul's own admission that "there is neither male and female" (Gal. 3:28). "Spiritual marriages" would have allowed men and women to live together without sexual intercourse. It is hardly surprising, therefore, that such well-intentioned practices sometimes encouraged the very thing they wished to avoid (see 1 Cor. 5). If such a lifestyle emerged from this "knowledge," then we can understand why the gist of the missing first letter mentioned in 1 Corinthians 5:9 was the admonition not to associate with sexually immoral persons.

Oral and Written Responses from Corinth

Chloe's people ("slaves"?) and perhaps others (1 Cor. 16:17) soon arrived in Ephesus from Corinth to report on the deteriorating situation in the home church (1 Cor. 1:11). Boasts about exclusive truth and pretentious claims to religious "knowledge" had brought on fiery antagonisms. Indeed, the circle of converts was perilously close to division, with each faction devoted to a different mystagogue—Paul, Peter, Apollos, or even Christ for the super Christians. Each faction claimed exclusive "knowledge" and divine intoxication from its leader. Each group claimed a glorified life apart from the cross. Each faction claimed full expression for its eschatological gifts, especially speaking in tongues, that secured a superiority over all others. The powerful signs to which it claimed privilege demonstrated, it boasted, the truth of its wisdom.

Such spiritual elitism fostered contempt of those with "lesser" gifts, led some to disdain the unimposing Paul, and cultivated a spiritual elitism that jeopardized the very existence of the church (see 1 Cor. 1:10–4:21). The cliques disrupted worship (see 11:17–34) and emboldened those with an eschatological preoccupation to celebrate the Lord's Supper as if it were the great messianic banquet reserved for the end of time. In their enthusiasm they stuffed themselves, saving nothing for others, perhaps Christian slaves whose arrival was delayed by assigned tasks. Some gorged themselves and drank; others had not a crumb for the "love feast." Such swollen self-indulgence and calloused indifference to the needs of others seem to have been rooted in the religious enthusiasm referred to in 1 Corinthians 1:10–4:21.

In 1 Corinthians 7:1 Paul shifts his attention to the concerns of the letter from the Corinthians ("Now concerning the matters about which you wrote . . ."). With the phrase "now concerning (*peri de*)," Paul introduced topics from the Corinthian letter. Indeed, by noting the appearances of *peri de* ("now concerning") we can reconstruct a rough outline of the Corinthians' letter to Paul (e.g., 7:1, 25; 8:1; 12:1; and 16:1). The membership of the Corinthian church was drawn mostly from the ranks of the underclass (1:26–28). As Paul described the church:

> Not many of you were wise by human standards, not many were powerful, not many were of noble birth. But God chose what is foolish in the world to shame the wise; God chose what is weak in the world to shame the strong; God chose what is low and despised in the world, things that are not, to reduce to nothing things that are.

Of these "weak" and "despised" ones, many were slaves (7:21–24) or the freed who had been released from bondage. Nevertheless, a sprinkling of leaders from the community did join the church. Chrispus, whom Paul baptized, was a synagogue leader (1:14; Acts 18:8), and Erastus, apparently a member, was the city treasurer (Rom. 16:23). The great majority of both poor and privileged were Gentiles. They may have attended the local synagogue, and some may have observed Jewish practices, but under Paul's leadership they located themselves in this "sectarian" Jewish movement that would someday be called "Christian."

The multiple writings of 1 and 2 Corinthians offer an extended record of a protracted and sometimes bitter set of exchanges spanning many years. Although persecution was a brutal reality in Thessalonica, Philippi, and Ephesus, no such grisly reality faced the church in Corinth, and no disillusionment darkened the mood of the converts. Paul's creative theologizing, however, was desperately needed to respond to the religious puffery and divisive pretensions of Corinthian converts, and to respond to suspicions and mistrust aroused by Paul's offering project and insurgent attacks from invading "super-apostles" (2 Cor. 3:3–18; 10:1–13:10). Fortunately, only in this exchange do we catch some sense of a provisional happy outcome (Rom. 16:23) when he spent the winter of 57–58 CE in Corinth enjoying the hospitality of Gaius (c. 56–57) and writing Romans. The offering project was ready for delivery to Jerusalem. The delegation had gathered to accompany the offering, and Paul's eyes were anxiously fixed on Jerusalem as his mind raced eastward and then boomeranged back west to Rome and beyond to Spain.

The exchanges begun here continued for several years, and though the history of that relationship is complex, one hypothetical reconstruction of its principal stages between 52 and 58 might be as follows:

1a. Paul's preaching in Corinth.

1b. Hearing before Gallio and Paul's expulsion/departure.

2. Letter A: Written by Paul to the Corinthians (1 Cor. 5:9) (missing).

3. Corinthians write to Paul (1 Cor. 7:1) (missing) and send oral communication (16:17) about deteriorating situation in the church at Corinth.

4. Letter B: Paul writes 1 Corinthians responding to both oral and written communication, and dispatches it with Timothy.

5. Letter C: Paul writes third letter, 2 Corinthian 8, and dispatches it by Titus and the anonymous "brothers" to complete the offering project. The effort founders and word comes of Corinthian suspicions about Paul's conduct and fitness for ministry.

6. Letter D: 2:14–7:4 (minus 6:14–7:1) reveals Paul's response to charges about his fitness for apostolic ministry and his lack of divine authority. After his disastrous ("painful") visit he left Corinth publicly humiliated by an antagonist and hurt by the defecting or passive church (2:1; 7:9, 11–12).

7. Letter E: Paul retreats, eventually arriving in Ephesus from whence he writes the slashing defense of his apostolic claim and gospel, and the attack on the "super-apostles" and their sympathizers (10:1–13:10). He sent Titus with this "letter of tears" in the desperate hope he could right the floundering mission and restore confidence in his ministry.

8. Letter F: Paul leaves Ephesus to rendezvous with Titus in Troas, in northeastern Asia Minor. He has no rest until he finally links up in Macedonia with Titus, who brings exceedingly good news. Paul's stinging rebuke and vigorous defense (obviously with Titus's able assistance) brought about a change of heart (repentance). Paul writes his reconciling letter from Macedonia (1:1–2:13; 7:5–16; 13:11–13) and probably dispatches it with Titus. Even though the storm clouds are past, some squalls remain, and to those Paul attends with a gentler tone than would have seemed possible just months before. Titus's assistance was still needed.

9. Letter G: Paul finally wrote 2 Corinthians 9 to all the churches of Achaia to set in motion the final phase of the offering for the "poor among the saints" in Jerusalem. He dispatches certain anonymous "brothers" with this letter and with instructions to prepare the churches for his imminent arrival with a Macedonian delegation.

10. Paul traveled south to Corinth, where he spent some weeks if not the winter, and wrote the Roman church from Corinth that the offering was ready, the delegation chosen, and the journey to present the offering was about to begin. So anxious was Paul about the presentation of the offering that he uttered a request for prayers of the Roman church that is full of pathos (Rom. 15:26–32).

Corinthian Letter to Paul

After dealing with the concerns offered in the oral report, in 1 Corinthians 7:1 Paul begins to treat one by one the major topics or the Corinthian letter to him. From the outline of their letter, recovered from Paul's response, I offer the following hypothetical reconstruction of the Corinthian letter to Paul:

(1) Concerning Marriage

Given the urgency of the times, we think married believers should refrain from sexual intercourse and virgins and widows should not consider marriage, in order to keep themselves in a constant state of readiness to meet Christ and to enjoy the company of angels. Given the urgency of the times, we remember how you said, "It is well for a man not to touch a woman." In this we are following your example. Moreover, you yourself said that in Christ there is "neither male nor female," and that the Lord said that in the kingdom men and women are neither married nor given in marriage [Luke 20:35]. As we await Christ's return, should not those of us who are married act as if we are not, and should not believers divorce any unbelieving partners?

(2) Concerning Contact with the World

You wrote us not to associate with the immoral, but to do that we would need to withdraw from the world. As you know, the world is full of immoral people. And how does this square with your exhortation to do "good to all"? And, did you not say, "for freedom Christ has set us free"? Don't we witness to Christ, by exercising our freedom in Christ? Also, if we are free and if idols have no real existence, what harm can come from eating idol meat? Also, we know that physical things cannot defile the spirit—"Food is meant for the stomach and the stomach for food." Must we decline invitations to eat with our unbelieving friends and family and forgo a chance to witness to Christ if the meat is not ritually pure? How can we witness to unbelievers if we offend them?

(3) Concerning Worship

Since all are one in Christ, the distinctions between men and women are artificial; such physical accidents mean nothing in the kingdom of God. It is entirely appropriate, therefore, for women to pray with heads uncovered and to share actively in the service. And why should you have reservations now about speaking in tongues? We are merely following your example. Those who are unable to speak the heavenly language of angels are less gifted.

(4) Concerning the Resurrection

Through baptism we have already passed from death to the resurrected life. If we have already died, and been raised with Christ, then, as you said, today is the day of salvation. Also, the whole idea of the resurrection of the body is disgusting. Which body? The old body or the young one? The sick body or the healthy one? How can you say we must prepare for the resurrection of the dead and the judgment of the resurrected? How can those who have already died with Christ and been raised up die again? Also, what do you mean by the "resurrection of the body"? The whole idea of the resuscitation of a rotten corpse is repugnant. Salvation brings release from our bodies; and did you not say that flesh and blood cannot inherit the kingdom of God? What good is salvation if we are still imprisoned in our bodies?

(5) Concerning the Collection

Although we are poor ourselves, we will contribute to the project for the poor in Jerusalem. It would probably be best if we sent someone from our church to deliver the offering. You would not want anyone to think you were skimming off part of the gift for yourself, would you? But some wonder why we must send an offering for the poor in Jerusalem. We have many, many poor here in Corinth; should we not attend to our own first? Many of us are slaves and destitute. We are very limited in what we can do.

(6) Concerning Apollos

Might you encourage Apollos to return to Corinth? He had a very effective ministry here. Some of our people miss his powerful witness, oratory, charismatic presence, and persuasive teaching of scripture. The brothers and sisters are always asking for his return.

Paul's Reply to the Oral Report from Chloe's People and to the Corinthian Letter[8]

In what we know as 1 Corinthians we see Paul's reply to two communications from Corinth, one oral and one written. Interestingly, Paul responded in kind, sending 1 Corinthians (which was really his second letter) from Ephesus by sea (1 Cor. 5:9, c. 53 CE) and dispatching Timothy by land (1 Cor. 4:17), probably with oral instructions. Paul's letter is intact, but for the sake of clarity I summarize his argument below.

Paul's Response to the Oral Report

(l) Concerning Division (1:10–4:21)

Why do you boast of your baptism in the name of people like me, Apollos, Peter, and even Christ? Is Christ divided? Were you baptized in the name of Paul? Does some special wisdom come in baptism through your union with Christ? Is that why you call yourselves wise, mature, and spiritual? Your boasting is silly and contrary to the ways of God. Divine wisdom looks like foolishness to society. Through a cross, or through a motley collection of people like yourselves, or through a frail and unimposing figure like me, God reveals wisdom not in strength and glory but in weakness and shame! Christ crucified, not Christ glorified, is the heart of my gospel, and this Christ forms the foundation of the church. All work laid on that foundation by Apollos or anybody else will be tested on the last day. To those inflated with their own self-esteem and heedless of the welfare of the church, let me say: if they destroy the church, God will destroy them. Is it because you think you are so spiritual that you presume to judge Christ's apostles and think you are above scripture [see 1 Cor. 4:6]? When I come, I will find out how really spiritual these people are.

(2) Concerning Immorality (5:1–6:11; 11:17–34)

a. Incest (5:1–13)

I hear that a man is cohabiting with his "father's wife," all in the name of the Lord Jesus, and worse, you condone it! You say Christians are above such trivial differences as those of sex, and that life in the kingdom transcends sexuality. You tolerate behavior that even pagans scorn. Expel this offender lest he poison the whole congregation. In doing so, he may be destroyed, but his spirit will be saved. When I wrote that you should not associate with immoral persons, I meant just such as this, not the outsiders.

b. Lawsuits (6:1–11)

I hear that some of you are defrauding others, and that someone has taken a case to the civil courts. How ironic that you who someday will judge the heathen, or even angels, now turn to the heathen for justice. Must the injured party turn to the civil courts? You claim to be wise (*sophos*): are you not wise enough to render a decision on such matters? Great harm can be done to the church and the mission by such internal strife.

(3) Concerning the Lord's Supper (11:17–34)

Each one eats disregarding the needs of others and only for self-satisfaction. You claim to be celebrating your life in the kingdom, but instead you profane the Lord's body. Do you not know that Christ is in his community? Your selfish and greedy behavior not only insults your brother and sister, it offends the Lord himself, who is present for judgment. That is why some are sick and some have died.

Paul's Response to the Corinthians' Letter

(1) Concerning Marriage (7:1–40)

I fear you misunderstood my remark that it is better for a man not to touch a woman and vice versa. Because you think you are equal to angels, you claim to be above such worldly things in order to keep yourselves in readiness for God's revelation.[9] The pure want to rid themselves of unbelieving partners. Continence within marriage is required, some believe. But abstinence from sex should be practiced only for a time of prayer. Widows and virgins are made to feel inferior if they marry. I encouraged all to remain as I am because of the special urgency of the times (the end is near), not because we have overcome the world. Not everyone has the gift of celibacy. It is better to marry than to be consumed with passion.

(2) Concerning Idol Meat (8:1–11:1)

It is true that there is no God but one, and that therefore idols have no real existence. Since idols do not exist, you ask, what harm comes from eating meat routinely offered to the gods in the marketplace? But what if my freedom causes a weaker believer to stumble? Freedom must always be subordinated to love. I am free, am I not? Yet I freely surrender my rightful freedom for the sake of others. Because you are washed and now eat supernatural food, do not think that you are infallible. Israel too was a sacramental community, and yet 23,000 died in a single day in the wilderness. You cannot worship the living God one day and share in pagan worship the next. One is bound to what is worshiped. You cannot share the cup of Christ and the cup or food of idols. Remember also that even if you are free in Christ, and even if all things are lawful, not all things are helpful. Eat in a way that strengthens yourselves and others.

(3) Concerning Distinctions between Men and Women (11:2–16)

Some of you say that in Christ there is neither male nor female. It is true that I encouraged women to prophesy in the service and that you were baptized into Christ, in whom there is "neither male and female," but you seek to obliterate all distinctions between male and female. Such are accidents of birth, you say, and after sharing in the new creation all such accidental distinctions should be ignored. You claim too much. While that is true for the future life, we are not yet angels. Women and men are interdependent. Woman was taken from the side of man (Adam), and now man is born of woman. Let men and women continue sharing in the service of worship, but let us maintain the distinction between and interdependence of male and female. Men, cut your hair, and women, cover your heads (or wear veils).

(4) Concerning Spiritual Gifts (12:1–14:40)

You claim to follow my example in practicing ecstatic speech. You do well to exalt the spiritual gifts, but if those who speak in tongues despise those who do not, how does that build up the church? Strive for the higher gifts like teaching and interpreting, which edify others. Allow all to contribute in their own way with whatever gift they have, and subordinate all of the gifts to love, the most excellent of all charismatic gifts (12:31).

(5) Concerning the Resurrection (15:1–58)

Remember the gospel that I preached: Christ died, was buried, and was raised. Christ's raising was the first of the general resurrection soon to be completed. You say you have already been raised up, that death is behind you, that only the life of glory remains, and that therefore there is no future resurrection for you. I hear also that the whole idea of the resurrection of the body is repulsive to you. Do you not know that God can give us a different body appropriate to that life? But death has not been completely conquered; that will come in the future when God puts all enemies underfoot, and the last enemy to be destroyed will be Death. Then and only then will we be able to say, "Death is swallowed up in victory."

(6) Concerning the Collection (16:1–4)

Have the collection ready when I come. I agree that someone from the congregation should accompany us to deliver the offering.

(7) Concerning Apollos (16:12)

I urged him to come, but it was not God's will that he come at this time. He will come later.

Paul Dispatched Timothy with Oral Instructions, and Timothy's Return

Three issues combine to stoke rising distrust and conflict between Paul and the Corinthians. First, there were the lingering conflicts created by a divisive spirit, religious puffery, spiritual elitism, and totalistic claims to salvation revealed in 1 Corinthians, which may have arrived in Corinth in the hands of or in advance of Timothy's arrival. When Timothy arrived in Corinth, he found the church shaken by internal disputes and gravely suspicious of Paul. Neither his presence nor the letter had healed the wounds opened by internal conflict. Second, certain Hellenistic Jewish Christian missionaries had arrived, bidding for the affection, loyalty, and support of the Corinthian church. They claimed to be "servants of Christ" (2 Cor. 11:23) and professed to be apostles (11:5, 13). They came armed with written testimonials to the success of their preaching elsewhere (3:1). These "superlative apostles" drew unflattering comparisons between their gifts and those of Paul. They said Paul lacked charisma, that he was unskilled in speech, physically weak, frail, and hypocritical—a bully in his letters but harmless in person (10:10). When Paul was in Corinth he had refused money, these men apostles of discord alleged, either because he was insecure in his apostolate (11:7, 9) or because he planned to skim off some of the Jerusalem offering for himself (12:16–18). For their part, these Jewish Christian missionaries boasted of their exploits in service of the gospel. With signs and wonders they demonstrated the power of their message, through visions they gained access to heavenly secrets, and for these divine gifts they sought support from the church and thus undermined Paul's efforts to collect an offering for the "poor" in Jerusalem.[10]

Third, Paul probably dispatched the highly commended Titus and the "brothers" with a letter of introduction and a specific program to complete the offering project in Corinth (2 Cor. 8). Rather than being eager and excited to participate in this highly symbolic gesture, the Corinthians were reticent. These doubts about the project and Paul's place in it combined with lingering internal problems and the invasion of itinerant missionary critics of Paul to fuel raging doubts about Paul's apostolic legitimacy, his motives, his duplicity, honesty, and the truth of his gospel. Paul's own converts, his "children," turned against him, or failed to come to his defense.

Paul's Painful Visit to Corinth

After writing a defense of his legitimacy (2 Cor. 2:14–7:4 [minus 6:14–7:1]) that was less than fully successful, Paul made a brief, "painful" visit to Corinth (2:1) that failed miserably. Once in Corinth he was insulted publicly by a Corinthian Christian (2:5–8; 7:12) and frustrated in his efforts to effect a reconciliation. He returned to Ephesus in humiliation and disgrace (12:21). His disastrous visit played into the hands of his critics. His hasty retreat lent substance to his critics' charge that he was cowardly. His position in the Corinthian church seemed more insecure than ever.

Paul's Fifth Letter to the Corinthians[11]

Humiliated, shamed, and angry, Paul limped away to Ephesus to ponder a response. Hunkered down in Ephesus after this public shaming, Paul scribed his fifth Corinthian epistle, or "tearful letter" (2 Cor. 2:4; 10:1–13:10) to try to patch up a relationship gone sour. That "tearful letter" catalogs the attacks of his rivals on his fitness for ministry, his honesty, steadfastness, sincerity, rhetorical sufficiency, and weak, "womanish" bodily presence. Hurt and angry, Paul summoned up some of the most brutal martial language he would use anywhere, turned it on his own converts (10:1–6, 10), and appended a section that demonized and stigmatized his rivals and their supporters (11:1–14).

Then with a flash of insight Paul appeared to realize the futility of playing the game of his rivals. A theological epiphany seems to have inspired some of Paul's most creative theologizing about the nature of power. While his critics mocked his bodily "weakness" (10:10), his "womanishness," Paul turned their word "weakness" to his defense. Using it in some form eleven times in one short treatise (11:21, 29, 30; 12:5, 9, 10 [bis]; 13:3, 4 [bis], 9), Paul takes on the persona of a "fool" who entertained and often mocked powerful figures at public events. While his critics mocked his bodily weakness, Paul found in the scars etched on his back not signifiers of shame or weakness but mystical links to the brutalized and crucified Christ. This radical ideology of power in weakness totally inverted and subverted the "dominant male discourse on the body" and elevated the trait of womanish weakness to become "the primary modes of identification and resistance," and directed the Corinthians once more to that which stood at the heart of his gospel from the beginning: "I decided to know nothing among you but Jesus Christ and him crucified" (1 Cor. 2:2).[12]

So anxious was Paul about the effect of this "severe" letter that he found it impossible to wait for Titus in Troas as planned. Instead, he set out to meet Titus (2 Cor. 2:12–13), finally linking up in Macedonia. Like a bright burst of sunlight after the passing of a storm, Titus's encouraging news brought joy to Paul: Titus reported that the Corinthians mourned their wrongs; they longed to see Paul (7:6–7). They had reprimanded the troublemakers and restored order. Paul's joy, optimism, and praise of the Corinthians blossomed. Expressions of "complete confidence" in the Corinthians (7:16) and generosity that would have seemed impossible just weeks before pushed aside the threats and warnings of the "tearful letter."

After hearing the good news, Paul sent Titus with a letter of thanksgiving to the Corinthian church (1:1–2:13; 7:2–16). The chief offender had been disciplined; Paul was sorry that his earlier letter was so severe, and he sought not punishment for him but forgiveness and restoration. A cooler conciliation and praise replaced the heat and hurt of the earlier letter. Now Paul's mind turned again to the offering project, as he penned one last, brief circular letter (2 Cor. 9) to the churches of Achaia to be carried by the "brothers" and to prepare for the arrival of Paul with the delegation from Macedonia.

Paul's Last Letter to the Corinthians (2 Corinthians 9)[13]

Filled with exhortation to complete this good work, Paul's mind races on ahead to the apocalyptic moment when the pilgrimage of Gentiles to Jerusalem would offer the gifts and praise that the prophets imagined would occur. Caught up in the ecstasy of that anticipated moment Paul inserted the reader into a great cosmic narrative. He shifted the gaze of his Achaian Gentile readers to set them in Jerusalem to blend their voices with the Jewish Christians in spontaneous praise. Paul gave play to his imagination and improvised a narrative so grand it almost takes the breath away. Thus he joined Gentile and Jew in the praise and glorification of God, and all of the past quarrels with Peter and James of the mother church were swept aside. Instead the prospect of this glorious outcome inspired Paul to a spontaneous cry: "Thanks be to

God for his indescribable gift" (2 Cor. 9:15). One can almost sense the quiet that would settle over the little house church cells in Achaia as this letter was read and as it bestowed on their offerings whether small or large a place in a scenario almost too great to imagine. With this offering the great reconciling work of God in Christ placed them on the threshold when Jew and Gentile believers would stand together in God's elect.

When we next hear from Paul, he is in Corinth with Gaius his host, a wealthy convert whom he earlier baptized on his founding visit (1 Cor. 1:14). The collection stood ready for delivery; the delegation from Macedonia and Achaia had gathered to set out in April with the return of the shipping season. The brilliance of Paul's earlier inspired moment had faded, and a somber Paul wrote the Roman church soliciting their prayers for a successful visit to Jerusalem. The world Paul created for his reader, however, was an unfinished one, a world that the realized eschatology could never provide. With the letter to Rome dispatched, this letter written, and the journey to Jerusalem about to begin, Paul's voice fell silent. But the story was interrupted at an opportune moment when hope for reconciliation burned brightly.

Summary of Paul's Interaction with the Corinthians

1. Founding mission in Corinth (51–52 CE).
2. Gallio hearing and expulsion/departure (52 CE).
3. Letter A to Corinthians (1 Cor. 5:9) (missing, 52/53 CE).
4. Corinthians letter (1 Cor. 7:1) (missing) and oral report (16:17, c. 53 CE).
5. Letter B: 1 Corinthians, response to oral and written communication dispatched with Timothy.
6. Letter C: 2 Corinthians 8 (offering) delivered by Titus and the anonymous "brothers." Arouses suspicions.
7. Letter D: 2:14–7:4 (minus 6:14–7:1), Paul's first defense; failed.
8. Painful visit (2 Cor. 2:1–4) and its disastrous ending (2:1; 7:9, 11–12).
9. Letter E: "tearful letter" (10:1–13:10) delivered by Titus.
10. Macedonian rendezvous with Titus. Reports reconciliation.
11. Letter F: conciliatory letter (1:1–2:13; 7:5–16; 13:11–13, c. 56 CE).
12. Letter G: round-robin offering letter (2 Cor. 9) to churches of Achaia. Anonymous "brothers" deliver (c. 56 CE).
13. Romans (57 CE).[14]

One might ask, does this discussion of the literary integrity of 2 Corinthians really matter? Why not simply read 2 Corinthians as it is? Why appeal to an unprovable hypothesis to make sense of this exchange? We do so, first, because there is no alternative. Since no text is self-interpreting, no interpreter simply takes the text as it is. One views a text through the optic one brings to it. Second, such constructions of the historical imagination assist our approach to the world of the text. Third, we engage in such acts of historical imagination to capture the dynamic and theological creativity that is revealed in the shrill and soothing exchanges between Paul and his churches. Such an act of conjuring the narrative of a text defies all facile solutions; nevertheless, it is necessary if one is to capture the dynamism of Paul's theology and the way it was refined in history's crucible. The hope and aim of the scholar is that her construction will reasonably explain the issues and problems the text presents, and that the conjured narrative will reveal the tensions and vitality of the interaction between Paul and this small cell of believers.[15]

Outline of 1 Corinthians
(Paul's Second Letter)

1. Address, Salutation, and Thanksgiving	1:1–9
2. Concerning Disunity	1:10–4:21
a. Dissension in the church (Related to boasting of special knowledge received in baptism)	1:10–17
b. God's wisdom vs. worldly (i.e., Corinthian) wisdom	1:18–2:16
c. Factions among the self-proclaimed wise (mature)	3:1–23
d. The church's judgment of Paul	4:1–21
3. Problems of Immorality	5:1–6:11
a. A case of incest	5:1–13
b. A lawsuit between Christians	6:1–11
4. Reply to Questions in the Corinthians' Letter to Paul	6:12–16:12
a. Introduction	6:12–20
b. Concerning sex	7:1–40
c. Concerning idol meat	8:1–11:1
d. Concerning distinctions between women and men	11:2–16
e. Selfish behavior at the congregational meal	11:17–34
f. Concerning spiritual gifts	12:1–14:40
g. Concerning the resurrection	15:1–58
h. Concerning the collection	16:1–4
5. Paul's Travel Plans	16:5–9
6. News of Timothy's Visit	16:10–11
7. Concerning Apollos	16:12
8. Conclusion	16:13–24
a. Closing paraenesis (ethical instruction)	16:13–18
b. Closing greeting, apostolic warning, and benediction	16:19–24

Outline of Letter Fragments from 2 Corinthians
First Offering Appeal (Letter 3, 2 Cor. 8:1–24)[16]

1. Address, Salutation, Thanksgiving	(missing)
2. Body of Letter	
a. Generosity appeal	8:1–15
(1) Macedonian example	8:1–7
(2) Apostolic appeal	8:8–9
(3) Advice for completion	8:10–12
(4) Gifting of equals	8:13–15
b. Commendation of Titus and the "brothers"	8:16–24

First Defense of Paul's Ministry (Letter 4, 2 Cor. 2:14–7:4)

1. Address, Salutation, Thanksgiving	(missing)
2. Defense of Ministry	2:14–7:4
a. Introduction	(missing)
b. Triumphal procession with God	2:14–17
c. Ministry adequacy defended	3:1–6
d. Ministry of new covenant	3:7–4:6
(1) Glory compared with glory	3:7–11
(2) Unveiled	3:12–18
(3) Concluding unit	4:1–6
e. Gospel: treasure in clay pots	4:7–15
f. Ministry validated in affliction	4:16–5:10
g. Ministry of reconciliation	5:11–6:10
h. Final appeal	6:11–13; [6:14–7:1]; 7:2–4
(1) An appeal for an open-armed welcome	6:11–13
(a) A non-Pauline insertion	(6:14–7:1)
(2) Concluding appeal	7:2–4

Second Defense—the "Letter of Tears"
(Letter 5, 2 Cor. 10:1–13:10)

1. Address, Salutation, and Thanksgiving	(missing)
2. Defense and Response to Antagonists	10:1–13:10
a. Rejoinder with language of war	10:1–11
b. Good and bad boasting	10:12–18
c. Persona of fool assumed	11:1–12:13
(1) Demonization of super-apostles	11:1–15
(2) Boasting contest	11:16–23
(a) Introduction to fool's speech	11:16–21a
(b) Power in weakness (womanishness)	11:21b–12:10
(3) Postscript to fool's speech	12:11–13
d. Final appeal and warning	12:14–13:10
(1) Apostolic visit and final defense	12:14–18
(2) Hopes and fears of the visit	12:19–21
(3) Closing threats and exhortations	13:1–10

Reconciling Letter (Letter 6, 2 Cor. 1:1–2:13; 7:5–16; 13:11–14)

1.	Salutation	1:1–2
2.	Blessing/Thanksgiving	1:3–11
3.	Letter Body	1:12–2:13;
		7:5–16
	a. Introduction	1:12–14
	b. Painful visit recall	1:15–2:4
	c. Discipline of the offender	2:5–11
	d. Anguished wait for Titus	2:12–13
	e. Paul and Titus rendezvous	7:5–16
	(1) Titus brings news of reconciliation	7:5–7
	(2) Good grief wrought by the "letter of tears"	7:8–13a
	(3) Consolation and confidence	7:13b–16
4.	Concluding injunctions and grace	13:11–13

Round-robin Offering Letter to Churches in Achaia
(Letter 7, 9:1–15)

1.	Address, Salutation and Thanksgiving	(missing)
2.	Final Offering Letter	9:1–5
3.	Divine Source of Sowing and Reaping	9:6–10
4.	Focus on Jerusalem and Eschatological Pilgrimage	9:11–15

GALATIANS (52–56 CE)[17]

Paul founded the Galatian churches from a sickbed. When illness overtook him on his way through Galatia, the local people took him in and nursed him back to health (4:13–16). During his recuperation, and after, Paul spoke to the Galatian Gentiles (*Keltai*, Greek for Galatians) of their adoption as children of God. No longer, he said, need they be slaves of this world's hostile, demonic powers (4:8–9). Through the Crucified One and the gift of the Spirit, they could be liberated from the clutches of demonic powers. After hearing this "good news" and witnessing the mighty deeds of Paul (3:5), the Galatians received his gospel with enthusiasm and revered the apostle himself. Their patient had become an "angel of God," or savior; even Jesus Christ himself they called him (4:14). Their devotion was so extreme that they would, if possible, have given him their eyes (4:15).

Opposition Developed

All was well when Paul departed, but later he learned that the Galatians had adopted another version of his gospel. His apostleship was under attack, and the church was in turmoil. Whether outsiders or insiders inspired the opposition is uncertain. In any case, the nature of that opposition is clear. Once Paul left Galatia, his converts learned from Jewish scriptures that the promises of God belong to the children of Abraham and that one became a son of Abraham through circumcision. Abraham, the father of many Gentiles (Gen. 17:5), had been circumcised when ninety-nine years old after receiving God's promise. Likewise, the Galatians might have reasoned that it was necessary for them, the spiritual descendants of Abraham, to be circumcised. Such a conclusion would have been natural in light of Genesis 17:10, which reads, "This is my covenant, which you shall keep, between me and you and your offspring after you: Every male among you shall be circumcised." Later in Genesis 17:14 divine proscription is placed on those who disobey the command: "Any uncircumcised male who is not circumcised . . . shall be cut off from his people." Word of the observance of circumcision by the Jewish Christians in Jerusalem may have strengthened the conviction of the Galatians that their males also should be circumcised. For whatever reason, by the time Paul wrote Galatians, the church was requiring all baptized males to be circumcised (5:2, 11; 6:12–13). Their zeal for God and the scriptures led them and perhaps women as well to keep other parts of the law (3:2; 4:21; 5:4, 18).

The Galatians thus attempted to revise Paul's gospel by adding circumcision to it. They also incorporated much from the local religion. They continued worshiping certain "elemental spirits" (4:9) and observing "days, and months, and seasons, and years" (4:10).

Of a piece with the modification of Paul's gospel were the questions raised about Paul himself, for it was impossible to separate the veracity of the message from the integrity of the messenger. The Galatians began to wonder if Paul were an interloper in the apostolic circle. Jesus' original followers, even Jesus' brother James, were leaders in the Jerusalem church. Their links with the Lord were biological, historical, and personal, and the authority for their leadership was unquestioned. Paul, however, was a newcomer, for it was only after Jesus' death that Paul learned of Jesus and his followers, and then only as their adversary. How could Paul claim to be the Lord's apostle when he had not known the historical Jesus? Many of Paul's traditions stemmed from followers of Jesus, not from Jesus himself. Thus Paul's gospel was second-hand and therefore deficient. However good his intentions or impressive his preaching, Paul's gospel required emendation, a supplement wider in scope, stricter in discipline, more firmly grounded in scripture and the apostolic tradition rather than some claimed vision. Their appeal to scripture was possibly developed in opposition to certain enthusiastic or libertine tendencies in Gentile churches like Corinth, or perhaps they saw a danger in Paul's preaching of salvation by grace alone. Note, for example, Paul's warning against the excesses of a freedom in the Spirit that drew few distinctions between moral and immoral behavior (Gal. 5:13).

Who Were Paul's Opponents?

Scholars hold three views on the identity of Paul's opponents.

a. One view is that Jewish Christians from Jerusalem (of Peter or James) trailed Paul from place to place as a kind of truth squad that sought to correct his dangerous innovation. The theory is that the Jewish Christian church in Jerusalem kept the law and sought to impose it on Paul's congregations who claimed salvation by grace apart from law and who had thereby grown morally lax.

This view, however, suffers from the lack of any reference to such opposition in Galatians. Although Paul was eager to show his independence of the so-called pillars in Jerusalem, Paul nonetheless referred to their endorsement of his Gentile gospel (2:9–10). If the pillars once endorsed Paul 's gospel, it is unlikely that they would then have actively opposed it. Moreover, the Galatian charge that Paul was dependent on the Jerusalem church for his gospel makes no sense if the Jerusalem leaders opposed him. And if Paul's opponents were Jewish Christians from Jerusalem, it is puzzling he should have to remind them that one who submits to circumcision is obligated to keep the whole law. Any Jewish Christian from Jerusalem would have known that it was an ancient Pharisaic principle, and it is not likely they would have neglected it. Finally, the reversion of the Galatians to the service of "elemental spirits" (4:9) and their tendency to turn Christian freedom into libertinism (5:13) could hardly have been the result of a campaign by Jewish Christians to bring all of Paul's converts into obedience to the law.

b. Followers of Johannes Munck, a distinguished Danish scholar, hold that Paul's opponents were members of the Galatian congregation.[18] According to Munck, Paul referred to the troublemakers as "those who are being circumcised" (6:13, AT), which would be singularly inappropriate if Paul meant to refer to Jerusalem Jews, who, of course, had been circumcised long ago. On Munck's side also is the absence of a single reference to the opponents as "outsiders" (unlike 2 Cor. 10–13; 3:1). In support of Munck's view, Lloyd Gaston has shown that there were Gentile Judaizers in Asia Minor, although from a somewhat later period.[19] According to Ignatius in his *Letter to the Philadelphians*, "If anyone interpret Judaism to you do not listen to him; for it is better to hear Christianity from the circumcised [such as Paul] than Judaism from the uncircumcised [e.g., Gentile Judaizers]."[20]

It would be natural for Gentile converts to conclude from reading Jewish scripture that circumcision was required of all believers (see Gen. 17:11,

14). Inevitably, this practice would cause some to wonder why Paul had not required circumcision. Paul's silence on this issue would have been especially perplexing in light of the practice of circumcision in the Jewish Christian church in Jerusalem. Had Paul deliberately misrepresented the gospel he got from Jerusalem by omitting the circumcision requirement? The issue is complicated by the fact that Paul, unlike Peter and James, had not known the earthly Jesus, and that might have inspired the quite logical question: Was not the gospel of the "pillars" more authentic than that of Paul?

Although Munck raised important questions about the identity of Paul's opponents, many scholars feel his thesis does not account for the references to behavior having nothing to do with Jewish faith and praxis. It is especially difficult to reconcile Munck's thesis with the references to the worship of elemental spirits in Galatia, to their observance of days, months, seasons, and years, and to their libertinism.

c. Walter Schmithals, a noted German scholar, has argued that Paul's Galatian converts were syncretists who combined features of Jewish praxis (i.e., circumcision) with items drawn from folk religion, and thus they tried to blend Paul's gospel with elements of their own religious and social context. Such a thesis allows for the amateurism of the Galatian observance of circumcision. For example, their unawareness of the principle that this cultic act obligated them to keep the entire law is surprising. But it does seem strange, if syncretism were the threat, that Paul should give it so little space while giving so much to the judaizing menace. Moreover, Judaism was no monolithic unity in the period, and syncretistic tendencies were quite evident in certain Jewish gnostic circles.

Paul's Response

The attempts to undermine Paul's authority and supplement his gospel evoked his fiery rejoinder. In place of the usual warm, friendly thanksgiving, Paul opened the letter with an expression of astonishment: "I am astonished that you are so quickly deserting the one who called you in the grace of Christ" (1:6). He then called down a twofold curse from heaven on his rivals who were preaching "another" gospel (1:7–9). Later he excoriated those who delighted in circumcising others and suggested with bitter sarcasm that they mutilate themselves (5:12). Using an ugly pun, he fulminated that those who receive circumcision are cut off from Christ (5:4). Finally, he audaciously warned those attacking him that they really oppose Christ (6:17).

The defense of Paul's apostleship with the defense of his gospel was natural, for in the mind of Paul and his readers the two were inseparable. When the Galatians thus located Paul's gospel in a human source, that is, the "pillars" of the Jerusalem church, Paul insisted that the call from Christ that initiated his apostleship was independent of the Jerusalem church. For three years after his call he did not visit Jerusalem, and when he did return it was only for a fortnight, and then not again for fourteen years. Even during his brief time in Jerusalem he maintained his independence, so he claimed, and then gained acceptance for his gospel; and later on one occasion he publicly rebuked Peter in Antioch for his duplicity on the issue of eating with Gentiles. Moreover, Paul appealed more often to his status as an Israelite than a Jew and thus showed a preference for a broader term than that of the Jerusalem church.[21] By arguing that Christ, not the Jerusalem leaders, commissioned him directly, Paul tried to neutralize the charge that his gospel was a human creation (1:18–2:21).

Paul disputed the scriptural basis of his opponents' opposition. His discussion centered on Abraham, a figure important to both him and his critics. As a son of Abraham according to the flesh (Rom. 4:1; 11:1; 2 Cor. 11:21b–24), Paul knew that Abraham was an uncircumcised *goy* or Gentile when he first trusted God's promise (Rom. 4). Abraham, Paul claimed, was thus the patron of all proselytes or Gentiles. Since God's promise was that through Abraham all the world's peoples (i.e., Gentiles) would be blessed, it is likely that the Galatians shared Paul's interest in the Abraham narrative, for in it they would have found grounds for requiring circumcision, and could point to the commandment to Abraham that all of his male descendants were to undergo circumcision (Gen. 17:9–11). Any uncircumcised male would "be cut off from his people" (Gen. 17:14). Against this interpretation of the Abraham narrative, Paul appealed to Genesis 15:6, where Abraham "*believed* the LORD; and the LORD reckoned [counted] it [his trust] to him as *righteousness*" (italics added). Therefore, Paul concluded, since Abraham was counted righteous on account of his faith before he was circumcised, it is faith, not circumcision, that links the children of promise with Abraham.

Paul then offered an exegesis of the Abraham narrative that some might think grotesque (Gal. 3:16): "Now the promises were made to Abraham and to his offspring. It does not say, 'to offsprings,' as of many; but it says, 'to your offspring' [singular]," which Paul read as a reference to Christ. Thus Paul implied that it was through faith in Christ, not law observance, that Gentiles became true children of Abraham. Given the benefit of modern exegetical methods, we know, of course, that Paul is unfaithful here to the intent of the Genesis material. But Paul's tendency to read himself and his community into those texts was common.

In light of Paul's positive statements about the law elsewhere, his almost totally negative characterization of it in Galatians is problematic. His statements here, however, must be read as exaggerations for effect—a polemical attempt to confute his critics. He vigorously opposed their effort to supplement his gospel with law observance for two reasons. First, it revealed a distrust in the adequacy of his gospel and the God who gave it. In Jerusalem Paul had defended his right to offer full salvation to Gentiles qua Gentiles to belong to God's elect; in this letter he met the attempt to assign Gentiles who entered the church through faith instead of the law to second-class status, which qualified Paul's offer of full participation.

The second reason for Paul's opposition was that the Galatian experiment with the law was amateurish. One senses Paul's disdain, if not contempt, for those who thought they could selectively observe portions of the law. Paul reminded the Galatians of a basic Pharisaic principle that evidently they had overlooked: "Every man who lets himself be circumcised . . . is obliged to obey the *entire* law" (5:3, italics added). Paul said this, however, not to urge those who were keeping part of the law to work harder to observe all 613 commandments, but to encourage his listeners to claim full membership in God's covenant people by grace and not as righteous proselytes via Judaism.[22] Since the Galatians came to enjoy life in the Spirit through "hearing with faith" free from "works of the law," Paul would have them continue in the way of responsible freedom (Gal. 5).

Outline of Galatians

1.	Address and Salutation	1:1–5
2.	Expression of Astonishment[23]	1:6–9
3.	Paul's Defense of His Apostleship	1:10–2:21
4.	Paul's Defense of His Gospel	3:1–4:31
	a. Spirit comes through gospel, not law	3:1–5
	b. Abraham: father of promise	3:6–29
	c. Law and grace	4:1–31
5.	The Gospel Applied: Freedom and Responsibility	5:1–6:10
	a. Stand fast in freedom	5:1–12
	b. Freedom to love	5:13–25
	c. The law of Christ	5:26–6:10
6.	Personal Exhortation and Conclusion	6:11–18

ROMANS (c. 56–57 CE)

Integrity of the Letter

There are, or once were, three different manuscript versions of Romans: one ending with chapter 14, one with chapter 15, and one with chapter 16. But which one went to Rome? The scholarly consensus is that it was not the shortest version (chaps. 1–14 plus the benediction in 16:25–27), used, if not created, by Marcion, a second-century "heretic."[24] Given Marcion's tendency to take the knife to disagreeable texts and given his distaste for the "Old Testament" (his term), Paul's praise of the Jewish scriptures in 15:9–12 and 15:21 may have inspired their amputation and the addition of a benediction (16:25–27). Since short versions of the letter do surface in late Latin manuscripts, however, Marcion may have simply adopted the shorter version.

More tenable, in the view of some, is that Paul's original letter to Rome contained only chapters 1–15 plus a concluding benediction that was removed to make way for chapter16. Some hold that chapter 16 was a later work, perhaps by Paul himself, and was probably sent to a church in the East. Because Paul spent so much time there, the leading candidate for that honor is Ephesus. Even if chapter 16 were written at the same time as chapters 1–15, it was not part of the same letter and can hardly be used to ascertain anything about the Roman situation.

The argument that the long version (chaps. 1–16) went to Rome raises a host of questions. Would Paul have known twenty-six Christians in Rome whom he could greet by name (16:3–15)? Since no other Pauline letter greets addressees by name, one wonders whether, even had Paul known twenty-six Christians in Rome, he would have greeted them by name. Prisca and Aquila were working with Paul in Ephesus when 1 Corinthians 16:19 was written (c. 53 CE). Had they now returned to Rome (c. 57 CE)? Paul greets Andronicus and Junia (Rom. 16:7), "fellow" prisoners, in Ephesus presumably. Had they also moved to Rome? Paul calls Epaenetus "the first convert in *Asia*" (16:5, italics added), but now he also is in Rome. While such a mass movement of Paul's acquaintances to Rome may sound improbable to us, it is certainly possible. Approximately three years before Paul wrote Romans, Nero had lifted the edict of Claudius (c. 49 CE) expelling Jews from Rome (see below). In that interim there was sufficient time for Jewish Christians to return to Rome from the East, and had they done so they might now offer a valuable bridge between Paul the apostle and the Roman churches. That return could explain the anomaly of Paul's final greeting.

Harry Gamble, however, has provided persuasive textual evidence that chapter 16 originally belonged to the textual tradition that has Paul send this entire letter to Rome.[25] The final benediction condemning false doctrine (16:17–19), however, points to a later situation in the East (see 2 Corinthians and Philippians).

Background of the Roman Church

We do not know who founded the Roman church or when. We know only that it had already been in existence "for many years" before Paul wrote Romans

(15:23), and that there was a church in Rome in the 40s when Emperor Claudius "expelled from Rome the Jews who were constantly stirring up a tumult under the leadership of Chrestus" (Suetonius, *Claudius* 25, in *The Lives of the Twelve Caesars*). Although Suetonius's report is vague, it probably refers to heated or even violent arguments in the Jewish community concerning Christ. Aquila and Prisca, Paul's coworkers in Corinth (1 Cor. 16:19), conceivably were among those expelled by Claudius. Meanwhile the Gentile Christians remained in Rome, unmolested by the ban of Claudius. After the death of Claudius, Nero lifted the ban in 54 CE, allowing Jewish Christians to return. But the return of the Jewish Christians may have instigated new tensions in the Roman church.

Problems within the Church

Scholars disagree about the purpose of Romans, and no single reason adequately accounts for its existence. Chapter 14 shows Paul was aware of conflict between Christians, possibly Jewish and Gentile.

One plausible explanation suggests that a Gentile emphasis on justification by grace apart from works of the law encouraged licentious tendencies (1 Cor. 5–6), and returning Jewish Christians, who like Paul tended to expect Gentiles to be morally lax, might have taken umbrage at the Gentile view that the gospel forbade the observance of dietary rules (chap. 14). In spite of Gentile disdain some Jewish believers ("weak") preferred eating no meat (14:2) to eating ritually unclean food (14:14). Similarly, abstention from wine routinely offered to pagan gods before its sale (14:21) avoided the sin of idolatry (14:2). It was better to risk being an overly scrupulous Jewish follower obedient to Torah than to offend against conscience; an overly scrupulous Torah observance was preferable to the risk of immorality encouraged by the Gentile gospel of justification by grace alone. For enough immorality existed among Gentile followers (cf. 1 Cor. 5–7) to lend substance to the salacious rumors that Gentile rejection of the law encouraged egregious lawlessness.

Paul had already objected to such charges with cutting rhetorical questions: "Should we continue in sin in order that grace may abound?" (6:1). "Should we sin because we are not under law but under grace?" (6:15). "Is the law sin?" (7:7). The accusation that Paul advocated "let us do 'bad things' that good may come" (3:8, AT) brought an angry snort from Paul.

Another plausible reason for writing was to answer the charge that his Gentile gospel suggested that "God's promises [to Israel had] failed" (9:6). Because they had been flung at him before, Paul was in a unique position to pose these questions with a strong negative answer implied: "No, no, absolutely not!" Jewish Jesus people, like Paul, active in both synagogue and church were continually exposed to ridicule and harassment from nonmessianist Israelites. Thus Jewish Christians were reviled by Gentile Christians for being overly scrupulous and were simultaneously charged by synagogue leaders with lax behavior. Why, these leaders might ask, do not the Gentiles first become proselyte Jews if they wish to become heirs of God's promises? Moreover, some Jewish followers claiming to be no longer "under law but under grace" may have abandoned the synagogue altogether and would have been dubbed apostates by their peers (6:15). They could legitimately ask, what kind of gospel was this that prompted believers to jettison the law as God's good gift and begin the slide into immorality? Incredulously they asked, how could anyone be law observant and also accept a gospel that rejected the law as unnecessary? More importantly, what kind of a God is it that would make promises but not keep them? The climax to the opening part of Romans 9–11 devotes itself entirely to this question.

It is possible also that Paul wrote to garner support for his Spanish mission, and though he clearly sought the support of the Roman church, it is unlikely that such heavy discourse was needed to serve that purpose only.

Finally, although the theologizing in Romans is profound, some would even say unsurpassed, the letter is not, as C. H. Dodd once claimed, a calm summary of his theology developed over a stormy apostolic career. The absence of a single reference in this letter to the cross is puzzling if that is the case.[26]

Paul's Response

Unlike Paul's other letters, Romans was written to a church he had neither founded nor visited. In Romans Paul named no adversary and attacked no opponent. Yet, like his other epistles, Romans is a genuine letter, not a treatise on systematic theology. Although its depth of insight is great—some would say unsurpassed—it nevertheless has the structure of a letter, breathes the warmth of a letter, deals with a real situation, and functions like a letter as a substitute for absence.

Written on the heels of Paul's heated exchanges with the Corinthian and Galatian churches, Romans echoes many of the concerns of those letters (e.g., references to Adam and Christ, the law, Abraham, the love commandment, the faithfulness of Jesus Christ, salvation for Gentiles, God's righteousness, the offering, election, and emphases on judgment and vindication). But Romans is also quite definitely distinct from them and is by no means, as several have suggested, simply a calm, cool, reflective summary of the wisdom Paul gleaned from his turbulent dealings with the Corinthian and Galatian churches. In this letter Paul mentions neither Judaizers (Galatians), nor enthusiasts (1 Corinthians), nor itinerant Jewish Christian apostles (2 Corinthians, Philippians), nor strangely the cross, the Eucharist, and except for 16:1–24, the church, or fierce critics (Philippians and 2 Corinthians). When Paul wrote, the Roman church was troubled, but it was not "sectarian." As Paul said, "I myself feel confident about you, my brothers and sisters, that you yourselves are full of goodness, filled with all knowledge, and able to instruct one another" (15:14). About some things, Paul wrote to strengthen and be strengthened by them (1:11–12). He hoped to reconcile a church divided to build a base from which to launch his Spanish mission (15:24, 28), to defend his gospel to the Gentiles, and to respond to criticisms threatening the future of his ministry (see 2 Corinthians and Galatians).

Since he had never visited Rome, the situation was delicate. The Gentile majority might resent his intrusion. The Jewish minority, after hearing that Paul was a dangerous and even reckless innovator, might understandably have been less than overjoyed at the prospect of a visit from this persona non grata from the East. In the discussion below we shall see how carefully Paul addressed the Roman situation. He opened the salutation with a defense of his apostolic credentials (deemed specious by some) and the truth of his gospel for *everyone* (Jew and Greek). In spite of the vituperation heaped on Paul by his critics in the East, Paul offered no apology: "I am not ashamed of the gospel; for it is the power of God for all those believing, Jew and Greek." Then Paul penned what served as the thematic head of the letter, "for in it [i.e., the gospel] the righteousness of God is being revealed out of the faithfulness [of Christ] unto faith [in Christ], and whoever is righteous out of faith shall live" (1:17, AT). Paul had to gain some endorsement of this basic premise of his gospel if he were to be received in Rome and if he were to have the support of the Roman church for his Spanish mission (15:22–24). For Paul, God's righteousness denoted no quality of divine being, but rather a divine action through Messiah Jesus to reclaim a crooked world, to raise up the fallen, and to offer liberation from the powers that be by faith or through God's acceptance, which was manifest in and through the faithfulness of Christ (3:21–26) to pagans (1:18–32) and Jews (2:1–3:8) alike.

Paul wrote that the coming of Christ exposed the historical failure of both Jews and Gentiles either to do the will of God or to render the thanks due. Therefore he asserted that boasting by the Jew and arrogance by the Gentile were both excluded: "all have sinned and fallen short of the glory of God." Since all "have sinned and fallen short" (3:23, AT), all stand in equal need of the means of grace offered through the faithfulness of Christ (3:21–24). Thus Paul's gospel included but transcended individual salvation and assumed cosmic proportions in the announcement of redemption from the tyranny of the cosmic, demonic, enslaving, and alienating powers of Sin and Death, and offered a remedy for this human bondage, brokenness, and alienation.

In 4:1–22 Paul invoked Abraham as a model for his inclusive gospel. In Galatia, his judaizing opponents appealed to the example of Abraham's circumcision (Gen. 17:9–14) to refute Paul's welcome of uncircumcised Gentile males into God's elect. But here Paul offered the Abraham story as support for his inclusive gospel (see Gen. 15:1–6, where Abraham received and believed in the promises of God before receiving circumcision). In Abraham's faith or trust in God, reckoned to him as "righteousness" while he was still a Gentile (i.e., before circumcision), Paul claimed support for his Gentile gospel and showed that his gospel did not overthrow the law (Rom. 3:31) but secured its deeper meaning. (Please note that the proclamation of a "righteousness by faith" either by Abraham or by a Gentile convert was no substitution of one work ["faith"] for another ["works by the law"]. Abraham's trust did not make him righteous, but instead his faith was the trusting acceptance of the efficacy of God's gracious or righteous work.) Later, in 5:12–21, Paul responded to the query as to how one man's act of righteousness, namely, that of Jesus, could redound to others. He argued from the first Adam to the last: just as through the disobedience of Adam others who sinned shared his fate, namely, death (Gen. 2:15–3:24), so now through "one man's act of righteousness" justification and life became available for all (Rom. 5:18). Paul's summary—where "sin increased, grace abounded all the more" (5:20)—inspired a slanderous jibe: "Should we continue in sin in order that grace may abound?" (6:1; cf. 3:8). Paul was keenly sensitive to the malicious charge that his Gentile gospel turned immorality into a pathway to grace. (Recall that in Corinth and Philippi at least, some had understood salvation by grace outside the law to mean that all things were lawful. In those cities certain libertines seemed to anticipate Herod's caricature of grace found in W. H. Auden's *For the Time Being: A Christmas Oratorio:* "I like committing crimes. God likes forgiving them. Really the world is admirably arranged.")[27]

Drawing on three metaphors—baptism, slavery, and marriage—Paul pointedly asked how anyone sharing the life of the new age could behave like a member of the old. Baptism represented more than the initiation into the new creation, liberation from Master Sin, and symbolic participation in the death of Christ with no preconditions whatsoever. Being raised up with Christ carried with it the requirement to walk in "newness of life" (6:4). Being liberated from the tyranny of slavery to Sin's cosmic power freed one to submit to the righteousness of God and to resist the dominion of Sin (6:12–23). How, Paul wondered, could a believer who had died to sin continue in its bondage (6:1–14)? Paul also pointed to the way the death of a husband freed the spouse to remarry and "bear fruit" (children) in a new relationship. Similarly, those who had died to the law, Paul asserted, were free from the law of marriage to join with and bear fruit for Christ in another relationship (7:1–6).

Drawing on these images, Paul aimed to correct the impression that his gospel encouraged immorality. He then rose to respond to the question raised by his last metaphor, namely, death to the law freeing the spouse to remarry: "Is the law [therefore] sinful?" (7:7). It is not bad Torah that brings sin and death, Paul bristled (7:12, 16, 21–23; 8:2) but rather the crooked human heart. Calling God's gift (Torah, law) "evil" questioned God's nature and implied a divine being whose will was so dark and whose nature so sinister as to offer malevolent gifts to children. Paul submitted that it was the creature's crooked heart that twisted the law into a grotesque caricature that brought death. The law may forbid one to "covet [desire]" (7:7), he argued, but it is human nature to most desire the forbidden. The fault is not in the law or the God who gave it, Paul claimed, but in the creature himself or herself. Thus it is the misuse of the law, not the law itself, that "brings death" (7:13).

Two problems face the reader in 7:13–25: (1) the ambiguity of the term "flesh" (*sarx*), (e.g., "nothing good dwells in my . . . flesh") and (2) uncertainty about how Paul employed the term "I." As an Israelite, Paul would have been unable to attribute evil to the flesh per se, for even if it were humankind's Achilles' heel, flesh was for Paul morally neutral. Through the flesh and the desires associated with it, humanity was vulnerable to Sin's assault, and after gaining a foothold, the evil impulse (*yetzer hara'*) that took up residence in the flesh could corrupt the whole person. It is possible for the flesh to be corrupted, but the flesh is not in and of itself a corrupting element. Paul referred to this corrupted element when he said, "nothing good dwells within me, that is, in my flesh" (7:18); when he did so, he hardly meant that the physical was inherently bad but that the person had fallen victim to the evil power of Sin. When Paul spoke of those who lived "according to the flesh" (8:12), he referred to those whose flesh was taken captive by demonic powers in the world.

The second problem concerns Paul's use of the term "I" in 7:7–25. His use of the first person singular coupled with the past tense and the apparent parallel he drew between himself and Adam (man) of Genesis suggest that Paul may be speaking autobiographically and thus referring to his own personal experience. It is more likely, however, that Paul used the first person singular to refer not just to his own experience but representatively to all human experience (e.g., note 1 Cor. 13, where the Greek emphatic "I" [*egō*] is not employed but the first person singular is clearly used). Therefore, the passage probably should not be read as if the allusions to anxiety and depression came from Paul's inability to keep the law in its entirety, for Philippians 3:4–6 suggests, on the contrary, that he claimed to be blameless before the law.

The "law of the Spirit" (8:1–2), Paul believed, offered a remedy from enslaving powers and freed one from the "law [here principle] of sin and death" (recalling Gen. 2:17) in order to walk "after the Spirit" (Rom. 8:4).

Paul's theologizing here is one of hope, enabling him to see God working *"in all things"* (8:28). While acknowledging human mortality and weakness, frustration and fear, and trauma and distress with clear-eyed honesty, Paul offered one of his most powerful assertions that believers in all of earth's vicissitudes were "more than conquerors through him who loved us" (8:37).

Then follows Paul's tightly reasoned climax to the first part of the letter. In the face of an accusing question perhaps inspired by the news of the tough position Paul took on law (Torah) in Galatians, he had to defend his Gentile gospel and answer the question—were God's promises to Israel trustworthy? Only here in the authentic letters does Paul respond to this hostile accusation that his Gentile gospel impugned God's fairness.

With deep pathos Paul recognized the rejection of Messiah Jesus by most Jews. He began with pathos, "I have great sorrow and unceasing anguish in my heart" (9:2). Echoing Moses' prayer that God would substitute his life for the sin of a wayward people (Exod. 32:30–32), Paul cried out, "I could wish that I myself were accursed and cut off from Christ for the sake of my own people" (Rom. 9:3). Avoiding any spiritualization of Israel's election that would qualify their historic privileges (9:5), Paul praised God for Israel's privileges, which included the glory, the covenants, the law, the worship, the promises (9:4), and the Messiah "according to the flesh" (9:5). Instead of qualifying or spiritualizing that history, Paul praised God for it (9:5). It will soon be obvious to the reader who carefully works through the complicated and passionate reasoning that follows that he aimed to insert his Gentile converts into that narrative.

After this introduction, Paul recalled the story of election to affirm God's freedom to choose Gentiles and emphatically denied that the "word of God had failed" or that the promises were unreliable (9:6). Paul then argued that God's godness required the freedom to choose and to include Gentiles qua Gentiles in the elect. But paradoxically, Paul asserted, God's temporary rejection was no contradiction of the divine promises to Israel, and divine election even if arbitrary he deemed not unjust or permanent (9:14–29), but *all* (Jew and Gentile) who turn to God will experience salvation (10:12–13). Finally, the Jewish rejection of the apocalyptic gospel, he claimed, was not final (11:1–32), for if the temporary rejection by the Jews led to the inclusion of Gentiles (11:7–32), then the normal order, Jew first and then also the Gentile, was reversed to allow Gentiles to go first, and that priority, he expected, would provoke the Jews to jealousy, leading to their salvation. Then God's strange and cunning game plan will have worked. But in the end, Paul emphatically asserted, "all Israel will be saved" (11:26), and "the gifts and calling of God are irrevocable" (11:29, AT).

Elsewhere I have argued that the unbearable tension of this argument was resolved through a racing metaphor that offered a radical and countercultural solution: winners in competition do not (contrary to the cultural dogma, theirs and ours) require losers.[28] That is, God's inclusion of Gentiles in the elect required neither the rejection of Israel nor the repudiation of promises God once made. The solution to this great dilemma was, Paul exclaimed, "hidden in the mystery of the Godhead itself" (11:25). And in the inspiration of the moment he launched into a soaring benediction:

> O the depth of the riches and wisdom and knowledge of God! How unsearchable are his judgments and how inscrutable his ways!
>   "For who has known the mind of the Lord?
>   Or who has been his counselor?"
>   "Or who has given a gift to him,
>   to receive a gift in return?"
> For from him and through him and to him are all things. To him be the glory forever. Amen.
>
> (11:33–36)

In this short summary of the argument in chapters 9–11 we glimpse tensions so great as to extend Paul's logic to its breaking point. The radical solution he proposed reconfigured the world in a dramatic way for both Jew and Gentile. This reconfiguration was no abstract exercise but came through Paul's creative reinterpretation of the election tradition. Paul's seminal mind thus offered a solution that affirmed the validity of God's promises to Israel while extending the scope of those promises. The summary of Paul's argument in his own words runs: "As regards the gospel they [the Israelites] are enemies of God for your [i.e., you Gentiles'] sake; but as regards election they are beloved, for the sake of their ancestors; for the gifts and the calling of God are irrevocable" (11:28–29).

Despite its radical depth, Paul's solution did not long go unchallenged, and he would probably have been heartbroken had he lived to see the outcome. His floundering Gentile mission succeeded beyond expectation, and in a century the Gentile majority abandoned Paul's conviction of the importance of its ties to Israel. By the second century Justin argued that Jewish Christians would be excluded from salvation (*Dialogue with Trypho* 47), and Jerome later ridiculed Jewish Christians who wished "to be both Jews and Christians . . . and are neither Jews nor Christians" (*Selected Letters* 112.13). While Paul's construction in Romans 9–11 was innovative and some might claim brilliant, his attempt to admit difference without ascribing otherness was more difficult to sustain than to create.

Paul was also alive to the charge that his gospel of salvation apart from the law encouraged immorality. He had already argued in Romans 6–8 that the freedom secured by the gospel provided no license for misconduct. Now in Romans 12–15 he extended that argument.[29] He admonished all addressees to present their bodies as "a living sacrifice, holy and acceptable to God" as their daily "spiritual worship" (12:1). He urged all with special gifts to use them to build up the church (12:3–8; cf. 1 Cor. 12); he exhorted all to genuine love, perseverance in suffering, generosity to outsiders, nonretaliation (Rom. 12:9–21), respect for governing authorities (13:1–10), and reconciliation between the "weak" and "strong" (14:1–15:21).

Paul's preoccupation with the outsider segued into his discussion of the believers' relationship to "governing authorities." The influence this passage has had on the Christian view of the state through the centuries requires our attention. In spite of the sometime charge that this passage from Paul's pen encouraged the acceptance of Hitler's rule by Christians, its appearance here forces us to ask how this discussion related to Paul's wider epistolary purposes. Paul had already declared Jesus as the head of the new humanity (5:18), and proclaimed him Lord (*Kyrios*) for the believer (5:15–16 and 10:9). He was painfully aware that eschatological enthusiasm had led believers elsewhere to disregard the claims of this world (see discussion of 1 Thessalonians and 1 Corinthians above). Perhaps believers in Rome had neglected or even abandoned the present, provisional order in favor of God's rule. By withholding taxes and civil service from the "earthly" kingdom, they may have dared to affirm a commitment to a kingdom not of this world (had not Paul himself written the Philippians that their *politeuma* ["citizenship"] was in heaven? 3:20). On the other hand, Paul may have been responding to the accusation that his gospel encouraged irresponsible disengagement from the political realm.

In response, Paul reaffirmed the otherworldly character of his gospel along with its this-worldly imperative. He exhorted, "Do not be conformed to this world" (12:2), and almost simultaneously added, "be subject to the governing authorities" (13:1), and "pay taxes to whom taxes are due" (13:7). There was no need for Paul to launch a campaign to reform the government. Why should he? His conviction that "the day of the Lord was at hand" (13:12) and that the "form (*schēma*) of this world" was passing away (1 Cor. 7:31) would bring revolutionary change. Far from canceling out civic duty, however, the nearness of the end gave it, so he argued, cosmic significance. As the grand assize neared, Paul held, the opportunity for witness became more limited and the need for it more urgent; therefore, believers were to seize the day to witness.

Although the state provided an orderly context for travel and witness, Paul's intention was to urge the use of the civic realm to give love concrete expression to the neighbor, so broadly defined, as to include "authorities" (Rom. 13:3) and persecutors (12:17), that is, outsiders, as well as the proximate "other" or offending, hostile insiders (14:1–15:13). In the 50s when Paul wrote all of his letters the Christians had not been targeted for a systematic persecution. One must wonder what Paul would have said had he lived to see the brutal and localized persecution by Nero a decade later.

In 14:1–15:13 Paul turned to deal with peace within the community of the faithful: "Welcome one another . . . as Christ has welcomed you," he admonished (15:7). He urged mutual respect and tolerance of difference between the "weak" and the "strong." He pleaded for the acceptance of those who were different—those with dietary scruples and those without them, and those with power and those without it.

The close of the letter allows the western horizon of Paul's mission to break into view: "I will set out by way of you to Spain" (15:28). With the mission in the East completed from Jerusalem to Illyricum (15:19), with the offering project for the "poor among the saints" collected, and the delegation gathered to deliver the collection (15:25–27), Paul's mind raced ahead from Corinth to Jerusalem then back to Rome and beyond to Spain. As the spring of 57 CE neared and the journey's launch approached, Paul grew ever more anxious and petitioned the Roman churches to pray for the success of the mission. His hopes for the success of the mission mingled with fears that it would fail. Paul had every right to be anxious. His last encounter with Peter in Antioch was bitter and angry. The people of James had followed him as something of a truth squad to correct his gospel (Gal. 2:12). His relationship with the synagogue was a tortured one—he reported receiving forty lashes less one from synagogue authorities five times (2 Cor. 11:24). Moreover, gift giving was a very complex and complicated exercise in the ancient world. The gift might not be deemed acceptable and both Jews and Gentiles might find the transaction insulting and controlling.

The letters themselves offer no information on how the offering was received. The Acts account suggests that the pilgrimage to Jerusalem did not end well (Acts 21:17–40). The attempt by Paul and some of his Gentile converts to present the offering in the temple, Acts claims, was judged to be provocative, and led to an accusation of their desecration of the holy place (Acts 21:28), and that in turn provoked Paul's arrest and dispatch to Rome for trial; but using Acts as a source requires care.[30] It is a later document, tends to blame Jews for causing trouble (see the stoning of Stephen, Acts 7:59), and claims a Roman citizenship for Paul that the letters nowhere report. It is significant that even Acts sets Paul on the way to Rome for trial, but interrupts the travelogue before Paul arrives.

So from Acts we do not know how the story ends. That was to come in a late-second-century legendary account, *The Acts of Paul and Thecla*, which placed Paul's trial and execution in Rome under Nero.[31] So perhaps it is best that we are left to conjure an ending consistent with Paul's gospel. He did indeed harbor a dream that one day God's elect Israel and Gentile converts would join to celebrate the world this offering symbolized and Paul envisioned in which there would be "neither Jew nor Greek" among the elect (Gal. 3:28). But Paul's apocalyptic vision sketched by the letters (e.g., 2 Cor. 9) envisioned an unfinished world "groaning" for fulfillment (Rom. 8:22) that a realized eschatology could not provide.

Finally, if chapter 16 were part of the original letter to Rome, came Paul's greetings. There Paul greeted 26 people, 10 of whom were important women in the church (16:1–23). The list includes such notables as Phoebe, who may have delivered and interpreted the letter to the Roman churches (16:1), and Junia, the only woman in the New Testament who is called an apostle (16:7). Is she now an apostolic presence in Rome? Then there was the couple, Prisca and Aqila, who had been coworkers of Paul but apparently now had relocated.

In any case, when Paul's ship moored for the last time, he left behind a rich legacy to be debated in the second century. Although his letters focus on contextual issues and thus have an ad hoc character, they bear witness to a fierce struggle to secure the legitimacy of a Gentile mission that did not negate Israel's special privileges. The multiple challenges Paul faced in the churches presented him with occasions for fresh theologizing. In Galatians and Romans Paul was pushed to the limit to articulate a vision that would hold the church together and be faithful to his gospel. The letter fragments in 2 Corinthians reveal what a dynamic and creative thinker Paul was, offering a revolutionary vision of the marks (power in weakness) of apostolic legitimacy. And nowhere more than in 1 Corinthians does a clearer picture emerge of the diplomatic and pastoral skills he needed to hold a fractious church together. While Paul found much in the churches that was repugnant— immorality, religious puffery, arrogance, greed, and simple selfishness—he preached a gospel that spoke of God's embrace of this lumpish lot *being saved* in Christ (i.e., a process). Through bitter struggles with rival apostles and errant churches, Paul's understanding of life in Christ, the Spirit's work, and the nature of apostleship received varying and sometimes brilliant interpretations and reinterpretations.

Outline of Romans

1.	Address and Salutation	1:1–7
2.	Thanksgiving	1:8–12
3.	Autobiographical Introduction	1:13–17
4.	God's Wrath Now Being Revealed	1:18–3:20
	a. Judgment on Gentiles	1:18–2:16
	b. Judgment on Jews	2:17–3:20
5.	God's Righteousness Revealed	3:21–5:21
	a. Through faithfulness of Christ	3:21–3:31
	b. Through Abraham, patron of Gentiles	4:1–25

PHILIPPIANS (c. 55/56 CE)

Paul wrote to the Philippian church from a jail probably in Ephesus (winter of 55–spring of 56).[32] From the time of its founding, the Philippian church had a turbulent history. Paul spoke of his shameful treatment and the fierce opposition he ran into there (1 Thess. 2:2). The church was hounded by outsiders (Phil. 1:29–30) and fractured by the pettiness and jealousy of insiders (3:2ff.; 4:2–3). Some there preached the gospel out of love and respect for Paul; others preached out of partisanship (1:15–17).

But throughout these difficulties, the relationship between Paul and the Philippian church remained warm, supportive, and affectionate. The Philippians supported Paul's mission financially in Thessalonica (4:16) and possibly also in Corinth (2 Cor. 11:9). They gave generously to the Jerusalem collection (2 Cor. 8:1–5), and they sent Epaphroditus to care for Paul in prison (Phil. 2:25). Paul was to return to Philippi on his way to Corinth (2 Cor. 2:13), and possibly again on his final visit to Jerusalem with the offering. When in prison, Paul wrote movingly of his love and longing for the Philippian believers (Phil. 4:1).

When Paul wrote the letter from prison, one judicial hearing had already been held, and either Paul's condemnation (1:20; 2:17) or his release (1:25; 2:24) seemed imminent. His mission continued, however, in spite of the chains. Some, both inside and outside the praetorian guard, were touched by Paul's witness (1:13). Some of the slaves and freedmen from Caesar's household were converted (4:22). Through the courageous example of the apostle, some timid believers became fearless (1:14). Word of Paul's imprisonment eventually leaked out to the congregation at Philippi, and considering their special reverence for him, the response was predictable, and the continued contacts understandable. Those exchanges may be reconstructed as follows:[33]

1. Having learned that Paul was a prisoner in Ephesus, the Philippians sent Epaphroditus with money for his support and with instructions for his care.
2. Paul sent a letter of thanks (now lost), and the bearer of this letter reported to the Philippians that Epaphroditus was very ill.
3. The Philippians wrote to Paul expressing:
   a. Their distress over the critical condition of Epaphroditus (2:26).
   b. A request for the return of Epaphroditus and perhaps an expression of regret that his illness prevented him from serving Paul as they intended (2:25–30).
   c. A report of a quarrel between two women in the congregation, Euodia and Syntyche (4:2–3).
   d. Concern over the efforts of local Jews to win (back?) converts that the church had gained from the God-fearers (3:2–16).
   e. Concern about immorality (3:17–20).
4. Paul sent the present letter (in whole or in part) with Epaphroditus (2:25–26).
5. A visit by Timothy to Philippi was planned; he was to report back to Paul (2:19–23).
6. Paul planned a visit to Philippi if or when he was released (2:24).

Opposition

Have no fear of "opponents" (1:28). Who were these opponents? What were they doing? What were they saying about Paul? Where did they come from? Although no precise description of the outlook of the opponents is possible, we can make a rough sketch of their thought. They were nagging Gentile followers to accept circumcision (3:2). They preach a partisan gospel designed to torment the imprisoned apostle (1:17). They reject the importance of the cross (3:18) in favor of a glorious resurrected life. And they make a fetish of self-indulgence: "their god is the belly" (3:19). Owing to the absence of any sustained discussion of the law, it is unlikely that the opponents were Galatian-type Judaizers. Given their proclamation of Christ (1:17) they probably were not but could have been from the synagogue, although Jewish opposition did exist in another form in 2 Corinthians.

The "opponents" were probably religious syncretists (see discussion above on a judaizing Galatian syncretism). To them Paul's gospel was just one ingredient among many in a religious potpourri. Circumcision was a sign and seal of the covenant. Initiation into the local mystery religion also allowed the neophyte to pass directly and completely from death to a mythic resurrected life. When added to Paul's gospel of grace and freedom in Christ, this religious stew could lead to an unusual configuration.[34]

An alternative view is that Paul addresses different types of opponents in this letter: Jews bent on winning back Gentile God-fearers, those who had slipped into immorality, and religious enthusiasts who were critical of Paul's gospel and its emphasis on the cross. Others suggest that Paul was slow to recognize the character of the opposition and was thus somewhat confused in his response. Given Paul's first confused defense of his apostolic fitness in 2 Corinthians 2:14–7:4 (minus 6:14–7:1), that is entirely possible.

Although both of these alternatives are tenable, they seem less persuasive than the first view. Given the range of Paul's opposition elsewhere, it is unlikely that he would have misjudged his opponents here. Moreover, if opposition were coming from such different groups, it is strange that the groupings are so indistinct in the letter.

Paul's Response

To those claiming to be already "saved," Paul spoke of "full" salvation as only a future possibility. In writing of sharing Christ's "sufferings" by becoming like him in his "death" in order to "attain the resurrection" in the future (3:10–11), Paul implicitly emphasized the provisional nature of present salvation and qualified the promise of his critics. A variation on the same theme appears elsewhere: "Not that I have already obtained this [resurrection] or have already reached the goal; but I press on to make it my own. . . . I press on toward the goal for the prize of the heavenly call of God" (3:12–14). Paul then called on the Philippians to imitate him, and thus implicitly rejected the claimed view of those professing too much (3:15–17). His emphasis on the future not only undercut the smug and self-assured, it also reassured those who stumbled while simultaneously exhorting them to "have this mind in you which was also in Christ Jesus. . . ." His recitation of the ancient Christian hymn in 2:6–11 enjoined obedience and looked forward to exaltation and triumph with Christ *in the future.*

Many read Paul's repudiation of his Jewish antagonists in 3:4–9 to mean that he rejected his Jewish past. Let us listen to his words: "Whatever gains I had [as a Jew], these I have come to regard as loss [dung] because of Christ" (3:7). This statement, however, is part of Paul's polemic against the "dogs," a term loaded with opprobrium on those seeking to modify his gospel and discredit him by appealing to circumcision as the prerequisite to the new life. Paul responded in total disgust. He called his considerable achievements—his Pharisaic inclination, his Abrahamic connection, and even his blamelessness before the law—"dung" (Phil. 3:8), which may sound like a total rejection of his Jewish ancestry; but given his positive statements elsewhere (e.g., Rom. 9:1–5; 11:1; 2 Cor. 11:21b–25; 2 Cor. 3:7) and affirmation of his Israelite heritage, Philippians 3:8 is less a repudiation made in the heat of an argument than a revaluation of all of his experience, even his religious experience, in light of Christ.

In spite of the competing claims, the internal strife, and external threats, there is a genuine warmth and human tenderness in Philippians that is refreshing when compared with the bitter clashes in Galatians and 2 Corinthians 10:1–13:10. Philippians shows that Paul was not always a stormy combatant or divine warrior. He was also a towering figure whose confidence in God's future led him to look past the worst that life could bring.

Outline of Philippians

1. Introduction, Salutation, and Thanksgiving — 1:1–11
2. Paul's Imprisonment — 1:12–26
3. Exhortation to Stand Firm against Opponents — 1:27–2:18
4. Travel Plans — 2:19–30
5. Letter Conclusion (beginning) — 3:1
6. Exhortation to Persevere in the Struggle against Judaizing Propaganda and Libertinism — 3:2–4:1
7. Conclusion (continuation) — 4:2–23
   a. Appeal for harmony — 4:2–6, 8–9
   b. Thanks for gifts (possibly a fragment of a separate letter) — 4:10–20
   c. Closing greetings and benediction — 4:7, 21–23

PHILEMON (c. SPRING OF 57 CE)

Perhaps after stealing money (v. 18), Onesimus, a slave, ran away from his rich Christian master, Philemon, and Apphia. By coincidence, he found Paul in prison, converted to Christ, and assisted Paul in some way (v. 10). Paul wanted to keep Onesimus with him, and, on the strength of his apostolic office, he felt entitled to claim his service. Instead, he returned Onesimus to his master with this brief letter. In it Paul urged Philemon to restore Onesimus to his "household," to treat him like a "beloved brother" (v. 16), and to refrain from meting out harsh punishment to which Onesimus was liable as a runaway and possible thief. That request gained weight in light of Paul's expectation of his own imminent release from prison and visit to Philemon (note his request: "Prepare a guest room for me," v. 22).

In Colossians 4:9 Onesimus is traveling with Tychus to Colossae, which might suggest that Philemon's residence was near Colossae. But that might be assuming too much, for the Pauline authorship of Colossians is doubtful; and even if Paul did write it, to find useful evidence in it for locating Philemon's home would require that the two letters were written about the same time and that the trip of Onesimus referred to in Colossians was the same as the one Paul spoke of in Philemon.

If, as many scholars hold, the Pauline authorship of Colossians is doubtful, then it is possible that the reference to Onesimus was scribed there under influence from Philemon. On this question it is best to plead ignorance and say honestly that we do not know where Philemon lived.

Outline of Philemon

1.	Salutation	1–3
	a. Paul as sender	1a
	b. Recipients—Philemon, Apphia, Archippus, and the church	1b–2
	c. Greeting	3
2.	Thanksgiving	4–7
3.	Body of Letter	8–22
	a. Return of Onesimus	8–20
	b. Apostolic Visit	21–22
4.	Conclusion	23–25
	a. Final greeting	23–24
	b. Grace and benediction	25

We have come to the end of our discussion of the letters as conversations. We have confined our treatment to the undisputed Pauline letters, for in those letters it is easier to see that we are dealing with real letters, highly personal in nature, intensely particular in their discussion of problems, and essentially conversational in talking with, not at, others. I hope that reading the letters as conversations will help the student appreciate their dynamic and interactive character and their theological depth and insight, and will assist in reading them as real conversations about matters of singular importance rather than static deposits of theological truth waiting to be mined for their treasure.

5

Paul and His Myths

To the person on the street the term "myth" is synonymous with "fiction" or "untruth." Because the old stories about gods, devils, witches, and talking donkeys and snakes seem quaint, they are shelved, assigned a place with other relics from humanity's infancy. But could it be that myths from the archaic past do not reflect primeval ignorance and superstition but reveal the heights and depths the human spirit reaches when it wrestles with questions about life and death, love and hate, fate and freedom, truth and falsehood, and so on? Could it be that myth and legend mirror not what happened in the ancestral period but rather the response in the soul of a people to what happened? So even if unhistorical, could myth be, like art for Picasso, "a lie that makes us realize the truth"? As important as it is to know "what really happened" in the ancient past, do we not also need to know how men and women responded to those happenings? Increasingly, anthropologists, historians of religion, and biblical scholars are turning their scrutiny to myth and legend because mythological materials often provide a living window on men and women of an earlier time expressing their inmost imaginings. Such expressions can sensitize people to the profundity and high originality of these people of old.

To avoid misunderstanding, we must distinguish myth from metaphor. The term "pig" is a graphic expression when applied to a male chauvinist, but it is hardly myth. When Paul calls himself a boxer who pummels his body into submission, he is using metaphor, and drawing on myth when he recites the eucharistic formula, "This is my body." Metaphor is descriptive and figurative language about an event, whereas mythological language is an event itself, transporting participants into a zone of sacred time and/or space. The breaking of the bread is more than picture language about Jesus' execution; it is an avenue through which a worshiper may mythically enter the presence of the Redeemer figure and become "a contemporary disciple."[1]

No definition of myth will entirely satisfy. Myth has been called a means of comprehending reality and of being apprehended by it, but this description is vague and too general. Henri Frankfort described myth as "a form of poetry which transcends poetry in that it proclaims a truth; a form of reasoning which transcends reasoning in that it wants to bring about the truth it proclaims; a form of action, of ritual behavior, which does not find its fulfillment in the act but must proclaim and elaborate a poetic form of truth."[2] Although Frankfort's statement is helpful and evocative, it is more a poem about a poem than it is a useful definition of myth. Gerardus van der Leeuw calls myth "a spoken word, possessing decisive power in its repetition."[3] Although myth, like all forms of communication, is tied to the word, can its power be restricted to the word? The three statements above are sufficient to show the difficulty of forging a satisfactory definition of myth. Because of this difficulty, most writers discuss instead myth's character and function. We will follow that approach here.

THE WORLD VIEWED MYTHOLOGICALLY

In the first century, the relationship of both peasant and philosopher to the natural world was closely personal. Where we see a landscape of things stiff and mute, they saw a world overflowing with life. Where we see objects passively waiting for our hands to put them to use, they saw "Thous" actively forcing themselves on the human consciousness. Where we see an order defined by abstract laws, they saw both order and chaos as vehicles of will and intent. When the cloud rumbled or the wind roared, they did so because they decided to, or because their master commanded: "Rumble!" or "Roar!"

The apostle Paul's experience of the nonhuman world was likewise a personal one. In Romans 8:22 he wrote of the world's participation in the final apocalyptic woes attending the birth of the new age and the birth of the new creation. The earth's share in this wretchedness goes back to the dawn of creation when as an innocent bystander it was forced to bear part of the pain that followed Adam's disobedience. Earthquakes and storms, plagues and drought, snakes and disease were seen as signs of the futility and decay that nature suffered because its destiny was linked from the very beginning with the destiny of humankind. In this view the creation shares not only the agony but also the ecstasy of the creature. For God acted in Christ to redeem not only the wayward creature but also the burdened creation. As its redemption neared, the creation stood on tiptoe waiting to share in the liberation of the human and nonhuman world (Rom. 8:19–21).

All through the ages the creation had worn an image of its Creator. In spite of its distorted nature, the image of the Creator's power and deity had remained recognizable. Notwithstanding humankind's efforts to deface the image, the marks of God's power and deity have never been completely erased (Rom. 1:20). The Gentiles have always been able to recognize the fingerprints of the Creator on the creation. Thus the creation, like the creature, suffered an alienation and dislocation that reached back to the primeval period; and nature, like human beings, continued to bear the image of its Maker even if in a twisted form. We see that the alienation and hope that creature and creation shared made them kin.

In spite of this feeling of kinship, however, the world also seemed alien to Paul. He spoke of breaking through the barriers that restricted his existence either by ascending to the third heaven (2 Cor. 12:2) or by being delivered from the struggles that attend life in the world (2 Cor. 5:8; 12:1–10). He saw his life unfolding in a world dominated by Satan (2 Cor. 4:4), and he perceived the unsteady footing of that world—"the present form of this world," he dictated, "is passing away" (1 Cor. 7:31). So Paul did not feel at home in the world as it was but looked forward to the time when the original order would be restored and all fear and dread between humanity and the world would be removed. As Paul thought, "When anyone is united to Christ, there is a new world; the old order has gone, and a new order has already begun" (2 Cor. 5:17 NEB).

MYTH AND CULT

In the secular West we tend to view time as an ever-flowing stream that bears its sons and daughters away. But in the cult, in Paul's day, time stood still. (The term "cult " as used here refers to corporate worship or religious rites rather than to a fringe group or sect.) Time stopped and was even reversed as the celebrant repeated the acts of God or shared in the sacred deeds of an earlier day. In the celebration of the Passover today, for example, one can witness Jewish families who are indistinguishable from their neighbors in the clothes they wear, the jobs they hold, or the cars they drive. Yet in recalling the deliverance of the Hebrews from Egypt thousands of years ago, they speak as if they lived in the second millennium BCE. Most will never have been to Egypt. Yet in drinking the wine and eating the unleavened bread, they imaginatively reexperience the slavery of the Hebrews in Egypt and their liberation from Pharaoh's bonds.

They recite: "We were Pharaoh's slaves in Egypt: and the Lord our God brought us out therefrom with a mighty hand and an outstretched arm. Now, if the Holy One, blessed be He, had not brought our fathers forth from Egypt, then we, and our children, and our children's children, would [still] be slaves to Pharaoh in Egypt."[4] While to the outsider it may sound strange for an American Jew to speak solemnly of sweating in Pharaoh's quarry long ago, to the insider who views that bondage through the eyes of myth, the liberation that was effected then is experienced once more.

Through the cultic act, the worshiper participates in what is real for all time. While the key occurrences of both Judaism and Christianity are historical, for those within the traditions these events possess a vitality that goes beyond the facts of the events themselves. The past was never a "dead past." As Jacob Neusner well said, "If we, too, the living, have been redeemed, then the observer no longer witnesses only historical men in historical time, but an eternal return to sacred time."[5] The great events that happened once upon a time continue to direct the course of the world and are experienced as current. Through the cult, the worshiper not only shares in the benefits of the primeval time but also finds an organizing center for the current disordered world. The old shepherd ritualistically jumps over his staff three times; the little girl regularly calls for her four "friends" (stuffed animals) and her drink before going to sleep; the Inuit woman routinely bows her head to offer thanks both before and after eating her diet of raw fish on the dirt floor of her hut. All are celebrating a tiny slice of life, and for each one these ritualistic gestures provide a structure for what otherwise would be an incoherent mass of activity.

In myth also an order is imposed. The order is not just any order but the order deemed true, the only order that is fundamentally real. In the Hebrew experience of the exile we see how even the terrors of history were integrated into a divine order and were thus made bearable because they were meaningful.

In 597 BCE the Babylonian army uprooted the Hebrews from Judah and exiled them to Mesopotamia. Eventually the temple was destroyed, the daily sacrifice interrupted, and Jerusalem was left in shambles. Babylonian troops were garrisoned in the "promised land" while the Hebrews were forcibly settled on the banks of the river Chebar near Babylon (in modern Iraq). There they raised their poignant cry, "How can we sing the Lord's song in a foreign land?" Yahweh had promised them via Abraham "the holy land." Now Babylon had robbed Israel of its divine possession. This historical event raised the problem of theodicy in the sharpest possible way. Was a God who would allow this to happen credible anymore? Had Yahweh forsaken the people or abrogated the promise? Since Israel's existence had been defined in relation to Yahweh, what would happen if there were a break in that relationship? Would Israel languish and die at the feet of its captors, or would it survive to stand at their grave?

Although a people may be powerless, it is hardly without power. In mythic ritual the Hebrews found strength in the celebration of the Sabbath to face and survive those historical terrors. The Babylonians could occupy the land, destroy the city, reduce the temple to ashes, burn the sacred objects, and exile its people, but they could not burn or destroy the Sabbath. On the Sabbath the Hebrews recalled how Yahweh had created the world out of formlessness and void, and how the Creator had crowned the creation with the Sabbath itself (Gen. 1:1–2:4a). Thus on each Sabbath the Hebrews celebrated an order that was real for all time, an order as old and fundamental as the creation itself, an order celebrating God's triumph over chaos. Empires might come and go, but this order would always remain. Each celebration of the Sabbath affirmed a faith that the God who in the beginning had brought order out of chaos would conquer captivity's historical chaos as well. So the Sabbath ritual was a deep source of strength and hope.

In Paul's letters also we see how the liturgy of the church served as a bridge between the past and the present. In all of the early Christian churches baptism served as the rite of initiation, and a sacred communal meal was eaten regularly—although how regularly we do not know. In both of these sacred rites the church shared in God's redemption of the world. Strangely enough, for Paul the death and resurrection of Jesus rather than his teachings formed the glowing center of emphasis. In passing through the water (baptism) and in eating the bread and drinking the wine, the believer established a continuity between the self and the death of Jesus that happened "once upon a time." In baptism the identification with Jesus was so complete that Paul spoke of being united with Christ in a death like his, of being baptized into his death (Rom. 6:3, 5), or even of being crucified with Christ (6:6). The immersion of the initiate in water simulated burial with Jesus; the emergence of the initiate from the water recapitulated Christ's resurrection. Through this rite the saving significance of the death and resurrection of Jesus was experienced within the community, and the believer was linked with that which was deemed real for all time. As the spiritual says, in baptism the initiate asked, "Were you there when they crucified my Lord?" At the literal level, the answer is absolutely obvious: "No, I was not there." At the mythic level, "Yes, I was there. . . ."

Eliade's observation that "every ritual has a divine model"[6] applies to the Eucharist as well as to baptism. In 1 Corinthians 11:23–26 the eating of the bread and the drinking of the wine commemorate Jesus' last meal with his disciples. The connection of this commemorative meal with the cross was thought to be so close that repetition of it spontaneously brought to mind Jesus' death. For example, Paul's recitation of the received eucharistic tradition placed the worshiper in a sphere of audacious power. Throughout the passage the emphasis is on Jesus' death and sets the worshiper in the presence of Jesus' betrayal, beating, and bloody death. Bread was broken, simulating the breaking of Jesus' body, and red wine was offered as a "new covenant in

[the] blood." Finally, to underscore this motif, Paul added the exhortation, "as often as you eat this bread and drink the cup, you proclaim the Lord's *death* until he comes" (1 Cor. 11:26, italics added). To "proclaim the Lord's death" obviously extended beyond a verbal announcement to suggest a mythic (or "spiritual") *participation* in the death as well.

Nevertheless, in 1 Corinthians 10:1–13 Paul countered the Corinthian belief that the Eucharist was a magical potion guaranteeing salvation. He reminded the church that just as its life as the sacramental community was prefigured in Israel's wilderness wandering, so also its punishment for the abuse of its status was anticipated in the judgment of Israel. Israel's status as the "sacramental" community did not exempt it from retribution. Its murmuring brought capital punishment. Immorality and idolatry brought the fall of 23,000 in a single day. Tempting the Lord brought destruction by snakes. Likewise, Paul warned, being in a sacramental community exempted no one from God's judgment. While to the modern reader such divine punishment appears unnecessarily harsh, Paul appropriated this tradition and assumed that the Corinthians shared his view of the power of the mythic realm celebrated in the ritual.

After citing the example of Israel and warning the Corinthians to "flee from the worship of idols," Paul offered: "The cup of blessing that we bless, is it not a participation [*koinōnia*] in the blood of Christ? The bread that we break, is it not a participation [*koinōnia*] in the body of Christ?" (1 Cor. 10:16, AT). The word *koinōnia* is used to denote everything from sensitivity groups to church campgrounds. When translated "fellowship," as is common, *koinōnia* is taken to mean a spirit of jovial camaraderie. But Ernst Käsemann proposed long ago that the word be rendered "falling into a sphere of domination."[7] Because this eating of the bread (flesh) and drinking of the wine (blood) placed the worshiper in the zone of the sacred, Paul urged the Corinthians to purify themselves lest they profane the "body" (1 Cor. 11:27–32). Even perfunctory obeisance to demonic powers, as in the pagan sacrificial meals, was incompatible with this mythic participation. Because some believers persisted in attending the pagan sacrificial meals, however, and neglected to rid themselves of the taint of such unholy alliances, illness and even death had entered the community. This sickness and death, according to Paul, was not from natural causes but from the judging presence of the Lord in the cultic meal (1 Cor. 11:30). The radicality of Paul is most obvious in the way he fixed on the death of Jesus as the locus of God's redeeming activity. In mythic participation in this death and resurrection, the believer already mythically tasted victory over the destructive, negative, and sinister elements in the world and already had a foretaste of the reconciliation, love, and newness of the new creation. Intimations of that promised reality came through participation mythically in an event in the past. But the promise contained in that past event awaited the future for its maturing. Thus the past, brought mythologically into the present, became the basis of the future hope.

DEATH AS MODEL

Jesus' death functions in Paul's writings not only as an earnest of God's future triumph but also as a model for action in the present world. In other words, Jesus' death was experienced not only in the cult but also in the daily round of work and play, eating and drinking, buying and selling, making love and social conversation. Paul connected his own activity with the death of Jesus. Shipwreck, beatings, imprisonments, conflict, and strife all serve as intimations of that death. Looking at the scars left by the "slings and arrows of outrageous fortune," to borrow from Shakespeare (*Hamlet*, III.1), Paul spoke of "carrying in . . . [his] body the death of Jesus" (2 Cor. 4:10). Scars on his back suffered in Jesus' service he called "marks of Jesus" (Gal. 6:17), an obvious allusion to the marks etched on Jesus' body by the beatings he suffered before his death and to the puncture wounds of crucifixion. Since the hunger, thirst, nakedness, homelessness, persecution, and slander Paul endured duplicated the suffering of Jesus, and since they were received in service to the Lord, Paul felt that his suffering shared mythically in God's redemptive work. Even the hurt and pain inflicted by the world was shouldered for the sake of that same world.

Drawing on his own experience, Paul urged the Corinthians to follow him and share "in Christ's sufferings" (2 Cor. 1:5 RSV). The Corinthian converts, however, believed that they had already overcome the world, that they were already "rich," "filled," and ruling (1 Cor. 4:8) and therefore had no need to share the world's incompleteness or futility and grief. Confident of their salvation, they celebrated their liberation from, not participation in, suffering. By citing his own humiliation and deprivation and calling on his converts to "be imitators of me," Paul undermined the claims of the Corinthians. He reminded them that neither their redemption nor the redemption of the world was complete. When Paul wrote, "I decided to know nothing among you except Jesus Christ, and him crucified" (1 Cor. 2:2), he stripped the Corinthians of their pretensions and brought them down to earth so that they could see the reality of the world's hurt and the power of the cross (see 1 Cor. 1:17–25). As in 1 Thessalonians, so also in 1 Corinthians, Paul mystically made suffering into a symbol of honor: "You became imitators of us and of the Lord, for you received the word in much affliction" (1 Thess. 1:6 RSV). In contrast, those who rejected Paul's example and indulged themselves were dubbed "enemies of the cross of Christ" (Phil. 3:17–18). It was not that sex and food were evil, but that an obsession with them rendered believers incapable of accepting either the suffering or the power that accompanied the way of the cross. It is possible that the sexual excesses and gluttony at Philippi were fruits of an accommodation of the gospel to old pagan ways, but most scholars believe they sprang from a perversion of religious freedom. In Paul's view, God had been revealed in the cross. Now the transforming power of that moment was to be apprehended anew as it was remembered in both the liturgy and the commonplace.

THE POWERS THAT BE

Although science has ostensibly freed us from superstition and fear, demons, monsters, and wormlike and larval beasts live on in our collective fantasy. Goblins and witches come out on All Hallow E'en (Halloween), crepe paper dragons snake their way down city streets in popular parades, monster movies and *Star Trek* serials punctuate weekly television calendars, and bizarre mutant creatures stalk the pages of science fiction. Despite our scientific better judgment, our fascination with these mythic beings persists. That fascination surfaces only sporadically, however, mostly in our moments of corporate play or in our personal dreams. For Paul, however, contact with such powers was real, insistent, and dreadful. Satan, the superhuman rulers of this world-age, the elemental spirits of the universe, the principalities and powers, the beasts at Ephesus, Death, Sin, and pagan deities all lived and contended for dominion and the loyalty of the world Paul inhabited.

The devil, for example, was an uncanny force, preying on the unsuspecting (1 Cor. 7:5), seeking advantage over Paul (2 Cor. 2:11), and stalking those excommunicated from the realm of the rule of Christ (1 Cor. 5:5). Likewise, Death for Paul was a personalized power that paid wages to its recruits and hosted an army that would be defeated only at the eschaton (1 Cor. 15:26, 54–55). These hostile powers, having crucified Christ, made false claims for their wisdom (1 Cor. 2:6–8). Moreover, in pagan cultic feasts, demons offered food and drink to the partakers, and weaned them from the table of Christ (1 Cor. 10:20–22). Both angels (even evil ones) and principalities, which included but transcended political power structures, vied for the loyalty of the believer (Rom. 8:38–39).

In Paul's view, therefore, those in Christ lived in a contested realm. In this field of competing forces there were no safe zones in which the uncommitted may live; there was no arena of thought free from the claim or dominion of some power. We see, therefore, why the term "Lord" is such a pregnant term for Paul. Informing the term was the belief that in the death and resurrection of Jesus, God had begun the final conquest of these hostile powers; the final moment when God would place all things in subjection, Paul promised, was imminent (1 Cor. 15:24–25). In the meantime, the fiery conflict between God and the hostile powers continued. Those once held captive were now being released from the clutches of the "powers that be," but they still looked forward to the complete triumph of God's righteousness when Jesus' lordship would be consummated.

The modern reader may find such views of personalized evil strange, dangerous, or offensive. However, our memory of Nazism and our continuing witness of racism make references to demonic forces comprehensible. And though Paul's references to apocalyptic terrors may appear surrealistic, we shall miss the power of individual passages and misunderstand the letters as a whole if we are insensitive to the way these mythological images inform Paul's thought and that of his readers. Life for some was simply empty; for others it was absurdly oppressed, and many felt helpless in the grip of forces too great for anyone to resist or comprehend. Paul's gospel spoke to the first of help, and to the second of salvation (rescue) from this ugly web, and thus he nerved women and men for their daily lives and for the final intense struggle.

THE LAST ADAM

Discussing Paul's use of the Adam symbol, Richard Rubenstein wrote: "Almost two thousand years before the depth psychology that his religious imagination helped to make possible, Paul of Tarsus gave expression to mankind's yearning for a new and flawless beginning that could finally end the cycle of anxiety, repression, desire, and craving—the inevitable concomitants of the human pilgrimage."[8] Whatever one thinks of Rubenstein's effort to link Paul with depth psychology, his observation was correct that the Adamic myth played a major role in Paul's thought. Paul could have joined Hamlet in saying, "The time is out of joint." In the apostle's view, this disjointed state represented a degeneration from a flawless beginning. The cosmic decline began when Adam revolted against the Creator's prohibition: "You shall not eat of the fruit of the tree that is in the middle of the garden . . . or you shall die" (Gen. 3:3; cf. 2:17). Before the fall man and woman lived in a state of innocence, unshamed by nakedness, strangers to want, freely taking from nature's breast without sweat or toil, and untroubled by anxiety over death. A friend of the animals, Adam was neither hunter nor hunted. Barely inferior to the gods, he shared in the creation by naming the animals and ruling the world without enmity or strife. Eve had the capacity to bear children without pain. But because of their disobedience, Adam and Eve were exiled from the garden to a life marked by toil and want, fratricide and fear, death and pain. Ever since,

Paul held, creature and creation have shared Adam's frustration and futility, and have suffered under the dominion of demonic powers. Even though Paul nowhere fully articulated this scenario, he took it for granted. For although the Hebrew scriptures and the Gospels rarely mention the Adamic myth, it occupied a prominent place in the letters. Three passages will receive our attention here: Romans 5:12–21; 1 Corinthians 15; and Philippians 2:6–11.

Romans 5:12–21

The belief was widespread in first-century Jewish thought that the original state that the world enjoyed would be restored in the end time. Paul obviously shared this view, but for him God's agent of this restoration was the Christ, whom he alternately called the "second Adam," "the last Adam," and "the Adam who is to come." In Romans 5:12–21 Paul contrasted this last Adam with the first. The two Adams were alike in that the action of each influenced the destiny of all humankind; they were different in that through the last Adam's act of righteousness came acquittal, whereas through the disobedience of the first Adam "many were made sinners" (Rom. 5:19). Through the last Adam came life (5:18), whereas through the first Adam came death (5:21).

Although Paul described Jesus as the antitype of Adam, he was uncomfortable with his comparison, for in Jesus, he added, grace has abounded more to humanity's good than did the sin of Adam redound to humanity's hurt and loss. While Paul did write that sin entered the human context through Adam, he did not create or endorse the doctrine of original sin as later known. He did believe, as did every rabbi, that sin was universal and that Adam was its genesis, but that it was perpetuated through repeated acts of disobedience, not by seminal transmission. With few exceptions (e.g., Enoch and Elijah, who were not known to have died and thus were judged sinless), all others become their own Adam. Paul here addressed those who wondered how it was possible for Jesus' acts of obedience and righteousness to benefit others. Those who comprehend what it is to be one with the first Adam, Paul argued, should have no difficulty understanding how one can be united with the last Adam.

1 Corinthians 15

In 1 Corinthians 15 Paul answered skeptics about the resurrection of the dead and even those who claimed to be already in a resurrected state. To many from a Greek tradition the whole concept of the resurrection of the body was totally repulsive. Apparently it was unclear to the Corinthians how or if the resurrection of Jesus applied to them. Paul argued that God's raising of Jesus was the "first fruit" of the end time and thus anticipated the imminent end when, in the spirit of Jewish apocalyptic thinking, believers would be raised (1 Thess. 4:13–17). Paul responded to those who wondered how a believer can be "in Christ" with an example that would have been familiar to any convert having a casual acquaintance with synagogue discussions or the scriptures: "For as through (*dia*) a man came death, so through (*dia*) a man has come also the resurrection of the dead. For as in (*en*) Adam all die, so [also] in (*en*) Christ shall all be made alive" (1 Cor. 15:21–22, RSV adapted). To be "in Adam" meant to participate in the destiny of Adam, with a mortality rate of almost 100 percent; whereas to be "in Christ" meant to share in the power and glory of the new creation. As Robin Scroggs put it, "Christ for Paul is not just an example of but the medium through which one shares in the resurrected life."[9]

The resurrection was to be for Paul a bodily resurrection. In 1 Corinthians 15:35–38 Paul probably addressed Greek Christians who found the whole idea of a resurrection of the body crude and ridiculous. Conventional Greek piety and the major philosophical movements denigrated the body as a living prison. Salvation meant release from, not perpetuation of, the body. In the rhetorical questions of 15:35 we may have an echo of their scorn: "How are the dead raised? With what kind of body do they come?" Paul responded by distinguishing among different kinds of bodies: human bodies and animal bodies, fish bodies and bird bodies, heavenly bodies and earthly bodies, sea bodies and landed bodies, and so on (15:3–40). In the classic Hebraic sense, the body was a synonym for the self. Thus Paul compared and contrasted the present earthly form with the future heavenly one. The form and substance that the self now has will perish, he noted, but the heavenly body will last forever (15:42).

Likewise, the first and last Adam belong to different spheres: As the Hebrew *ʾadamah* suggests, the first man, Adam, was "earth man," i.e., he came from *ʾadamah*, earth. The second Adam is from heaven (15:47). This contrast of "the earth man," who is perishable, with the heavenly man, who is "a life-giving spirit" and eternal, makes his point (15:45). Both are bodies—one earthly, the other heavenly. This tortuous route leads Paul to conclude with the affirmation, "Just as we have borne the image of the man of dust [Adam], we will also bear the image of the man of heaven [Jesus]" (15:49).

Philippians 2:6–11

In Philippians 2:6–11 Paul quoted a Christian hymn in which many scholars see a contrast of Jesus with Adam. Although the hymn nowhere explicitly mentions Adam, a contrast between Jesus and Adam seems implicit. The first strophe of the hymn refers to Jesus, who, "though he was in the form of God, did not regard equality with God as something to be exploited [or 'snatched at']." The mention of "form" (*morphē*) evidently refers to the image of God, which both Jesus and Adam (Gen. 1:26) bore. Unlike the first Adam, however, the last did not try to usurp the place of God (see Gen. 3:5) but instead took the role of a slave. Whereas Adam sought to exalt himself, Christ humbled himself; whereas Adam rebelled against the Creator, Jesus was obedient unto death. The conduct of the last Adam was a model of selflessness, obedience, innocence, and sacrifice that Paul exhorted his converts to emulate: "Let this mind be in you, which was also in Christ Jesus" (2:5 KJV). We see, therefore, that the second Adam is not only the agent of redemption, reversing the decline of the cosmos, redefining hardship and death, but also the model of the true Adam before the fall. In this presentation, Christ retains untarnished the image of God, and he will rule as Adam was meant to rule until all things are placed under him (1 Cor. 15:24–28). The last Adam, thus conceived, served as both the medium and the model of restored humanity. Of the three examples, the case for having this one refer to Adam by implication is weak.

Our discussion of the function of myth in Paul is far from exhaustive, and is intended only to show how, for Paul, even the distant past was neither a "dead past" nor the future an unreal one, but both met and embraced through myth in the present. I hope, however, the treatment will show how mythic materials grow and change. And observing the way myth and symbol receive energetic and creative use in the letters provides a clue to Paul's primary concerns. Our purpose has also been to go beyond an investigation of what happened ("external history") and to learn how Paul and his converts experienced those happenings ("internal history"). H. Richard Niebuhr first used this distinction between internal and external history and offered a succinct summary:

> To speak of history in this fashion is to try to think with poets rather than with scientists. That is what we mean, for poets think of persons, purposes and destinies. It is just their Jobs and Hamlets that are not dreamt of in philosophies which rule out from the company of true being whatever cannot be numbered or included in an impersonal pattern. . . . Hence we may call internal history dramatic and its truth dramatic truth, though drama in this case does not mean fiction.[10]

I hope that we are in agreement when I use "myth" where Niebuhr uses "drama," for through myth also we see how events are apprehended from within the community, how history is a lived experience, and how persons interpret the way events shape their destiny. In the cult the believer was in Christ and Christ was in the believer. In the daily life of the Christian the sacrifice of Christ was replicated. In the attack on the demonic powers, the paradise once lost was being regained. In his ascent to the third heaven, Paul was breaking the confines of this world and experiencing what defied articulation (see 2 Cor. 12:1–6). The only way to speak of it would be mythically, and since the church frequently spoke of such events, it had to be careful. In speaking mythically, the church constantly risked being called (and indeed becoming) a lunatic fringe interested only in subjective, individualistic experiences. It avoided that by insisting that any experience of what happened be judged by the church's memory of what indeed did happen. Moreover, recollection had to be corporate, to weed out the faulty or the fanciful. In this sense the mythological experience of the tradition is different from the private experience of a mystic, and thus Paul spoke not just of his own experience of history but of the experience he shared in and with the Christian community.

6

Interpreters of Paul
in the New Testament

Within the New Testament itself there are almost as many disputed as undisputed letters of Paul (six vs. seven). That persons would write under the name of other significant figures shocked no one in the ancient world. Within the Old Testament itself appear pseudonymous writings like Daniel, the "books of Moses," Second and Third Isaiah, and some of the psalms, and in the period between the Testaments they flourished.[1] In the New Testament as well, the use of pseudonyms was a common literary device (see the epistles of Peter, James, and John). While such a practice opened the door to an abundance of pseudonymous works in the second and third centuries CE, literary abuse of the method did little to discredit or discourage writing under an assumed name in the late first century. While many factors influenced the adoption and use of a pseudonym, at least two things are clear: (1) The desire to locate oneself within a tradition linked to an important figure (e.g., Peter, James, John, and Paul; later Philip, Thomas, Mary, et al.). Thus those who wrote letters under a pseudonym sought to interpret, defend, or expand the theology of venerable figures for a later time. (2) The attempt to gain credibility, authority, and acceptance for a later interpretation. As some of the earliest writings for the instruction of the Christian church, Paul's letters established a precedent that was readily adaptable to a variety of later challenges when Paul's Gentile gospel was still contested. The existence of a collection of Paul's letters within two generations of his death points to his importance and, therefore, invited the use of his letters as a metric for the accuracy or truth, at some level, of other traditions. Moreover, since Paul was the most apt founder and most eloquent defender of the Gentile mission, the selection of his name was a natural and practical choice under which to write. Thus the appeal to Paul's name and the adoption of ideas, theology, language, and emphases from his letters served to guarantee the truth or authenticity of his traditions. In the late second century after Paul's legacy had been vigorously contested and revised by Ignatius, Marcion, Irenaeus, Tertullian, and others, the inclusion of Paul's letters in the canon was a burning issue. By then he was such an influential figure and had assumed such importance for the church that the rather unusual step was taken to include letters in a collection of scriptures for the church. Although all letters ascribed to Paul were not included (e.g., the *Letter to the Laodiceans*), the thirteen included are treated here, and that decision dictates the need to deal with certain letters in the disputed category.

COLOSSIANS

The Question of Authorship

Of the deutero-Pauline letters, Colossians and 2 Thessalonians make the strongest claim to authenticity. But as far back as 1839 the German scholar Mayerhoff questioned the Pauline authorship of Colossians. Reservations about its authenticity have persisted into our own time. The unusual language, style, and theology of the letter are the principal reasons for this skepticism about its genuineness. While none is decisive by itself, these reasons when taken together make the case against Pauline authorship weighty indeed.

Linguistic Evidence

One can easily cite the appearance and omission of language that is unusual for Paul, the absence of favorite Pauline words and expressions, and the presence of certain stylistic features that are rare or missing altogether in the undisputed letters. In Colossians one finds thirty-three words that occur nowhere else in the New Testament and fifteen words that are used by other New Testament writers but fail to appear in the undisputed Pauline letters.

In addition Colossians contains a number of unusual expressions that Paul never used elsewhere. References to "blood of his cross" (1:20), "evil deeds" (1:21), "forgiveness of sins" (1:14), and "*the* faith" (2:7, italics added) appear in Colossians but go missing in the undisputed letters. Likewise, the contrast of the visible and invisible in 1:16 was made nowhere else by Paul. While an argument from silence is hardly decisive, it is strange that the author of Colossians does not use such characteristic Pauline words as "salvation," "righteousness," and "justification." Such omissions in light of the legalistic tendencies of the addressees are striking. Moreover, the absence of such favorite Pauline words as "my brothers [and sisters]" seems peculiar.

Style

If the presence of non-Pauline language and the absence of favorite Pauline expressions raise questions about the Pauline authorship of Colossians, its style causes further doubt. Even a casual reading of the letter will detect a redundant style. Expressions such as *"praying* for you and *asking"* (1:9), *"endure* everything with *patience"* (1:11), "firmly *established* and *steadfast"* (1:23, AT), "the *ages* and *generations"* (1:26), *"teach* and *admonish"* (3:16), and *"psalms, hymns,* and spiritual *songs"* (3:16, italics added to all) are common in Colossians but less pronounced in the undisputed letters. Moreover, there is a greater tendency in Colossians to string together dependent clauses and phrases into long, rambling sentences. Note, for example, that the thanksgiving that begins in 1:3 continues without interruption for five verses (1:3–8).

In assessing the evidence cited here, few would quarrel with the observation that significant differences exist between Colossians and the undisputed Pauline letters. The disagreement arises over the assessment of this evidence. Those inclined toward assigning the letter to Paul would argue that the differences can be explained by factors unique to the composition of Colossians itself. The peculiarities of language and style can be attributed to the hymnic style of the letter,[2] evoked by circumstances unique to Colossians, created by an aging, mellow, contemplative apostle waiting in prison for his trial, or caused by a secretary (or amanuensis) taking liberties with the apostle's dictation. But it is difficult to understand how a hymnic style would account for the omissions noted earlier, or how an altered context could effect the stylistic changes here present. Moreover, even while Paul's thinking indisputably changes over time, there is little evidence even in Paul's later letters (e.g., 2 Cor. 9 and Romans) of a mellowing process. Finally, if the scribe is responsible for the significant shifts in style and language in the letter, then the scribe has in some sense become the author. In any case, while it is important, linguistic and stylistic evidence alone is less than decisive when considering the question of authorship. So usually, as here, the linguistic argument is linked with theological evidence.

Theology

At many points the theology of Colossians agrees with that of the undisputed letters, but in its concept of apostleship, Christology, and eschatology there are significant differences.[3] In Colossians Paul appears as the apostle who through his preaching *and suffering* takes the gospel "to every creature under heaven" (1:23). Although in the undisputed letters Paul does represent himself as the apostle to the Gentiles who shares in the suffering of Christ (e.g., 2 Cor. 11:21b–12:10), nowhere in the authentic letters does Paul speak of the vicarious character of his suffering. In Colossians, on the other hand, the apostle gladly suffers, he tells his hearers, "for your sake" (1:24). Thus the suffering of the apostle for others complements the suffering of Christ, which also was for others (see especially Rom. 3:24–26).

In the undisputed letters, Paul sought to elicit and nurture faith in Jesus as Messiah, but the apprehension of the new life, Paul held, was always partial in nature. In 1 Corinthians especially Paul scoffed at those who claimed to be mature (3:1–4). In Colossians, on the other hand, Paul appears as the apostle whose message offered "in all wisdom" (1:28) served to make everyone "perfect" (*telios*) in Christ. In the Hellenistic world such *telioi* ("perfect ones") were those deemed worthy of divine illumination and truth.

Finally and most significantly the sense of apocalyptic urgency and immediacy is missing altogether. No longer was the apostle driven to complete his work before time ran out. No longer did the apostle write under the shadow of the world's imminent denouement. No longer was apostleship itself seen as a gift of the end time. So, while in some respects the understanding of apostleship in Colossians resembles that of the undisputed letters (e.g., as a mission to the Gentiles), in its view of the suffering of the apostle, its understanding of the apostolic preaching as wisdom for the perfect, and its diminished sense of apostolic urgency, this epistle differs significantly from the undisputed letters.

Moreover, the Colossian view of Christ, like that of apostleship, is unusual for a Pauline letter. Instead of the body of Christ, as in 1 Corinthians 12:12–27, the author viewed the church as the trunk of the body of which Christ is the head. He viewed this Christ as a cosmic figure whose universal rule was *already* expressed within the church. Such a view, which most scholars feel comes from Hellenistic philosophy, would surely be unusual if not unique for Paul.

The above emphases distinguish Colossians from the undisputed letters of Paul. However, the most radical difference between this letter and the authentic letters is in its understanding of eschatology. In other letters, the apostle's belief in the imminent return of Christ profoundly informed his thinking. He viewed the harassment, beatings, misfortunes, and imprisonment that he suffered for the gospel as apocalyptic "woes," which, like birth pains, announced the imminent arrival of the end time. In 1 Corinthians 7:31–32 Paul discouraged normal, wholesome, human attachments to a marriage partner in light of the imminent apocalyptic trauma. He encouraged support for civil authority (Rom. 13:11–12) because, he believed, it would restrain the evil powers loosed in the last days, for he exclaimed, "the night is far gone, the day is at hand." The believers who now taste salvation, Paul adamantly held, would experience it fully in the near future (1 Thess. 4:17). The offering for the Jerusalem church that assumed such a prominent place in 1 and 2 Corinthians and Romans and carried powerful eschatological significance for Paul (2 Cor.

9) must be viewed against an apocalyptic horizon that is missing from Colossians. The apostle prosecuted his mission and the offering with feverish intensity to complete it before history's finale. Paul's view of the end was central to his understanding of the church, his instruction for believers, his personal sense of mission, and the ethical imperative he advocated for his converts.

In Colossians, on the other hand, the mood of expectation is subdued. No longer does the prospect of the imminent end of the age influence the perception of all human relationships. Rather than the full experience of salvation being a future prospect, the author believed that already God *"has rescued* [past tense] us from the power of darkness" (1:13), a theological concept almost impossible to ascribe to Paul. The mystery hidden for ages has "now *been revealed* [past tense again] to his saints" (1:26). The author reminded his readers: "When you *were buried* with him in baptism, you *were also raised* with him" (2:12), and "you *were dead* in trespasses . . . God *made you alive*" (2:13). The author assured those *"once estranged"* that they were *"now reconciled"* (1:22, italics added to all). The italicized words of these quotations, with their emphasis on salvation already achieved, hardly harmonize with Paul's understanding of salvation as a work in progress. The full experience of salvation, reserved for the future in the undisputed letters, now moves into the present or even the past. The future dimension almost disappears.

In this shift of emphasis from the future to the present, the concept of hope also changes. In the undisputed Pauline letters, where hope sprang from faith and was linked with the anticipation of the end of the age (a temporal category), hope in Colossians was stored up in the heavenly realms. Thus a special category has replaced a temporal one, and a symbol of anticipation is replaced by hope as a symbol of assurance.

While it is possible that these theological departures from the outlook of the undisputed letters can be explained by changes in Paul's thinking (for we know that Paul's thinking did change), the context, or sources, that seems improbable. It is more reasonable to assume that the alterations in language, style, and theology were the work of a later interpreter or school of interpreters who sought to bring the Pauline tradition to bear on a new situation. By the way the author integrated major theological motifs and literary devices from the undisputed letters, we know he was acquainted with the traditions and letters of Paul. But the deviation in language, style, and outlook suggests that the author belonged to a time perhaps twenty years after Paul 's death.

The Context of the Letter

Like the undisputed letters of Paul, Colossians gives the impression of being a real letter, that is, a real conversation between its author and believers in a concrete situation. As in the study of the undisputed letters, we must search the letter itself for clues to the content of that conversation. Even though their identity is debated, we learn from Colossians that "false teachers" were present. The letter does hint at the substance of a "philosophy" (2:8) that was hardly a system of clear, logical thought or speculation, but rather a special religious tradition, a revealed knowledge, or a way of life through which the ultimate ground and secret meaning of the universe were grasped.

The "Philosophy" of the Opponents

Fixed on the cosmic powers or "elemental spirits of the universe" (2:8), the scope of this philosophy was expansive. Rather than merely material elements such as air, earth, fire, and water, these "elemental spirits" were divine beings who exercised control over the world and required special devotion. Angel worship (2:18) linked with obeisance to the elemental spirits or "principalities and powers" (2:15 RSV) offered a visionary experience of the heavenly *plērōma* ("divine fullness" or mystery) that assured one's place among the perfect ones (*teleioi*). Those possessed by divine power the author graphically characterized as "vainly puffed up by the mind of the flesh" (2:18, AT). Ascetic or world-denying by nature (2:18), they passed judgments on the basis of "food and drink" and on the observance of "festivals, new moons, or sabbaths" (2:16). The world-denying commands, "Do not handle, do not taste, do not touch" (2:21), promoted a certain "self-imposed piety, humility, and severe treatment of the body" (2:23), which simultaneously encouraged a contradictory overindulgence (3:5). Is it possible that through their asceticism, these believers hoped to strip "off the body of the flesh," a spiritualized, mythic form of circumcision (2:11)? And was their prodigal self-indulgence a demonstration of their defiance of the world and the values of the culture? Perhaps, but we cannot be certain.

The cosmic speculation linked with world-denial suggests a gnostic background to many. The reference to the observance of new moons, Sabbaths, and the submission to regulations or *dogmata* (2:20), coupled with the worship of cosmic forces, an appeal to visions, asceticism, and indulgence led Gunther Bornkamm to assert that there is "no doubt that the heresy was a variety of Jewish Gnosticism."[4] Others, however, see the teaching as an expression of Hellenistic Jewish piety or even Neo-Pythagorean spirituality.[5] An emerging consensus views the philosophy as a syncretistic form of Hellenistic Judaism open to popular religious piety. Certain features of this piety (such as cosmic speculation and asceticism) tend toward a gnostic speculation that later received a bewildering array of forms. However this teaching may be known, it is significant for our study that its main contours are not in dispute.[6]

Response to the "Philosophy"

To confront this teaching the author summoned a collection of Paul's letters known to "him." The Paul of this letter is sketched as a powerful figure with a universal vision. He is said to bring the gospel "to every creature under heaven" (1:23); as an apostle to the Gentiles ("nations," NRSV; 1:5–8, 24–29), this world-renowned figure attended to this little church in the remote Lycus River Valley in Asia Minor; he shared the limelight with none of the inner circle in Jerusalem, he suffered on behalf of the churches, and he ministered with "divine" credentials (1:25). By appealing to Paul, our author hoped to secure a hearing for his teaching and to gain a certification for the correctness of his gospel. This attempt to establish the validity of his teaching was especially important if he were to refute the false teaching. Unfortunately, we have nothing from the "teachers," who doubtless could have and may have found support in Paul's letters for their philosophy.

In response to the cosmic speculation and veneration of the elemental spirits, our author subordinated all powers to a cosmic Christ, or head of the church exercising dominion over all principalities and powers. He, and no other, the author wrote, is Lord over the *stoicheia* ("cosmic forces") worshiped by the Colossians. As the "head of all rule and authority," he, the author held, is the *plērōma* or divine fullness (2:10). He disarms and subjugates the celestial powers worshiped by the Colossians (2:15). Through him and his reconciliation the whole cosmos is brought back into the divine order. *In Christ*, the author added, "the fullness of God was pleased to dwell" (1:16). *In Christ*, he asserted, reside the true "treasures of wisdom and knowledge" (2:3). *In Christ* is found a circumcision "made without hands" (2:11). *In Christ* is the resurrection realized here and now (2:12). *Through Christ* the aliens are reconciled (1:22).

In this way our author set the Pauline teaching about Christ over against the Colossian "philosophy and empty deceit" (2:8), and contradicted those who delude and beguile the innocent (2:4). Their ascetic commands he called "human commands and teachings" (2:22). Moreover, from a practical point of view, these regulations, our writer said, are ineffective in restraining indulgence (2:23). In contrast to those who are "puffed up" (2:18), or arrogant and assertive, he admonished the believers to "clothe yourselves with love" for the sake of church unity and to teach one another "in all wisdom" (3:14, 16). In contrast to the regulations that are essentially world-denying ("Do not handle, do not touch," etc.), our author juxtaposed a set of rules adopted from Hellenistic Jewish circles that were world-affirming in some sense: "Husbands, love your wives. Children, obey your parents. . . . Fathers, do not provoke your children" (the so-called household rules or *Haustafeln*, 3:18–4:1). Although the author has access to some of Paul's letters, it is interesting to see what he ignores in this small collection of "household rules" that reaffirmed a social hierarchy that required a subordination of women (3:18)—"wives be subject to your husbands"—that at times Paul repudiated (cf. Gal. 3:28; Rom. 16:1, 7; 1 Cor. 11:5). The requirement that women be subordinate has caused some to wonder if the rhetoric here used to fix women in their lower place might have been a reaction to some of the more liberal tendencies in Paul.

Unfortunately, we have no further word to or from the church at Colossae. It was eclipsed in importance by Laodicea and ultimately failed to survive one of the many earthquakes that regularly devastated the Lycus Valley. So we are left, as is the case so often in the New Testament, not knowing how the struggle ended. While we do not know what happened to the church, we do know that the letter survived, and very soon profoundly influenced another New Testament writing—the letter to the Ephesians.

Outline of Colossians

1. Address, Salutation, Thanksgiving, and Prayer for
   Growth   1:1–11
2. Body of Letter: Theological Foundation for Ethics   1:12–2:23
   a. Christ hymn and application   1:12–23
   b. Apostle's message and application of divine mystery   1:24–2:5
   c. Relationship of cosmic lordship of Christ to church
      at Colossae   2:6–23
3. Paraenesis or Ethical Instruction   3:1–4:6
   a. Theme—"Seek the things that are above"   3:1–4
   b. Things "below" to avoid (vice list)   3:5–11
   c. Things "above" to seek   3:12–17
   d. Household rules   3:18–4:1
   e. Concluding paraenesis   4:2–6
4. Parousia of Tychicus   4:7–9
5. Final Greetings and Conclusion   4:10–18

EPHESIANS

Ephesians and Colossians are literary siblings. Almost one-third of Colossians appears in Ephesians, and approximately one-half of the sentences in Ephesians include some language from Colossians. Although Ephesians borrows more from the undisputed Pauline epistles than does any other New Testament epistle with the exception of 2 Thessalonians, the literary relationship to Colossians is so close as to suggest a direct dependence. In the household rules taken from Colossians 3:18–4:1, for example, the author of Ephesians changes, expands, and sharpens his Colossian source to fit a new situation.

Where wives are asked to "be subject to your husbands, *as is fitting in the Lord*," in Colossians 3:18 (italics added), Ephesians has the more demanding, "*as you are to the Lord*" (5:22). Given the completely different understanding of such key words as "mystery" and "stewardship" in these letters (cf. Col. 1:25–28; 2:2; and Eph. 3:3–6; 1:9; and 5:32), it is unlikely that they came from the same hand. What is more probable is that the author knew a collection of Pauline letters that included Colossians when he penned Ephesians.

The Question of Authorship

If Colossians is judged to be deutero-Pauline and the author of Ephesians heavily relied on Colossians, then it follows that Ephesians is also deutero-Pauline. It is important, however, to consider linguistic and theological issues that also influence that judgment. Even if direct dependence is asserted, it is important to take note of the ways the author of Ephesians changes, expands, and sharpens whatever sources he appropriated to address a different situation.

Language and Style

The language and style of Ephesians are unusual for a Pauline letter. Nowhere else in the New Testament is there such an interest in the saintliness of an apostle (thirteen references) nor does Paul in the undisputed letters ever refer to himself as a saint (*hagios*). Instead of the "least of the apostles" (1 Cor. 15:9), Paul now appears as "the very least of all the *saints*" (Eph. 3:8). References to "the heavens" (plural, five times), "the beloved" (referring to Christ, 1:6), "flesh and blood" (6:12), "commonwealth" (2:12), "holiness" (*hosiotēs*, 4:24), "debauchery" (*asōtia*, 5:18), "compassionate" (*eusplanchnos*, 4:32), and "favor one with" (*charitoō*, 1:6), occur in Ephesians but nowhere in the undisputed letters. The absence of this language in the undisputed letters of Paul plus its presence in later post-Pauline writings both within and outside the New Testament argues for placing Ephesians in the postapostolic period, after 80 CE.

Stylistically Ephesians also shows certain idiosyncrasies. Long, complex sentences abound in the Greek (e.g., 1:3–10; 1:15–23; 3:14–19). The heaping up of synonyms is frequent, such as the "energy of his great strength" (1:19, AT), the "aeon of this world" (2:12, AT), and "prayer and supplication" (6:18). While Paul also builds long, convoluted sentences and multiplies synonyms, even a casual reading of Ephesians will spot excesses uncharacteristic of Paul.

Theology of the Letter

More than the vocabulary and style, the theology of the letter points to someone other than Paul. In at least three important areas the outlook of Ephesians differs from that of the undisputed letters: its eschatology, its view of the church (ecclesiology), and its understanding of apostleship. As our discussion of Colossians noted, a feverish expectation of the imminent end of the age informs the undisputed letters. The tension between the "now" and the "not yet" so common in the undisputed letters is muted in Ephesians. The approaching end and impending judgment are alluded to only in the most general way (1:4). The urgency that drove the apostolic mission has left, and no interest in the Parousia (second coming) of Christ is expressed. The temporal dimension, as expressed in Paul's statements about the past (or salvation history, Rom. 9–11) or the future expectation, are displaced by spatial categories. Christ appears in Ephesians as the head of the cosmos "far above all rule and authority and power and dominion" (1:21). Those "far off" have been "brought near" (2:13). Believers are given the power to comprehend "the breadth and length and height and depth" (3:18). In these three statements about Christ, salvation of the Gentiles, and the understanding of the believers, space rather than time is the controlling category.

An emphasis on the church provides the integrating center of the letter. Against 1 Corinthians, which offers the church as the body of Christ, Ephesians presents the church as a sphere for the activity of the cosmic Christ, who exponentially expands the boundaries of the church. Now the church universal rather than the church local receives emphasis. The great Christ mystery is no longer God's gracious work through an ignominious cross but the embrace of both Jew and Gentile by the church universal. Founded on "the apostles and prophets" (Eph. 2:20), this church becomes in Ephesians the seat of the cosmic Christ, and differs markedly from the struggling, messy local congregations of the undisputed letters. While the term *ekklēsia* can refer to the wider community in the genuine letters, a subtle shift has occurred. Whereas the undisputed letters view the church in light of Paul's Christology, Ernst Käsemann was quite correct that in Ephesians "Christology . . . is interpreted almost exclusively by ecclesiology [not the reverse]."[7]

View of the Apostle

Finally, the understanding of apostleship in Ephesians differs significantly from that of the authentic Pauline letters. In Ephesians the apostles provide the foundation of the church (2:20), a statement that would have made Paul wince. The undisputed letters emphatically assert that the mission of the apostle is to proclaim the gospel to the Gentiles (e.g., Gal. 1:16; 2:7). In Ephesians, on the other hand, Paul's apostolic task was to affirm the unity in the church of Jews and Gentiles (3:2–6). This shift of emphasis reflects a situation that developed after Paul when the Gentile church, no longer a struggling minority movement in this Jewish sect, was in control and the first hints of discrimination against the Jewish Christian minority were beginning to appear.[8]

We see, therefore, that its language, style, eschatology, view of the church, and understanding of apostleship place Ephesians in the deutero-Pauline category.

The Context of the Letter

As we saw in chapter 4, the undisputed epistles of Paul are real letters address-ing real people in real situations. In each letter we noted a concrete situation evoking the letter. Ephesians, on the other hand, only grudgingly yields clues to its purpose, and thus the attempts to reconstruct the setting of the letter have been disappointing. J. Paul Sampley may be correct that the "purposes of its author are hidden from the modern reader," but before we surrender our quest let us offer some possibilities.[9]

The Problems Evoking the Letter

Ephesians resembles a religious tract more than a letter, and the general nature of the instruction has invited a number of theses about its purpose. More than a generation ago E. J. Goodspeed argued that Ephesians was written as a summary of Pauline theology to serve as a cover letter for a collection of the Pauline epistles.[10] While such a thesis would explain the general nature of the letter, it does not explain the absence of references to prominent motifs that appear in the undisputed letters (e.g., the Parousia and the cross). Moreover, if Ephesians ever stood at the head of a collection of Pauline letters, all evidence for such a position has been lost. Nils Dahl, a distinguished Pauline scholar, once suggested that Ephesians was written to instruct new Gentile converts on the meaning of baptism.[11] With some plausibility Henry Chadwick thinks the letter addressed a crisis created by the success of Gentile Christianity and its drift away from its moorings in the Jewish tradition.[12] Others have seen an attempt to counter the influence of Gnosticism or a popular religion of the day. A very old thesis that enjoys little favor today is that Ephesians was a defense of Paul against competitors from Johannine and Petrine circles. From this short list of hypotheses it is easy to see the confusion that persists about the purpose of this letter. Perhaps the difficulty lies in the attempt of scholars to find a single purpose behind the writing, when in a postapostolic work, no less than in a writing of our own, a letter, an essay, or a tract may serve many purposes simultaneously.

Adaptations of two of the proposals mentioned above continue to be attractive to scholars: (1) that our author wrote to urge the Gentile Christian majority to accept a Jewish Christian minority and to affirm its ties with the ancient Hebrew traditions, and (2) that in the ethical admonition the author corrects libertine tendencies stemming from gnostic influence or from the popular religion of the day (mystery cults, Neo-Pythagorean philosophy, folk religion, etc.). Let us now look at each in turn.

1. During and after the Roman-Jewish War (66–70 CE) that left Jerusalem in ruins, tensions increased between Jews and followers of Christ. Before the war, as we know from Paul's letters, it was possible to believe that Jesus was the Messiah and remain active in the synagogue. By the time Matthew's Gospel appeared (c. 85 CE), harsh exchanges were traded between church and synagogue, and when the Fourth Gospel appeared a decade later, belief in Jesus as the Messiah could mean expulsion from a synagogue, at least for the evangelist's community.[13]

While it is risky to generalize from these two examples, one can easily construct a scenario in Asia Minor that exacerbated these hostilities and under Paul's name evoked Ephesians. True to their pacifist teachings, the Jesus people who refused to support the Jewish revolt against Roman occupation were open to the charge of being traitors and cowards. Gentile converts viewed as Jewish messianists until the war, might want to dissociate themselves from the nationalistic cause of the Zealots, if for no other reason than to avoid Roman reprisals. Thus there would be in both Jewish messianist and Gentile Christian circles an emphasis on a particularity apart from a Jewish tradition dominated by a radical, revolutionary posture. While understandable, such a posture would have made it increasingly difficult to confess Jesus as the Messiah and continue living as a Jew. The pressure, whether subtle or overt from the Gentile majority, would be to encourage either assimilation or withdrawal into a Jewish Christian sect. The threat of a rupture between Jewish and Gentile followers was real. The danger of isolation from or even repudiation of the Jewish tradition in the Gentile church was ever present. This imagined scenario is plausible, if hypothetical at this point, but from second-century writings (Marcion and Justin) we are privy to a rupture that was already well under way. The book of Revelation at the end of the first century offers some testimony that likewise points toward an emerging split. But in any case the ugly divorce came after Paul's death in the 60s. If what I propose is credible then it would appear that the author of Ephesians was alarmed by this emerging split and attempted to speak to the crisis.

2. More than a decade ago, scholars observed that both the language of the author and the outlook of the addressees showed some gnostic coloration. Given the proto-gnostic desire to escape the prison of the body to ascend to a higher realm, the command of the author to "put off your old nature . . . and put on the new nature" (4:22, 24 RSV) rings true to the gnostic or pre-gnostic outlook. The libertine inclinations of the audience or the temptation "to practice every kind of impurity" (4:19) resemble later gnostic traits. But whether the ideology ("every wind of doctrine," 4:14) that informed these

tendencies came from organized gnostic circles or from the mysteries, popular religions, or folk piety tinged with Gnosticism is difficult to establish with any certainty. Although the exact contours of the conceptual landscape are unclear, apparently a concrete situation provoked this document.

The Response to the Problems

In this response to the concrete situation the author tapped one or more undisputed letters of Paul and the deutero-Pauline Colossians. Moreover, paraenetic materials showing a family resemblance to some Qumran scrolls may have shaped the thinking of the writer as well. The later instructions, or "household rules," derive from Hellenistic Jewish circles (via Colossians), and his perception of Christ as the head of the cosmos and of the sexual union of Christ and the church betrays both gnostic and Hellenistic traits. Working out of those materials the author affirmed a unity that derived from Christ, in whom the whole cosmos, he thought, found its unity and purpose; and in a faintly Platonic sense, the author proclaimed the mystery of the unity of the church as a cosmic, divine mystery. Thus we can see how in Christ's reconciliation of the cosmos the author found a model that joined Jew and Gentile in one community.

In the undisputed letters Paul repeatedly argued for the right of Gentiles to be included in the church qua Gentiles without first converting to Judaism (see Rom. 9–11 and Gal. 1–3). In spite of his protestation, the Jerusalem church continued to exert a powerful influence on Paul. But with the war and a growth of the Gentile church that Paul could hardly have imagined, the symbiotic relationship between Gentile and Jewish factions of the church or even between the gospel of Christ and the Jewish traditions could no longer be taken for granted. Since Paul had argued for the inclusiveness of the church and since he had come to a position of respect and honor (at least in some circles), the use of his name and teaching seemed entirely apt. Under these altered circumstances, the author of Ephesians uses Paul's name to argue for the inclusion of Jewish believers in the community without assimilation to the views of the Gentile majority. While Paul had argued for the inclusion of Gentiles as Gentiles, the author of Ephesians argues for the inclusion of Jewish believers as Jewish believers.

The appeal to the suffering of the apostle for the church is intended to inspire a willingness to follow the instruction in the letter out of gratitude to the "apostle." Paul appears as "a prisoner for Christ Jesus for the sake of you Gentiles" (3:1) and as a "prisoner in the Lord" who encourages the recipients "to lead a life worthy of the calling to which you have been called" (4:1). In 3:13 the hearers are asked to "not lose heart over my sufferings for you." While in the undisputed letters (especially 2 Corinthians) the emphasis on suffering is stronger, only in the deutero-Pauline letters does the suffering have a vicarious dimension; it is *"for you."* One can easily imagine how reverence for Paul and careful observance of instructions from him would be fostered by the awareness that the apostle was suffering for the readers.

In the undisputed letters Paul argued that his call and apostolic commission legitimated his gospel to the Gentiles (Gal. 1:15–16; Rom. 1:5). Although the apostolic call remained important in Ephesians, it was understood differently. No longer was it seen as the puzzling way the grotesque cross revealed God's nature or the numinous divine presence, but rather the inclusion of Jews and Gentiles in one church uncovered a "mystery." Since the unity derived from the Christ in whom the whole cosmos found a unity and purpose, in a faintly Platonic sense the mystery of unity of the church shared in that divine, cosmic mystery. Thus in Christ's reconciliation of the cosmos the author found a model for the reconciliation of Jew and Gentile.

In presenting the apostle as the "least of all the *saints*" (3:8) who belongs to the "holy apostles" of God through whom Gentiles become fellow heirs (3:5), the author rhetorically affirmed the importance of this message and invoked the name of the now revered apostle Paul to lend authority to this tractate. This elevated view of Paul, which borders on reverence, would have surely secured a hearing for an attempt to deal with a crisis that threatened to fracture the church and to cut it loose from its spiritual moorings. Quite appropriately he appealed to Paul in order to encourage tolerance of and respect for Jewish followers of Christ as Jews and to discourage participation in the popular religions of the day. He urged the church to resist erroneous doctrine (4:14) and to shun immorality or libertine behavior. Most scholars agree that the paraenetic material comes from many sources, but our author fashioned that material to emphasize the importance of unity, order, and mutual respect. In a characteristic Pauline fashion, the closing reaffirms the major concern of the letter. There the church is urged to reaffirm its support for Paul (through prayer) and the mystery (i.e., the unity of the church) (6:18–20).

Outline of Ephesians

2 THESSALONIANS

The Question of Authorship

This letter has few pages, but many problems. In addition to the question of authorship stand questions of the identity and function of the *katechōn* ("restrainer" or "oppressor" in 2:7), the literary relationship to 1 Thessalonians, the purpose of the letter, and its context, all of which are stubborn, intractable problems facing the interpreter. Although included here in our discussion of deutero-Pauline letters, 2 Thessalonians has received strong support for inclusion among the authentic letters. Persuasive arguments can be marshaled both for and against its authenticity, but I included it here because its authenticity is in doubt.

The case against Pauline authorship includes the linguistic, literary, and theological arguments seen elsewhere. First, the language and style of this letter differ from the undisputed letters in significant ways. Nowhere else does Paul speak of being made "worthy of the kingdom of God" through suffering (1:5), or of the "restrainer" (or "oppressor," 2:7), or of "good hope" (2:16), "eternal comfort" (2:16), "good resolve" (1:11), or of being "shaken in mind" (2:2). Nowhere else does Paul speak of his readers as those whom God chose to "believe the truth" (2:12d–13). While such language sounds strange when put on Paul's lips, words or phrases elsewhere in 2 Thessalonians echo those of 1 Thessalonians. For example, the salutation of 2 Thessalonians is nearly identical to that of 1 Thessalonians, the thanksgiving in 2 Thessalonians 1:3–4 closely parallels that of 1 Thessalonians 1:2–3. Similarly, the expression, "brothers and sisters, we ask and urge you," in the first letter (4:1) resembles "we beg you, brothers and sisters," in the second (2:1). The expression, the "Gentiles who do not know God" (1 Thess. 4:5), is nearly identical to "those [unbelievers] who do not know God" (2 Thess. 1:8); and "Finally, brothers and sisters" (1 Thess. 4:1) is repeated exactly in 2 Thessalonians 3:1. The reference to the "labor and toil" of Paul and his coworkers and that they worked "night and day" of 1 Thessalonians 2:9 are almost exactly duplicated in 2 Thessalonians 3:8.

While the language in 2 Thessalonians agrees rather closely with that of 1 Thessalonians in places, scholars dispute the significance of those agreements. Some argue that if Paul wrote 2 Thessalonians either shortly before or soon after 1Thessalonians their verbal agreement is hardly surprising. But such a temporal proximity would make their differences harder to explain. Others notice that most of the parallels appear in the letter opening and closing, traditionally the most stereotyped parts of the letter. These would thus be the epistolary sections easiest to duplicate. So the linguistic arguments tend to cancel each other out. The issue of authorship, therefore, must be decided on other grounds.

Second, taking up the literary question, the unusual form of the letter poses more of a problem for Pauline authorship. The thanksgiving especially has been singled out for scrutiny, because all of Paul's authentic letters save Galatians have a thanksgiving, and except for that in 2 Corinthians all of the letters except for 1 Thessalonians have one thanksgiving, which has two. Birger Pearson has made a compelling case that the second thanksgiving (1 Thess. 2:13–16) was added later to tie the early persecution of Christians to the destruction of Jerusalem by the Roman onslaught in 70 CE.[14] The break in the material, the unusual language, and the veiled allusion to the destruction of Jerusalem support the argument that the second thanksgiving was added after Paul's death. The second thanksgiving was inserted to reflect the developing tensions between nonmessianist Jews and followers of Christ, Jew and Gentile, after the war. Second Thessalonians takes over this unusual dual thanksgiving and closely duplicates its form (e.g., 1:3–12 and 2:13–17). It is possible then, if not likely, that a later writer using the edited version of 1 Thessalonians with two thanksgivings imitated its form and some of its content. It follows, obviously, if such were the case, then Paul could not have written 2 Thessalonians.

One other small clue points to an author other than Paul. In 2:2 the author urges his hearers not to be disturbed by letters "purporting to be from us" (RSV). Given Paul's status as a persona non grata in many regions, it seems strange to have a pseudonymous letter circulating in his name. From what we know of pseudepigraphy elsewhere, most often the names used belong to some venerated figure from the past (e.g., Moses, Enoch, Abraham; or in the New Testament, Peter, Paul, James, or John). We have no instance of a pseudonymous letter being written in the name of a living person. From a practical point of view we can see why. It would be risky for a person to adopt the name of a contemporary when the risk of being exposed would be high; it would be rather easy to check the authenticity of the letter with the person in whose name it was written. Moreover, a special problem intrudes when one argues, as many do, that Paul wrote the first letter only a few weeks before the second. While such an argument would explain the similarity of the letters, it is difficult to see how in only a few weeks after the writing of the first letter a pseudonymous letter could appear bearing Paul's name. The conclusion of the letter, "I, Paul, write this greeting with my own hand" (3:17), appears to be a brazen attempt to establish the credibility of the letter against the claim of rivals in a post-Pauline period when other deutero-Pauline letters were appearing. In any case the claim ascribed to Paul to write 2 Thessalonians "with my own hand" is hardly proof of the letter's authenticity.

Third, the theological outlook of 2 Thessalonians differs from that of 1 Thessalonians in important ways. In the first letter Paul expects that some of his readers will still be alive at the Parousia of Christ (4:17). This emphasis on the imminent return persists throughout the undisputed letters of Paul. Even in Romans, one of the last letters, Paul asserted that salvation (or the end) "is nearer to us now than when we became believers; the night is far gone, the day is near" (13:11–12). It seems strange, therefore, in 2 Thessalonians to see an apocalyptic timetable that allows for a postponement of the end. Before the "day of the Lord" (2:2) the believers will witness the appearance of the "restrainer" (2:7), the "man of lawlessness" (2:3), and a period of apostasy from the faith (2:2–12). Although the end of the age still lingers on the horizon in 2 Thessalonians, the delay effected by a timetable is unique in Paul's letters. Gerhard Krodel has noted how the use of the apocalyptic timetable here functions in a way quite different from that of the eschatological allusions in the Corinthian letters.[15] Before the Parousia of Jesus there must come first the apostasy of believers, the arrival of the rebel, and the disappearance of the restrainer. Presupposed by this timetable is a delay. In 1 Thessalonians, on the other hand, Paul uses an imminent eschatology to counter the discouragement of his addressees.

In addition to the altered eschatological strategy in 2 Thessalonians, other prominent Pauline emphases are subdued. The Pauline view of the cross, resurrection, and Spirit play a diminished role. Instead of asking his hearers to imitate his suffering as their share of the cross, "Paul" invited his addressees to copy his work ethic, that is, to earn their bread by sweat and toil as does he (3:7–13).

For these reasons, therefore, I incline toward including this letter among the deutero-Paulines. In the generation after Paul's death there was a need to understand the delay of Christ's return (note especially Matt. 25). However, no scholarly consensus exists on this question. Fortunately, the problem the epistle addresses is much clearer than the identity of the author. It is to that issue that we now turn.

The Context of the Letter

Second Thessalonians addressed two problems: apocalyptic enthusiasm and persecution. The suffering that the readers endured (1:5) some understood as a sign that the end had already come. Some were disturbed and others alarmed by a bogus Pauline letter announcing that "the day of the Lord is already here" (2:2). Moreover, "wicked" people allegedly preyed on this anxious congregation, deceiving some and exploiting others (3:2). This period of feverish expectation of the world's denouement, created by a bogus letter and by false teachers, led some to quit work and wait for the end (3:6). They idled away their time, sponging off the workers (3:11–12), and their claim to liberation from work's sweat and grime disturbed the exploited in the church (3:11).

In response our author promised relief and/or rest to terror's victims. He offered consolation and hope to the tortured and harassed, and confidently predicted the demise of the faceless oppressors. Recalling the *lex talionis* that exacted "an eye for an eye, and a tooth for a tooth," the author predicted affliction for those afflicting the church (1:6) and rejection for those rejecting the gospel (1:8). He assured the oppressed that he, the "apostle," was praying for them, exhorted them to persist in good resolve (1:11) in order that "Jesus may be glorified in you" (1:12). He promised God's comfort for those who remained calm and resolute in persecution (2:1) and exhorted them all to hold fast "to the traditions" (2:15, a strikingly un-Pauline phrase). The author promised that the Lord would strengthen them for their struggle and would guard them from evil (3:3).

By establishing an apocalyptic timetable, the author sought to modify the intense apocalyptic enthusiasm threatening the church. The author warned those who insisted that "the day of the Lord" had come (2:2) to remember that the "day" will arrive only after the apocalyptic rebellion, after a period of apostasy, after the judgment of "the man of lawlessness" (2:3), and after the exposure of his signs and wonders as false (2:9). Even though the identity and function of the *katechōn* or "restrainer" (2:7) was probably known to the readers, he/they are veiled from us. The identity stands hidden in the haze of its Jewish apocalyptic background. The precise role this figure would play in history's final apocalyptic drama also is unknown.

Through the skillful use of these traditions in 2:3–12, however, the author sought to qualify and modify the enthusiastic eschatology of his readers. By speaking of the delay of the "end" and the apocalyptic reversal of the position of the oppressor and oppressed, he offered encouragement and consolation to the persecuted and exhorted the idle to work. The apostle toiled and labored, even while he preached the gospel, offering his own example as a model worthy of imitation (3:7–12). Members of the community were commanded to shun all idle busybodies and thus sought to reclaim them for the church (3:6, 11, 14–15) by publicly shaming them.

We see, therefore, how our author drew on 1 Thessalonians and the Jewish apocalyptic tradition to address both persecuted persons and enthusiasts. Relying heavily on both the form and content of 1 Thessalonians, and the apostle's example and name, he offered comfort and correction. Although his strategy differed from that of the Paul of 1 Thessalonians in his use of a timetable metric marking the way to the end, the author correctly understood Paul's resistance to religious enthusiasm, the apostle's emphasis on "work with the hands," and his suspension of the believer in an energy field between "the now and the not yet."

Outline of 2 Thessalonians

1. Address, Salutation, and First Thanksgiving   1:1–12
2. Encouragement in the Face of Eschatological Trauma   2:1–12
3. Prayers and Exhortations   2:13–3:5
   a. Second thanksgiving and intercession   2:13–17
   b. Prayer request and intercession   3:1–5
4. Paraenesis   3:6–16
   a. Avoid the idle   3:6–7
   b. Paul's example   3:8–10
   c. Earn your own living   3:11–13
   d. Shun the slackers   3:14–15
5. Letter Closing   3:16–18

1 AND 2 TIMOTHY AND TITUS (THE PASTORALS)

The Question of Authorship

Ostensibly written from a "pastor" to "pastors," these letters gained the name the Pastorals some 350 years ago. For much of the time since, it has been simply taken for granted that these letters, written under his name, were by Paul. In the early nineteenth century, however, biblical critics took notice that the language, style, and content of these letters differed markedly from the authentic Pauline letters. With few exceptions, modern scholars agree that Paul did not write the Pastorals. While their absence from an early manuscript (Chester Beatty papyrus number 46, P46 for short) can be discounted because part of the papyrus appears to be missing, it is more difficult to explain why Marcion omits the Pastorals from his collection of Paul's letters (c. 150 CE). One could object that the anti-gnostic polemic in the Pastorals was offensive to Marcion and thus led to their rejection. But it is harder to explain why they were eventually tacked on as an appendix to the letter collection in the church's first canon of scriptures. This subordinate position suggests that though they were included, their acceptance was somewhat tentative. The church could not say no to the Pastorals, but it was unable to utter a resounding yes.

As with the above letters, the more compelling arguments against Pauline authorship are linguistic and theological. Excluding proper names, about twenty percent of the vocabulary appears nowhere else in the New Testament, and approximately thirty percent of the language of the Pastorals is altogether absent from the undisputed letters. More decisive than the quantity of unusual words, however, is their distinctive character. The vocabulary of the Pastorals more reminds one of a Hellenistic Jewish philosophical treatise than a Pauline letter. Such words as "piety" (*eusebeia*, 2 Tim. 3:5), "irreligious" (*anosios*, 2 Tim. 3:2), "way of life" (*agōgē*, 2 Tim. 3:10), "truth" (*alētheia*, 2 Tim. 2:15), "in accordance with piety" (*eusebeia*, Titus 1:1), "loving good" (*philagathos*, Titus 1:8), "temperate" (*sōphrōn*, Titus 1:8), "self-controlled" (*enkratēs*, Titus 1:8; all ATs) are more characteristic of the popular Hellenistic writings of the day than of the letters of Paul.

Moreover, some of the vocabulary that is integral to the undisputed letters appears nowhere in the Pastorals. Such words as "uncircumcised" (14 times), "to die" (35 times), "to proclaim the good news" (*euangelizesthai*, 18 times), "spiritual" (18 times), and "body" (59 times) are absent altogether from the Pastorals. Also, an important theological word—"righteousness" (45 times)—appears in the Pastorals only five times and carries a theological meaning unknown to Paul. While an argument from silence is suspect if used alone, when taken with the other positive evidence cited above it raises insurmountable objections to Pauline authorship.

While statistical evidence is valuable, seldom is it decisive by itself in questions of authorship. A comparison of the outlook of the Pastorals with that of the genuine letters is more instructive. First, the understanding of the church in the Pastorals is markedly different from that of the authentic Pauline letters. The institutional forms we see in the Pastorals are clearly more developed. Through the laying on of hands, we are told, "Paul" ordained Timothy to a ministerial task (2 Tim. 1:6), and Timothy in turn was to pass on the apostolic charisma to others (2 Tim. 2:1–2). Thus the church received an ordained clergy that claimed apostolic authority and with that authority the responsibility to maintain "sound teaching." Timothy and Titus, who stood in the apostolic chain, also appointed "elders" who governed the church and proclaimed the word. They chose deacons who are sober, unselfish, married only once, and good managers (1 Tim. 3:8–13). They installed deacons who managed the church and administered charity; the elders governed and preached. They charged the leaders with protecting "sound teaching" from false interpretation or compromise to assure institutional health.

Both internal and external threats to the church are met in the genuine letters with vigorous and often heated rhetoric. In the Pastorals, however, there is little independent argumentation. For Paul the mission of the church is expansive; the posture of the Pastorals is defensive.

The emphases of these letters depart significantly from those of the undisputed letters. For Paul church leadership was charismatic or Spirit-endowed; for the Pastor (the author of the Pastorals) the leadership was institutional. For Paul "faith" was usually understood in an active sense (e.g., trust in God, acceptance of God's work in Messiah Jesus), but for the Pastor "faith" was a body of Christian truth to be guarded and defended. For Paul the church was the body of Christ; for the Pastor the church was a fortress that defended the "deposit" (1 Tim. 6:20; 2 Tim. 1:12, 14). For Paul error was corrected by forceful debate; for the Pastor the correction came through a calm comparison with truth. For Paul the imminent return of Christ suffused all of his thought; for the Pastor the Parousia, or second coming of Christ, played an insignificant role. We see, therefore, that in their understanding of the church, its organization, purpose, and function, Paul and the Pastor were poles apart.

The paraenetic materials in the Pastorals also vastly differ from those of the Pauline letters. Martin Dibelius, an influential German scholar, once referred to the paraenesis of the Pastorals as a bourgeois ethic.[16] By that he meant the deeds and rules prescribed in the Pastorals encourage a type of piety that was indistinguishable from that of the cultural ethos. When Paul borrowed ethical material from hellenized circles, he normally placed his own stamp on it. The Pastor, on the other hand, hardly exerted such a masterful reshaping of his material.

The Pastorals depart significantly from their Pauline model in their reaffirmation of a gendered hierarchy. In describing the role women exercise in the church, Paul spoke approvingly of the ministry of women. He noted with appreciation the contribution of his coworker Prisca; Paul recognized the important charismatic role of female prophets in the interpretation of scripture in Corinth; Phoebe served as a deacon (not deaconess); Paul acknowledged the important leadership role of Mary, a servant of the Roman churches (Rom. 16:1, 3, 6); and he recognized with appreciation the important role of Junia, the female apostle (Rom. 16:7; not the masculine Junias as in the RSV). In Galatians Paul cited with approval a baptismal formula that announced that in Christ there is "no longer Jew or Greek, there is no longer slave or free, there is *no longer male and female*" (Gal. 3:28, italics added). In the Pastorals, on the other hand, the accepted cultural norms prevail. Although the Pastor assigned some role to widows over sixty, he forbade a woman to teach or "to have authority over a man"; rather, the woman was "to keep silent." She was to earn salvation by bearing children, "*provided* [she] continued in faith and love and holiness, with modesty" (1 Tim. 2:12, 15, italics added). It is hardly possible to harmonize the Pastor's thinking about women of faith with that of the undisputed letters.

We see, therefore, why the Pastorals should not be ascribed to Paul; however, in their own time the Pastorals played an important role. Some kind of institutional order needed development in the emerging Jesus movement. Given the delay of Jesus' Parousia, the threat posed by Marcion, the ascendancy of gnostic teaching, and episodic persecution or harassment, some development of Pauline theology was required. To that development we now turn.

Context of the Pastorals

The Problem within the Community

Although the Pastor refrained from aggressive confrontation with the false teacher, his contrast of sound doctrine with erroneous teaching offers an interesting picture of the teaching or "heresy" he opposed. Subscribing to Jewish "myths," "genealogies," and "commandments of those who reject the truth" (1 Tim. 1:4; Titus 1:14), the Pastor's opponents also engaged in certain ascetic practices. They repudiated marriage and avoided certain foods (1 Tim. 4:3). In claiming a presentist experience of the resurrection (2 Tim. 2:11), they effectively removed the eschatological reservation at the core of Paul's theology (2 Tim. 2:18). They claimed "knowledge" (*gnōsis*, 1 Tim. 6:20; Titus 1:16), and they possibly claimed the total freedom of expression by men and women in the service of worship. The emphasis on asceticism, aeon speculation, a realized eschatology, a higher salvific knowledge, and a libertine behavior linked with law observance suggests that this version of "Christianity" was a form of Jewish Gnosticism. The "false teachers" had enjoyed some success with the "naive" and unstable (2 Tim. 3:6–7 and Titus 1:11); they had enriched themselves at the expense of the credulous. In the paragraphs below, we shall note the Pastor's assured response to these challenges.

The Pastor's Response

The Pastor juxtaposed his reading of Paul's letters to those of his adversaries. His corrective had two facets. First, he sought authority for his interpretation of his "teaching" against that of the "errorists" by invoking the name of their hero—the once much maligned but now revered and rehabilitated apostle (especially by Marcion and Valentinus). He also adopted and wrote in Paul's name. By selecting and interweaving traditions from Paul, whom he presented as a patriarchal figure whose ministry was linked with the church's origin, he offered a corrective to false teaching.

Second, by appropriating those chosen and trusted by Paul, namely, Timothy and Titus, the Pastor claimed authority for commissioning deacons and elders to guide the church and legitimized them with this historical linkage. The Pastorals have "Paul" write Timothy, a coworker and "loyal child in the faith" (1 Tim. 1:2), and Titus, "my loyal child in the faith we share" (Titus 1:4), and authorize them to "appoint elders" (Titus 1:5) and "deacons" (1 Tim. 3:8–13). Thus, through Paul's students in ministry, the Pastor cleverly forged a historical link with Paul that said, "mine is better than yours." In the dispute with the later gnostics this chain of authority evidently proved useful. Although the link with the apostle was forced, there was a certain aptness in the appeal because Paul had opposed gnostic tendencies in Corinth. Though his strategy would have been different, Paul might have agreed with the Pastor on the seriousness of the threats posed by the rival teachers.

In addition to his appeal to authority through Paul, the Pastor also provided a substantive alternative to the rival emphasis on asceticism, aeon speculation ("myths"), realized eschatology, and superior knowledge (*gnōsis*). Instead of seeking to discredit the views of the "false teachers" through direct confrontation, the Pastor simply contrasted their "silly myths" with his "sound doctrine." A "knowledge of the truth" (Titus 1:1), "sound doctrine" (Titus 1:9), what is "sound in *the* faith" (Titus 1:13, emphasis added), or "teaching" (1 Tim. 4:16), was contrasted with the *gnōsis* of the adversaries. The "sound words of our Lord Jesus Christ and the teaching that is in accordance with godliness" (1 Tim. 6:3) were compared to the claims of those swollen with conceit (1 Tim. 6:4). The "good confession" (1 Tim. 6:12) belonged to those who "rightly [handle] the word of truth" (2 Tim. 2:15), and confuted those who engaged in "wrangling over words" (2 Tim. 2:14) or in "profane chatter" (2 Tim. 2:16).

Thus not only did the Pastor avoid a pitched battle with his adversaries, he also advised his addressees to refrain from any direct challenge to the "false teachers." He urged them instead to abstain from "stupid and senseless controversies" (2 Tim. 2:23, and their "godless and silly myths" [1 Tim. 4:7 RSV]) and admonished them to correct their "opponents with gentleness" (2 Tim. 2:25). One feature that shines through all of his response is the Pastor's remarkable confidence that this soft approach to the errors of those "of corrupt mind" (2 Tim. 3:8) would be recognized by all and would lead to reform.

In his attempt to counter the ascetic tendencies of the gnostics, the Pastor suggested that all foods were to be received with thanksgiving (1 Tim. 4:3). Against those who forbade marriage,[17] the Pastor recommended it for young widows and presumably for the unmarried as well. Against those who claimed to have already experienced the resurrection, a pale copy of traditional Pauline eschatology was held up that assigned "the last days" and the resurrection to the future. Appealing to Pauline teaching, the Pastor said, "If we have died with him, *we will also live with him*" (2 Tim. 2:11, italics added; that does sound Pauline). Finally, it seems possible, if not probable, that the traditionally subordinate position assigned to women in the Pastorals was a reaction against alternatives in vogue elsewhere.[18]

We saw in our discussion of the Corinthian correspondence that religious enthusiasts promised an existence transcending sexuality to those fully experiencing salvation in the present. In their glorified state some Corinthians held that all distinctions between men and women were erased. Agreeing with Paul, and following his celibate model, they could say that in Christ "there is no longer male and female" (Gal. 3:28). A similar viewpoint was likely shared by the gnostics of the Pastor's communities. The Pastor attempted to refute such claims by imposing on women the traditional social restrictions that the gnostics had abandoned in the name of liberation.[19] The Pastor commanded women to avoid alluring attire and to "learn in silence with full submission" (1 Tim. 2:11). They were forbidden to teach (as they did in Corinth) or to exercise authority over men, as Phoebe would have done, and they were to earn their salvation by bearing children (i.e., the church was to grow by propagation and evangelism, 1 Tim. 2:12–15).

It is tempting to suggest that these letters lack the vitality and interest of the undisputed Pauline letters. The Pastor's static view of faith and his demeaning view of women offend our modern sensibilities. He could be faulted for his bourgeois ethic, which has had a significant impact on Pauline interpretation over the centuries and into our own time. One could easily point to the Pastor's lack of intellectual rigor and theological creativity. But however harshly we judge his strategy or ideology, in retrospect we know that the ideology and strategy of the gainsayers was formidable. Had Gnosticism or the teaching of Marcion dictated the future and theology of the church,[20] the history of the whole Western world would have been very different. Had Gnosticism triumphed, the church as we know it would be unrecognizable.

In our survey of the deutero-Pauline letters, we have seen various interpretations of the Pauline tradition for later contexts. The Gentile mission had succeeded so well that the Gentile church was in a position to determine its own agenda, to create its own theological idiom, and to chart its own course, heedless of the views of the Jerusalem circle or the sensibilities of a shrinking Jewish Christian membership. The Roman-Jewish War had exacerbated tensions between Jews and non-Jews, which further threatened the relationship between Jewish and Gentile Christians. The growing theological disputes and animosity between synagogue and church were waving them steadily toward a decisive rupture. The loss of confidence in traditional religious forms, combined with a growing disenchantment with social institutions, was to spark off a vast array of world-denying movements (Gnosticism was the most notable among them). The Parousia, or return of Jesus, so eagerly expected by Paul, had not come even though Jerusalem lay in ruins and Roman Christians had suffered severe persecution. None of these events was foreseen or addressed by Paul. It is a tribute to him, nevertheless, that in his teaching, personality, and example, others in a vastly different age found instruction and encouragement, consolation and hope. Given the benefit of our perspective, we can see certain differences or even contradictions when comparing the deutero-Pauline letters with the undisputed epistles of Paul. But the very use of the Pauline tradition is proof that the deutero-Pauline authors chose to associate themselves with the tradition of an apostle who in spite of being viewed as a pariah in some circles was also seen as a prodigy in others, and they chose to associate themselves with the traditions of the prodigy in order to complement it, not to contradict it.[21]

Outline of 1 Timothy

1.	Address and Salutation	1:1–2
2.	The Theology of the Opponents	1:3–20
3.	Instruction for Prayer and Worship	2:1–15
4.	Requirements for Bishops and Deacons	3:1–16
5.	The Ethics of the Opponents	4:1–10
6.	Instructions for Directing the Church	4:11–6:19
7.	Letter Ending	6:20–21

Outline of 2 Timothy

1.	Address, Salutation, and Thanksgiving	1:1–5
2.	Advice to Timothy	1:6–4:5
	a. Do not be ashamed	1:6–14
	(Example: Onesiphorus)	1:15–18
	b. Be strong in suffering	2:1–7
	(Example: Paul)	2:8–13
	c. Strategy to be used against the "heresy"	2:14–4:5
	(1) Avoid godless chatter—rightly handle the word of truth	2:14–19
	(2) Shun passion and controversy—seek love and peace	2:20–26
	(3) In struggle with false prophets, follow Paul's example in teaching, endurance, and love	3:1–17
	(4) Preach the word—endure suffering	4:1–5
3.	Paul's Situation	4:6–18
	a. Imminent martyrdom	4:6–8
	b. Final instructions for Timothy	4:9–15
	c. Paul's trial and rescue	4:16–18
4.	Letter Closing	4:19–22

Outline of Titus

1.	Address and Salutation	1:1–4
2.	Qualifications for Elders (Bishops)	1:5–9

7

Currents and Crosscurrents

In death as in life, controversy swirled around Paul, the pariah. During his Gentile mission heated exchanges with believers punctuated his letters. Conflict with public officials, arrest, and incarceration interrupted his ministry. Harassment and beatings at the hands of his synagogue critics sapped his energies and grieved his spirit. But even after his mission was cut short by death, Paul's power to provoke continued. More than a century after his burial, his interpretation of the gospel still raised the hackles of some Jewish Christians. In one circle of believers he was tagged with the unflattering epithet "Simon Magus," a demonic magician of some notoriety in Christian apocryphal materials.[1] More recently Paul was accused of diverting Christianity from its source in Jesus' teachings into the stagnant backwater of church dogma.[2] Paul's name is still anathema to some who view him as a male chauvinist.

Although Paul has always had his detractors, he has also had his defenders. If the test of profound and seminal thinking is its ability to generate debate, then certainly Paul's thought would qualify as profound and seminal. His letters meant enough to merit their collection and preservation. The vigorous and imaginative understanding of his gospel spawned a whole family of letter imitations. The writers of these deutero-Paulines (Colossians, Ephesians, 2 Thessalonians, 1 and 2 Timothy and Titus) were so impressed by Paul that they adopted his name to authorize their message. Paul's shadow also fell across Acts, Hebrews, and various noncanonical Christian writings. Among these extrabiblical materials appears the *Acts of Paul* from the late second century. Allusions to Paul and quotations from his letters abound in writings of the early church. Pivotal exegetes like Augustine and Luther found in Paul the optic through which they read all scripture. We see, therefore, Paul's power to provoke and excite continued through the centuries.

In the following pages I shall sketch key topics of the continuing dialogue about Paul. In viewing the currents and crosscurrents in the history of Pauline interpretation, we gain a better appreciation of the subtlety of Paul's thought and how certain prickly passages continue to challenge and frustrate the interpreter. Although such an appreciation is no magic formula for easy mastery of these ancient documents, it is nonetheless helpful for any reader seeking to understand Paul's thought.

We shall focus on five issues that have dominated Pauline interpretation. In chronological order, they are (1) Gnosticism: the problem of evil in the world; (2) Pelagianism: the problem of sin; (3) the relationship of Paul and Jesus; (4) the relationship of Paul to his background; and (5) Paul and women.

GNOSTICISM: THE PROBLEM OF EVIL IN THE WORLD

The feud over the proper relationship of the Christian to the world smoldered for almost a century and then erupted in blazing fury in the late second century. Even in the first century the author of Colossians attacked those in the early church who scorned the world below against the world above. The worship of angels (Col. 2:18), the elevation of visionary experiences, and the promise of an apotheosis for those who acquired divine or cosmic knowledge (2:18, 20) all reflect the otherworldly preoccupation of these marginal groups. Their special disdain for the world manifested itself in such prohibitions as "Do not handle, do not taste, do not touch" (2:21). A reckless abandon was paired with an ascetic emphasis. Those condemned for treating the world with disgust were accused also of "fornication, impurity, passion, evil desire, and greed" (3:5). A strange logic held world denial and physical indulgence together. World rejection demonstrated one's deliverance from the world, and indulgence in the world manifested one's triumph over it. Some Christian gnostics later felt obligated to transgress all moral strictures that earthlings impose in order to assume a place in a higher divine order.

In the second century the Pastorals (1 and 2 Timothy and Titus), written under Paul's name, were summoned to authorize the subversion of gnostic or gnosticizing opponents, and offer a more revealing sketch of these opponents than does Colossians. In 1 Timothy, for example, those who have "missed the mark as regards the faith" (6:21) claim knowledge (Greek *gnōsis*, from which the term "gnosticism" derives). More than just intellectual apprehension, this *gnōsis* was synonymous with salvation for these "heretics,"[3] who claimed a present enlightenment (2 Tim. 2:18) that bestowed a euphoric sense of triumph over the evil world. Although these opponents were called "Jews" (Titus

1:10), they rejected the Jewish belief in the fundamental goodness of the creation (1 Tim. 4:4). Their adherence to "godless and silly myths" (l Tim. 4:7 RSV) and their use of "endless genealogies" (l Tim. 1:4) imposed a hierarchy of angelic mediators to bridge the gulf between the good God and the evil world. Against the gnostic appeal to Paul's letters for support, the Pastorals offered a counterweight.

Second-century Gnosticism almost conquered under Paul's banner.[4] Although Gnosticism was multifaceted, certain themes and emphases occur with some regularity. Gnostic sects everywhere held the material world and things of the flesh in contempt, and this disdain spilled over onto the world's Creator. If the earth is evil, they reasoned, its architect must also be evil. Christian Gnosticism, consequently, often contrasted the creator God of the Old Testament with the God revealed in Christ. They viewed one as the "god of this world" (2 Cor. 4:4) and therefore diabolical, and the other as the God of the highest heaven and therefore gracious and good. Salvation, naturally enough, was understood as liberation from this earthly prison and as rescue from the worldly flesh.

The gnostic myth held that through some tragic failure a spark of the divine was planted in some (but not all) persons. With the memory of this divine origin erased, humanity sank into an ignorant stupor until the high God of mercy sent Christ to awaken the "spiritual" who were ignorant of their divine origin, to remind them of their true divine origin. Salvation was synonymous and synchronous with this *gnōsis* moment; an awareness of the divine origin of the true self illumined all existence. More than an instant of mental recall, this epiphany brought a reunion with one's heavenly origin through which came experiences of transcendence or of ecstasy. In dreams, visions, tongues speaking (angelic speech), and heavenly journeys (see 2 Cor. 12:1–6) came an intimation of one's divine parentage and its fullness. As the gnostic *Gospel of Philip* later said: "Those who say that the Lord died first and (then) rose up are in error, for he rose up first (then) died. If one does not first attain the resurrection, will he not die?" (56:15–19).[5] Moreover, since the body shared the taint of this depraved world, the idea of the resurrection of the body was repugnant to gnostics. Their world rejection was matched by a preoccupation with heavenly things—divine mysteries, esoteric wisdom, manifestations of the power of the Spirit, and libertine demonstrations of freedom from the body. As "spiritual" beings they worshiped the spiritual person, Christ, but they conveniently ignored or possibly even cursed the earthly Jesus.[6]

Marcion was a key second-century figure at the center of the raging controversy about Paul. Whether he was a gnostic, strictly speaking, is questionable; certainly his outlook shared features of the gnostic vision and was, perhaps mistakenly, associated with them. Although he was excommunicated from the church at Rome in 144 CE, the movement he founded dominated Syria until the beginning of the fifth century. Orthodoxy prevailed over Marcionism only after Bishop Rabbula (411–435) promoted the destruction of their churches and their property was "acquired" by the triumphant church. Thereafter, the zealous bishop "gently" persuaded Marcionites to give up their "error," be "baptized," and submit to the "truth."[7]

Interestingly enough, Paul's letters along with the Gospel of Luke formed the heart of Marcion's Bible; he was the first to call these scriptures the "New Testament." None of the "Old Testament" (also his term) books were included. It may seem strange that the gnostics were so fond of Paul unless one notices that certain statements of Paul, isolated from their immediate and broader context, do seem to buttress gnostic claims. For example, in 1 Corinthians 9:26–27 ("I punish my body and enslave it"), Paul spoke of the body as an enemy to be beaten into submission. Elsewhere Paul spoke pejoratively of the flesh (e.g., "nothing good dwells . . . in my flesh," Rom. 7:18). In Romans 7:24 Paul begged for deliverance from "this body of death." Romans 8:23 resonated with the gnostics: "we ourselves, who have the first fruits of the Spirit, groan inwardly while we wait for adoption, the redemption *of* our bodies," which tempted gnostics to read, "redemption *from* our bodies" (emphasis added). Since they despised the body, the gnostics could easily join Paul in saying, "flesh and blood cannot inherit the kingdom of God" (1 Cor. 15:50).

In other passages, too, the gnostics claimed Paul advocated views they cherished. They were preoccupied with "spiritual things" and with divine mysteries. Paul also, they discovered, spoke of "what no eye has seen, nor ear heard, nor the human heart conceived" (1 Cor. 2:9). Moreover, Paul boasted of a vision in which he was "caught up into Paradise and heard things that are not to be told, that no mortal is permitted to repeat" (2 Cor. 12:3–4). They too aspired to fly to the third heaven (or higher) to receive special visions and to taste the ambrosial food and drink. They found useful Paul's division of people into the "spiritual (*pneumatikoi*)" and the "fleshly (*sarkikoi*)" (1 Cor. 3:1).

The gnostics also found support in Paul for the radical dualism between the world above and the world below. In 2 Corinthians 4:4 Paul referred to the "god of this world [who] has blinded the minds of the unbelievers." While Paul was here probably referring to Satan as the "god of this world," the gnostics could read the passage to mean the "creator God" (Yahweh) who made this fallen world. They concluded from this reference that it was the evil God, Yahweh, who "blinded the minds" of humanity so that mortals could no longer remember the true, extramundane, changeless God or even their own celestial origin. The stubborn insistence of the gnostics that Yahweh was the evil "god of this [evil] world" clashed with the classic Hebrew view that Yahweh was just and merciful and that the creation was good. The Jew delighted in the pride that Yahweh took in this handiwork: "God saw everything that he had made, and indeed, it was very good" (Gen. 1:31). The gnostic rejection of the Old Testament as the revelation of a base, pretender God in favor of Christian writings about a gracious higher God drove a wedge between Hebrew scriptures and Christian tradition. This threat of divorce sharply posed the question of the relationship between Jewish and Christian tradition.

Early in the second century the church fathers[8] took up their cudgels against the gnostic position. Central to their attack was the conviction that the Hebrew scriptures and Christian writings belonged together. They vehemently denounced as a grotesque caricature the gnostic teaching that Yahweh was wicked. They argued instead that the God of the creation and Israel was the same God revealed in Jesus Christ. They tirelessly maintained that there was no basis in Paul for the dualism of the gnostics. Origen persistently objected that there was no evidence in Paul's letters to support the view that matter per se was evil. Irenaeus, a second-century bishop of Lugdunum (Lyons), attempted to rob the gnostics of their base of support in Paul. He knew of the gnostic use of Paul's statement that "flesh and blood cannot inherit the kingdom of God" (1 Cor. 15:50) that it might be read to support the gnostic repudiation of the body. But against such a position Iraeneus submitted four reasons for his belief in the resurrection of the physical, fleshly body, all of them drawn from Paul's letters.

Causing the greatest challenge for the fathers was Paul's interpretation of the law. The gnostics had gathered grist for their mill from passages such as Romans 3:2, where Paul appears to repudiate the law: "But now, apart from law, the righteousness of God has been disclosed." The gnostics read this and similar passages as support for their rejection of the Hebrew scriptures. The fathers were justifiably puzzled by the ambiguity and shifting emphases in many of Paul's statements about the law. Origen, for example, noted six different ways Paul used the term "law."[9] The fathers admitted that Paul's characteristic emphasis on grace seemed to relegate law to a subordinate role, yet Paul's own recasting of the law in messianic terms as the "law of the spirit" (Rom. 8:1) and the "law of Christ" (Gal. 6:2) demonstrated his positive assessment of law.[10] Following these cues the fathers overcame the most serious objection to reading the letters in the light of, rather than in opposition to, the Jewish tradition. Their position prevailed, and in time the gnostic threat diminished. Nevertheless, the relationship of God to the world and the church to Judaism were hot issues, not only because those questions were important for understanding Paul, but also because they stood so near the heart of the life of the church until the modern period. Christian theologians still wrestle with the problem of how to be open to the surprises embedded in God's new acts without repudiating the old ones.

PELAGIANISM: THE PROBLEM OF SIN

Even during the controversy between Christian gnostics and the Roman church favored by Constantine, other disputes were brewing over the proper interpretation of Paul. Whereas the gnostics longed for deliverance from the evil world, other believers fixed on the problem of sin and release from its burden. Thus salvation from sin—the justification of the unrighteous—held the attention of Christian theologians from the fourth century to the present. The principal figures in the early debate were Augustine and Pelagius, both churchmen of the fourth and early fifth centuries. We know Augustine from his *Confessions* and other writings. Pelagius, a brilliant theologian and serious biblical exegete, wrote major commentaries on Romans, 1 and 2 Corinthians,[11] and shorter ones on all the other letters in the Pauline corpus. At issue between Augustine and Pelagius was the understanding of the nature of sin, its origin and remedy. Long before the first ink flowed from his pen against Pelagius (in 412 CE), Augustine had already tagged humanity as a "lump of sin" that could do nothing toward its own salvation.[12] Meanwhile Pelagius was teaching that humanity had the ability to live a sinless life, but simply decided not to do so.

His exegesis of Romans led Pelagius to reject the idea that sin was seminally transmitted. The British monk Pelagius argued that the transmission of sin from Adam to all humankind was not by propagation but by imitation.[13] In his painstakingly careful exegesis of Romans 5:12, Pelagius found support for the view that human beings are sinners not by birth but by choice. He concluded that the doctrine of original sin held by Augustine was false and contradictory: if "sin is natural, it is not voluntary; if it is voluntary, it is not inborn. These two definitions are as mutually contrary as are necessity and [free] will."[14]

Pelagius thus raised questions about the scriptural basis of the doctrine of original sin and the anthropology implicit in it; he also asserted that such a view undermined the Christian doctrine of God. How, he asked, could a just God create sinners and then condemn them for sinning? How could a righteous God command, "You shall be holy, for I the LORD your God am holy" (Lev. 19:2), after making the human being congenitally incapable of holiness? How could the Son of God command the believer to be perfect, "as your heavenly Father is perfect" (Matt. 5:48), if humanity should be so stained by sin at birth that it would be rendered incapable of perfection?

Pelagius quickly saw the implications of this understanding of Paul for the practice of infant baptism. Since he rejected the doctrine of original sin, he denied that babies were in need of cleansing from the stain of sin. Although he endorsed infant baptism, he balked at the suggestion that it was necessary for the salvation of the infant.

Given the position of Pelagius, it is easy to understand why he was infuriated by Augustine's prayer: "Grant what You command, and command what You will."[15] Such an attitude, Pelagius argued, would undermine moral striving and sanction the immorality that he saw on every side in Rome.[16] Now that it was socially acceptable to become a Christian, Pelagius feared that the high ethical imperative in Paul's gospel would be fatally compromised.

Not surprisingly, Pelagius and Augustine soon engaged in a public fight. In 412 CE Augustine began writing to expose the "errors" of his rival. He attacked both Pelagius's understanding of sin and his doctrine of human nature. He disputed Pelagius's claim that God, not people, could be blamed for the existence of sin if it were imputed at birth. On the contrary, Augustine objected, God made Adam and Eve free and innocent. It was through their rebellion, not by God's design, that they and all after them became sinners. Adam was able to introduce sin into the human context, but he was unable to remove it. It was inconceivable to Augustine that the disobedient Adam could produce innocent offspring. Consequently, in his view the whole human experiment begun by God suffered blight through Adam's fatal error.

Augustine believed that Romans 5:12 supported his understanding of sin. Working from a Latin text, he read this verse to say that "death came to all, in whom [in quo, i.e., Adam] all sinned." Also his Vulgate text inspired him to read the Latin in quo as masculine even though quo could be read as neuter, changing the meaning entirely. He was apparently unfamiliar with the Greek text, which would have required reading the Latin in quo as neuter, giving the passage a completely different meaning more consonant with the typical Jewish reading: "death came to all because all sinned" (emphasis added). Paul was obviously indebted to the Jewish tradition that held that each person became his or her own Adam by choice, not through propagation. The apostle did recognize that social context exerted pressure on people to act selfishly, but he hardly held the view of "original sin" as we know it. Thus Paul could grant that there was a cultural or "worldly" bias toward sin without calling it a necessity. Moreover, both Augustine and Pelagius seemed to misunderstand Paul's view of sin as Sin—a cosmic power competing with God for control of the world.

Augustine further argued that Pelagius underestimated the power of sin and also overestimated the human power to conquer it. For once Adam introduced sin into the human framework, the trap was sprung. Creatures in the grip of this cosmic power, like drug addicts, were judged powerless to free themselves; deliverance had to come from outside. True to Paul's view, Augustine held that this remedy was provided as a gracious act of God through Jesus Christ. Thus he endorsed infant baptism, because at birth infants need redemption. To Pelagius's objection that such redemption could be effected only by faith, and therefore was not available to untutored infants, Augustine retorted that faith is no human work but a gracious gift of the Creator. For salvation all mortals are dependent on God, and there is nothing they can do to effect their own redemption.

The charge by Pelagius that total reliance on God sanctioned moral indifference brought an angry reply from Augustine. Like the ancient rabbis, he placed statements about God's grace and human responsibility side by side without sensing any tension between them. Pelagius saw the Christian life as a cooperative affair: One half of the responsibility belonged to God, who endowed people with the ability to do right; the other half of the responsibility rested on individuals to exercise that ability. Appealing to Paul, Augustine on the other hand viewed the work of divine grace and human response in paradoxical and total terms: All is given by God, yet all is required of human beings.

In the opinion of Augustine, Pelagius's confidence in human achievement took the power to direct history out of the hands of God and placed it in mortal hands. For if the creature is the maker of its destiny and has the ability to direct the course of history, the doctrine of the sovereignty of God is needless, or worse. Pelagius's emphasis on human freedom and responsibility virtually eclipsed the traditional stress on divine providence. In response, Augustine resorted to the use of the paradox once again to hold the two motifs in balance. Drawing on Paul's discussion of predestination in Romans 9:14ff., he coupled opposing statements: All things are predestined by God; the human is totally free and responsible.

The debate between Pelagius and Augustine raged for six years. Finally, in 418 CE Pelagius was officially condemned by the Synod of Carthage in North Africa and dropped out of sight. The debate continued, however, in spite of the official condemnation because it was thought to be about a core issue of Christian faith.[17] More than a thousand years later Martin Luther argued that the anti-Pelagian tracts of Augustine still addressed the most urgent doctrinal question of his time. Augustine and Luther were clearly intellectual brothers in their assessment of human depravity and divine grace. Both came to their understanding of the gospel after searing personal struggles, and both found their way out of their distress through Paul's letters. Luther's own tortured autobiography colored the way he read both Paul and Augustine, and led him to regard Pelagius's confidence in human beings to keep God's commandments as vain and naive. With great poignancy Luther described his collision with Romans 1:17 and its obstinate refusal to surrender its meaning. He was galled by Paul's statement that "the justice of God is being revealed from heaven against all ungodliness and wickedness" (AT), and he was angry at God for exacting justice even if it were through the gospel. For no matter how hard Luther tried, he still failed to fulfill God's just demand. If salvation depended on performing the impossible, how could one ever be saved,

Luther groaned? Near despair, he noticed the context of Romans 1:17. With astonishment he read the words, "the just shall live by faith" (KJV). Luther's moment of enlightenment came when he saw that it was through faith, not works, that one came to a proper relationship with God. This emphasis on God's justification of the sinner held enormous implications for the interpretation of scripture and gave the interpretation of Paul a critical place in the theological debates that followed.

In assessing these men and the implications of their thought for our understanding of Paul, we should remember that Pelagius, Augustine, and Luther were all committed Christian intellectuals eager to discern and properly interpret the Pauline tradition. Pelagius did raise questions about troublesome passages whose truth could not be decided by some independent arbiter suspended somewhere above the rough-and-tumble of this world. Augustine misread and misunderstood Romans 5:17, but Pelagius failed to appreciate fully the cosmic and mysterious power of Sin (not sins). So which was the more faithful to Paul? Without realizing it, most American Christians, Protestant and Catholic, come to the letters with spectacles provided by Luther, or Augustine, or even Pelagius. Justification by faith, which was at the heart of the thought of all three, has traditionally assumed a dominant place in Western Christianity. This motif stood near the center of Paul's argument in Romans and Galatians. But it is mentioned infrequently or not at all in the other letters. We need to be careful in reading these other letters lest our preoccupation with the guilt of the individual and God's grace blind us to the great variety and scope of Paul's concerns elsewhere. Some scholars feel that Paul's thought should be viewed in a broader cosmic frame that includes but transcends the emphasis on individual salvation.[18] Others argue that justification by faith was the center of gravity of the whole body of Pauline letters. These unresolved issues continue to make the reading of Paul an exciting and challenging experience.

THE RELATIONSHIP OF PAUL AND JESUS

"Jesus was not a Christian, he was a Jew." So spoke the influential German scholar Julius Wellhausen in 1905.[19] Many would still heartily agree. They view Jesus as a charismatic Galilean who had an uncanny feel for the essence of true religion. Trusting completely in God, he lived a life free of anxiety and devoid of pretense. He cared little for religious rules or rituals, and he stepped across social barriers to befriend criminals, prostitutes, the poor, and little children. But somehow the primitive and beautiful religion of this Galilean peasant has been spoiled by the professionals, obscured by theological overlay, cluttered by dogmatic assertion, and robbed of vitality by institutional forms. Usually in this scenario it is the apostle Paul who is seen as the initial corrupter of this vital, true religion. According to this view, Paul's insistence on the Jesus of the cross totally eclipsed Jesus the teacher in parables. Paul pushed aside the "gentle Jesus, meek and mild," in favor of the vindictive Judge coming with God's angels in flaming fire. He forced Jesus' simple announcement, "your sins are forgiven" (Mark 2:5), to give way to theological speculation about guilt and redemption. This interpretation holds that the history of Christianity would have been entirely different had Paul's influence been limited to only a small circle of converts. Paul's interpretation was decisive, however, because his influence was so far-flung. As the Johnny Appleseed of early Christianity, he planted the seeds of his gospel from Antioch to Rome. As the founder of churches, he locked the religion of Jesus in an institutional case. This Paul, many feel, cut Christianity off from its roots in the life and teachings of Jesus, the Galilean holy man.

This contemporary juxtaposition of Jesus and Paul has a long history. As early as the seventeenth century, John Locke, an English Deist, saw such a cleavage. He reached this conclusion after beginning a search for a "reasonable Christianity" free from the "shackles of dogma."[20] He wanted to make a fresh appraisal of the New Testament independent of the bias of a Christian orthodoxy inspired by Paul. This independent study convinced him that a great chasm ran through the New Testament between the simple gospel of Jesus and the complicated, obscure theology of Paul. The gospel *of* Jesus, according to Locke, came from the lips of Jesus himself, but the gospel *about* Jesus was the invention of later interpreters like Paul. The implications of Locke's study were clear. If one is to recover the message of Jesus in its pristine purity, one must strip off all dogmatic distortions whether of the Church of England, of the Council of Nicaea, or of the apostle Paul himself. The four Gospels must be used as the primary and even exclusive source if the simple gospel of Jesus is to be reclaimed.

This tendency to divorce the teaching of Jesus from the theology of Paul reached its apogee in the thought of Wilhelm Wrede (1859–1906), a brilliant German biblical scholar. In his view, Jesus was a simple, pious Galilean peasant whose prophetic insight, moral sensitivity, empathy for the oppressed, and strong sense of the divine presence meant nothing to Paul. Although Jesus was remembered by the apostle as a real historical figure, the particulars of his earthly life meant little to Paul. Before Paul came, Wrede argued, Christianity was only "an inner Jewish sect," but after Paul we have "a Christian Church."[21] According to Wrede, the religion of Jesus is true Christianity, but the religion of Paul is a fabricated and institutionalized dogma.

Geza Vermes, a reader in Jewish studies at Oxford University, tried once again to untangle the Jesus of history from the Christ of dogma. His study of the Dead Sea Scrolls and the Talmud persuaded him that Jesus was fully understandable only within the framework of first-century Galilean Judaism.[22] He found in Galilee a strong interest in the Elijah miracle tradition and in meditation, which would explain Jesus' acceptance there and his mixed reception in Jerusalem.[23] Religious enthusiasm and ignorance of rabbinic tradition, Vermes concluded, were viewed differently in Galilee and Jerusalem. Placing Jesus in this Galilean setting, Vermes contended that Jesus probably did not claim to be the Messiah, that he certainly did not claim to be divine, and that he would have been outraged by the incarnation formula, "true God from true God, . . . and was made man," as the Nicene Creed affirms. Vermes believed that it was Hellenistic paganism, not Paul, that led Gentile Christianity astray; nevertheless, it was church doctrine that spoiled the simple religion of this pious Galilean peasant and his Jewish followers.

It is difficult to understand why Paul should escape blame since he enjoyed his greatest success in interpreting the Christian gospel for the Hellenistic mind. Vermes's approach avoided some of the mistakes of former scholars, but the jury is still out on his case. It would seem, however, that the challenge his thesis posed has already been met by two earlier developments in this century: (1) the advent of form criticism, and (2) the studies of Albert Schweitzer.

Rudolf Bultmann and Martin Dibelius first taught that the traditions of Jesus circulated orally in certain forms (e.g., parables, sayings, miracle stories, and passion narrative) long before they were assembled and edited by the Gospel writers. Through his careful study of the forms and their use of the Gospel writers, Bultmann proved that the church not only kept alive the Jesus materials through oral tradition, but also shaped and interpreted them to address changing needs in the churches.[24] Gradually scholars have come to accept that the Gospel writers further shaped, edited, and interpreted the materials that they appropriated from the oral stream to speak to their own times. Exegetes now realize that the Gospel writers were not composing objective historical biographies of Jesus but were writing their own story of Jesus' life with a strong theological emphasis. Mark, for example, underscored the importance of Jesus as the suffering and dying Son of Man. Matthew emphasized Jesus' role as the eschatological teacher. Luke spoke of Jesus as the bearer of the Spirit, the friend of the poor, and the fulfillment of Israel's hopes. Through form criticism we have learned to appreciate the Gospel writers as creative interpreters who left their imprint on their work through their selection, arrangement, and interpretation of the oral tradition. Once one realizes that the Gospel writers as well as Paul had strong ideological interests, the old view that the Jesus of the Gospels was free of dogmatic interpretation is no longer defensible. If any transformation had taken place, it clearly was not the work of Paul alone.

When Albert Schweitzer died in 1965 he was aptly eulogized as one of the great human beings of the twentieth century. As a missionary doctor in Lambaréné in French Equatorial Africa, a concert organist, and winner of the Nobel Peace Prize, he captured the imagination of the Western world. But it was his biblical scholarship that led him in the first place to give up promising careers in music, theology, philosophy, and a university professorship to enroll in medical school and found a hospital in Africa when he completed his medical study. When Schweitzer went to Africa in 1913, he carried with him a book-length manuscript on Paul. Fifteen years later he found time to prepare the manuscript for publication. When his *Mysticism of Paul the Apostle* appeared, it was revolutionary. Scholars still consider familiarity with Schweitzer's work to be an absolute requirement for an intelligent discussion of scholarship on Jesus and Paul.[25] In this book he argued that the apostle likewise understood Jesus in the light of Jewish apocalypticism. In the first century, Jewish apocalyptic communities not uncommonly held that God's eschatological rule would soon be ushered in by a period of intense suffering. Jesus, Schweitzer argued, identified his own rejection and death with that final trauma that would provoke God's rule. Paul likewise saw the cross as the pain accompanying the birth of the new age. Schweitzer concluded from this that in their common reliance on Jewish apocalyptic thought and in their understanding of the passion, Paul and Jesus were in perfect agreement.

Even while recognizing his groundbreaking scholarship, few scholars if any now accept Schweitzer's thesis that Jesus deliberately courted death to hasten God's final denouement, and the mystical solidarity with or participation in Christ initiated in baptism was hardly the essence of Paul's thought. But all would agree that Schweitzer opened up new dimensions and raised profound questions concerning the relationship of Paul and Jesus. Whatever faults Schweitzer's work may have had, there is no escaping his essential point that both the character of Jesus' life and ministry and the proclamation of Paul were eschatological through and through, and both must be assessed in the full light of the Jewish apocalyptic thinking of the day.

Unquestionably, however, Paul's letters differ from the Gospels in style and emphasis. Long, involved discussions weave complicated patterns and make complex arguments in the epistles. Short, pithy sayings dart from the lips of Jesus. Paul's letters are heavy with thick abstractions (e.g., the righteousness of God). Authentic Jesus materials such as the parables bear the unmistakable aroma of this earth, but the frequent allusions to Jesus' return (Parousia) as in

Paul would have sounded unnatural on Jesus' lips. The postresurrection situation and Paul's worldwide mission summon forth themes that were muted in or absent altogether from Jesus' ministry. Paul reflected long and deeply on the meaning of the Christ event and the cross. But even though Paul modified the traditions and created new centers of meaning in Christian thought, his theology does not contradict the proclamation of Jesus. His work is an extension and even a reformulation of the meaning of the Christ event, but he and Jesus are no more incompatible than are Bartok and Beethoven.

THE RELATIONSHIP OF PAUL
TO HIS NATIVE JUDAISM

Paul's theology is often portrayed as the antithesis not only of the teachings of Jesus but also, paradoxically, of first-century Judaism. When Paul entered the Jesus movement as an apostle, many assume that he repudiated his ancestral religion, recalling it only in order to throw his gospel into bold relief. In the conversion experienced by Augustine, Luther, and the Pietists of the early sixteenth century, it is generally believed, we have a carbon copy of Paul's own spiritual biography.

"Pick it up, read it. Pick it up, read it," Augustine reportedly heard a child singing. When he took up the Bible to read, his eyes fell on Romans 13:13–14: ". . . not in reveling and drunkenness, not in debauchery and licentiousness, not in quarreling and jealousy. Instead, put on the Lord Jesus Christ, and make no provision for the flesh, to gratify its desires." Augustine reported: "Instantly, as the sentence ended, there was infused in my heart something like the light of full certainty and all of the gloom of doubt vanished away."[26]

So ended Augustine's long, dark night of the soul and his experimental profligacy. His experiments with philosophy and Manicheanism had left him empty and restless. His excursion into hedonism was unsatisfying, and with his conversion to Christianity Augustine felt his period of blind and aimless groping had ended. The change in Augustine was dramatic. In a sensitive discussion of his pilgrimage of faith, he contrasted the dissatisfaction and fruitless searching before his conversion with the peace and purpose he felt afterward. Even the birds knew, he said, that he was a Christian. In many ways Luther's experience paralleled that of Augustine. Restless and dissatisfied, Luther left the study of law and philosophy at the university in Erfurt, Germany, hoping to find peace in the Augustinian monastery. But despite herculean efforts to live a blameless life, he felt condemned, empty, and wanting. Release came for his troubled soul through his discovery of Paul's emphasis on salvation by grace. A total reorientation in his self-understanding and theological outlook occurred. Energies once sapped by anxiety and guilt burst forth anew in highly creative ways.

The Pietists of the late sixteenth and seventeenth centuries likewise found support in Paul for a strong emphasis on conversion. In Romans 7 and 8 they thought they had found evidence that Paul divided life into two stages, one falling before, the other after conversion. They read the first-person singular references in Romans 7 as autobiographical statements that Paul made about his life as an unconverted, frustrated, guilt-ridden Pharisee. They pointed to 7:9–10, where Paul wrote, "I (*egō*) was once alive apart from the law, but when the commandment came, sin revived and I died." In verse 15 they believed they found a Paul distracted and utterly confused: "I do not understand my own actions. For I do not do what I want, but I do the very thing I hate." This inward struggle, they believed, finally erupted in a cry of defeat in verse 24: "Wretched man that I am! Who will rescue me from this body of death?"

In this view, chapter 8, on the other hand, referred to Paul's Christian life after conversion. After the light of Christ had illumined his night, Paul exclaimed triumphantly: "Who will separate us from the love of Christ? Will hardship, or distress, or persecution, or famine, or nakedness, or peril, or sword? . . . No, in all these things we are more than conquerors through him who loved us" (vv. 35, 37). The Pietist gushing over Paul's conversion was further supported, they believed, by Paul's appeal to his Damascus road experience reported in Acts (9:1–9; 22:6–11; 26:12–18). Upon conversion Paul, the zealous Pharisee, finally acknowledged that his efforts to keep the law had failed. Now he openly admitted what he had tried to conceal by frenetic activity. Now the ethical crisis was overcome in a dramatic conversion by which he found release from enormous psychological tension.

The numerator in the experiences of Augustine, Luther, and the Pietists was in each case different, but the denominator was the same. All spoke poignantly of a rescue from a dreadful past. All viewed life under grace as the exact opposite of a former life. And all found in the letters of Paul the inspiration and direction for a metamorphosis. Given the pattern of their experience, it was natural for them to see in Paul the same rupture as they experienced between the way of unbelief and the life of faith. Paul the Jew was called the unbeliever; Paul the emissary of Christ was made the model of faith. Paul the devotee of law was cast as a wayward, guilt-ridden Pharisee; Paul the recipient of grace became the apostle of freedom. Understandably such an assessment tended to drive a wedge between Paul's life in Christ and his life under the law.

Without question the idea that Jesus was the Messiah was rejected by most Jews, and Paul himself endured conflict with the synagogue. Moreover, in Philippians he dismissed as "dung" (*skyballa*, 3:8) his considerable achievements under the law. To the end of his life he expressed remorse for his persecution of followers of Christ before he reversed himself to become an apostle to the Gentiles. Finally, he wrote movingly of the revelation of God's righteousness "apart from law" (Rom. 3:21). All of this would seem to argue for a radical discontinuity between Paul the "Christian" and Paul the Israelite.

A growing number of scholars, however, question this reading of Paul. They point out that Paul nowhere suggested either that he found the law intolerable or that he felt conscience-stricken because his frenzied attempts to keep it failed. On the contrary, in Philippians 3:6 Paul said just the opposite: he was "under the law, blameless." Furthermore, Romans 8:2 hardly meant that Paul held the two eras to be incompatible. Instead, Paul wrote of two laws: "The law of the Spirit of life in Christ Jesus has set you free from the law of sin and of death." Whatever life in the Spirit was for Paul, it was not lawless. Did Paul here, like Jeremiah, suggest that the gap between God's requirement (Mosaic law) and the human tendency to resist had been overcome? If so, he may not be repudiating the law but rather announcing the arrival of the day when the gulf between God's speaking and the human response was overcome. Jeremiah heard God say, "I will put my law within them, and I will write it on their hearts" (Jer. 31:33). For Jeremiah that hardly meant that God's Torah would be repudiated, but that human resistance to the divine will would end. Evidently Paul believed that that time had arrived. In that day God would etch the law of the Spirit on the human heart, and human resistance would vanish so there would no longer be a chasm between hearing and doing, or divine command and human resistance, but God's people would freely do what God had inscribed on the heart.

Also misleading, if not erroneous, is the view that Paul rejected his past when he became an apostle. Until his last letter (Rom. 9:4–5; 11:1) Paul continued to locate himself in the people of Israel (see also 2 Cor. 11:21b–26). He often wrote of the coming of the Messiah (Christ) as the fulfillment of God's promise to the Jews "first." He quoted from the prophets, who, he held, anticipated God's new day in Jesus, and he believed that salvation not only emerged from the Jews but would also embrace them in the end time (Rom. 11:26).

In addition, Paul's eschatology closely resembles that found in Jewish apocalyptic literature. In his eager waiting for God's final visitation as well as in the way he imagined the end to be, Paul was at one with much of first-century Judaism.[27] The difference is found in his conviction that in the death and resurrection of Jesus the end had already begun. The time clock read differently but the numbers on the face were the same. We see, therefore, that although there were differences between the views of Paul and those of his Jewish contemporaries, the distinction was not total. Even Paul's reference to his achievements under the law as "rubbish" (Phil. 3:8) was not so much a repudiation of his past as it was a revaluation of it in light of his encounter with the new age inaugurated by Christ.

Almost daily we are made painfully aware of the separation of Judaism and Christianity. History books are replete with reports of bitter and shameful strife between Jews and Christians. Synagogue members go to their worship on Friday night and Saturday; Christians gather on Sunday. Vandals desecrate Jewish cemeteries and spray paint swastikas on synagogue walls. The memories of *Kristallnacht* and Auschwitz linger and haunt both Jew and Christian. Time and again these ugly acts stain human hands and painfully aggravate divisions and distrust. All of Western history and much of the present experience underscore the difference between these sister faiths. We should be careful, however, when we project these patterns of discrimination, prejudice, and hooliganism back onto Paul. Nowhere does Paul speak of "Christianity" as an entity separate from Judaism. Everywhere he envisions his Gentile mission as part of God's promise to Israel to include all peoples in a final redeemed human family. As we read the letters of Paul, therefore, it is best to guard against the too-common assumption that Paul rejected the tradition he once loved.

Not only does this dislocation of Paul do violence to his thought, it also distorts our picture of first-century Jewish faith. Indeed, a rather poor likeness of first-century Judaism has often been drawn by merely reversing everything Paul says about his life in Christ. Paul's gospel was joyful, so Judaism is depicted as joyless. Paul was liberated from sin and death through grace; Jews, so it was said, were yoked by the law to sin and divine wrath. The God of Paul is sketched as a God of grace; the God of the Jews is cast as a severe taskmaster. Paul was self-giving; the Jews were self-seeking. As official warders of the law, the Jews became insufferable religious snobs. If they observed the law's letter, they ignored its spirit (cf. Matt. 23). And if they did not keep its letter, they were engulfed in a fog of guilt and anxiety.

The more we know about first-century Judaism the better we realize that the common reconstruction above is an absurd and even dangerous parody. Through the scrolls left by the Qumran community near the Dead Sea, we have gained a better understanding of both the variety and the nature of first-century Hebraic life and thought.[28] The community attended to God's law, but it knew itself also as the beneficiary of God's grace. The rule for the community best summarized the view of the community: "If I stagger because of the sin of flesh, my justification shall be by the righteousness of God which endures forever. . . . He will draw me near by His grace, and by His mercy will he bring my justification" (*Community Rule* 11:12). The community opposed insincerity and hypocrisy, and its piety although intense was hardly joyless (e.g., see the *Hymn Scroll*). We see, therefore, that the religion of Israel invoked to display Paul to greatest advantage bears little resemblance to the historical evidence from his own time.

Reading Paul by the light of the total reversals of Luther and Augustine not only sets Paul adrift from his moorings in the Hebrew religion, but also focuses our attention too narrowly on the salvation of the individual. With our attention riveted to this motif, as important as it is, we sometimes neglect other emphases in the letters.

Most scholars would readily agree that Paul's theology is multidimensional. Disagreement exists, however, about what was really the dominant motif in his theology. Scholarly opinion has fluctuated from the view that Paul's message was individualistic to the core, to the belief that his gospel was communal throughout. One focuses on the individual; the other encompasses the whole range of salvation history.

Perhaps the works of Rudolf Bultmann and Johannes Munck best pose these alternatives. Bultmann, possibly the most influential biblical scholar of the twentieth century, found the key to Paul's theology in his understanding of the human (i.e., in Paul's anthropology).[29] In formulating Paul's anthropology, Bultmann leaned on existentialist thought for guidance. Paul was aware, he believed, of the one question that forced itself on all humanity: Can a person be open to the future that stretches out ahead? Each person yearns, he believed, to be free enough to be open and honest in each encounter. In spite of this longing for truth in the inward being, however, each person feels that his or her life lacks the integrity, authenticity, and fulfillment that belong to its true nature. The creature begins, therefore, with a deep sense of emptiness. Each person wants authentic existence, but each refuses to believe that such comes only as a gift from God, as a reprieve from self. Each tries to secure authentic life by human efforts, not realizing that self-assertiveness always ends in self-deception and doubt.

This self-reliant, self-assertive spirit manifests itself in many ways, religious as well as secular. To attain to oneness with the cosmos, some perform sedulous religious duties as a form of self-aggrandizement, and become self-righteous and alienated from the self and others. Others labor for recognition, cash, authority, children, and power only to find that in truth they are working solely against a sense of personal inadequacy. One's best efforts fail to secure what one wants, precisely because they are efforts, premeditated and self-conscious. The authentic existence one searches for is as elusive as the end of a rainbow. Yet each is also unable to accept life from God because God is out of one's control. To enjoy freedom the individual would have to surrender autonomy, but that risk is too great. Fear and anxiety attend this fruitless search. The more insecure one is, the more one turns in on himself or herself; the more one turns in on the self, the more insecure one is. Humanity is trapped, unable to break out of this vicious circle.

This tangled web over the human is cut through only with the proclamation of the word of God, or rather, the question of God. God's grace comes to the individual, but not to support efforts at regularizing the future; God's grace comes as a question: "Will you surrender, utterly surrender, to God's dealing?"[30] Through the acceptance of grace, one rests secure in the knowledge that one is loved. Thus he or she is released from self-preoccupation to be open to the future. Now one is free, risk is possible, anxiety is overcome. But this authentic existence is not realized once and for all; it must be continually re-presented in the question of God and the renewed acceptance by humanity.

It is clear from this brief summary that Bultmann saw salvation for the individual as the governing theme of Paul's theology. Understandably, therefore, Bultmann takes scant notice of the broad historical themes in Paul's letters (e.g., Rom. 9–11).[31] For this brilliant scholar, decisive history is not world history but individual history.

Juxtaposed against Bultmann's understanding of Paul stands the work of Johannes Munck, *Paul and the Salvation of Mankind*.[32] The book opens with a study of Paul's Damascus road experience. In the traditional view, that experience is seen as a release from pent-up frustrations accumulated through Paul's repeated, unsuccessful, and obsessive attempts to keep the law and from guilt heaped up by his compulsive hatred and fanatical persecution of innocent Christians. Like a boil opening to release its poison, so this theory goes, through conversion Paul's life was cleansed of its gangrenous infection. Munck objected that neither Acts nor Paul's letters offer even a hint that Paul's preconversion history groaned under any such heavy psychological burden. Instead, Munck argued, Paul's Damascus road experience conformed rather closely to the pattern of Old Testament prophetic calls. Paul, like Jeremiah and Isaiah, scribed that God "set me apart before I was born" (Gal. 1:15; see also Rom. 1:1; Isa. 49:1; Jer. 1:5). In Galatians 1:15–16, as also in Isaiah and Jeremiah, the call "from the womb" was linked with the mission to the Gentiles.

Just as the prophets served under constraint, so Paul was under compulsion to fulfill Christ's commission. According to Munck, these similarities place Paul among the ranks of the prophets. And like those prophets, he had a peculiar role to play in the history of God's people. Unlike the Old Testament prophets, however, Paul's role was to be acted out during the final scene in God's historical drama. Indeed, as the apostle to the Gentiles, Paul was assigned the lead role before the curtain was to fall. The end of the age was delayed, Paul believed, so that the Gentiles could be brought into the community of God's people. In other words, the end of the world stood waiting for the completion of Paul's mission.

Romans 9–11 assumed pivotal significance for Munck's thesis. In traditional Jewry the question was often asked, "What is holding back the coming of the Messiah?" The usual answer was that only when Israel is converted can the messianic age come. Paul's mission to the Gentiles enunciated in Romans 9–11, therefore, becomes essential for the success of God's plan. The strategy was to use the conversion of the Gentiles to arouse jealousy in the Jews and thus lead them to salvation. Paul's conviction that his role was crucial for the redemption of all humankind lent energy and urgency to his entire mission and gospel.

Even the offering that Paul collected for the "poor among the saints" in Jerusalem Munck wedged neatly into this scheme. This act, like the prophetic signs of old, was pregnant with meaning. From Hebrew prophecy, Israel expected that in the messianic age Gentiles would stream to Jerusalem bearing tribute and uttering praises to Israel's God. Therefore, when Paul, along with a delegation from the Gentile churches, gathered in Corinth to embark with the offering for the "poor among the saints" in Jerusalem, they were inserting themselves into a suspenseful and divine drama with powerful eschatological significance. The offering aimed to symbolize the arrival of the messianic age to all, Jews and Gentiles.

In this brief résumé of Munck's thesis we have passed over many stimulating features of his work. Even this short summary, however, shows where he and Bultmann separate. Whereas for Bultmann the dominant emphasis in Paul was on the salvation of the individual, for Munck everything in Paul was subordinated to the eschatological mission. The purpose of this mission was not the conversion of the individual but the reassertion of God's dominion over the entire creation.

Whatever the blemishes of his work (and there are many),[33] Munck at least identified the danger of melting Paul's thought down into a single element, or a singular preoccupation with the individual and his or her salvation. Perhaps a swing to the opposite extreme is equally unwise. Paul was concerned with the salvation of the individual (1 Cor. 5:5) but never in isolation from wider historical and corporate concerns. Paul's theology does bracket themes as large as the cosmos itself (Rom. 8:19ff.), but the individual is not thereby reduced to the status of an insect.

Given our emphasis today on the gospel as a resource for the "inner life," and given our tendency to view matters of faith as private affairs, it is hardly surprising that we look for the individual emphasis in most things we read. I do not wish to speak against the dignity or worth of the individual, but such an emphasis if taken alone stands in real tension with the outlook of Paul. God's call, for Paul, was more than a summons to enjoy salvation; it was an invitation to participate in a divine narrative that was bigger than oneself, namely, the salvation of the entire human and nonhuman world (cf. Rom. 8). It is well to remember that for the apostle there was simply no separation between individual fulfillment and group participation. To be in the community of God's people was in and of itself fulfillment on the highest level. So although in a certain sense Paul's message was personal, it was never private. For Paul the individual was first, last, and always a social being.

PAUL AND WOMEN

Paul, according to George Bernard Shaw, is "the eternal enemy of Woman."[34] In Shaw's view, Paul insisted that the wife "should be rather a slave than a partner, her real function being, not to engage a man's love and loyalty, but on the contrary to release them for God by relieving the man of all preoccupation with sex just as in her capacity of housekeeper and cook she relieves his preoccupation with hunger."[35]

A popular view of Paul suggests that his words about women, were, to say the least, patronizing. This popular outlook draws on the deutero-Pauline letters to cast Paul as a patronizing authority who, even while urging mutual love and respect between husband and wife, commands the woman to be submissive to her husband (Eph. 5:21ff.). He officially forbade women to exercise authority over men (1 Tim. 2:12), and decreed that women were to fulfill the divine purpose by having children and continuing in faith (1 Tim. 2:5). He commanded them to be silent in the churches (1 Cor. 14:34). He admonished others—men and women—to celibacy (1 Cor. 7:7).

Robin Scroggs, a respected Pauline scholar, once issued a significant caveat against this popular caricature.[36] He correctly noted that the primary support for the view of Paul as a male chauvinist comes from deutero-Pauline materials (1 and 2 Timothy, Ephesians, and Colossians). He joined other scholars in arguing that 1 Corinthians 14:33b–36 ("women should be silent in the churches") was inserted by a later hand to harmonize 1 Corinthians with 1 Timothy. Elsewhere in 1 Corinthians Paul assumed women were to be vocal participants in church as prophets (11:5). Moreover, Scroggs sided with John Hurd[37] and the recent translators of the NRSV that 1 Corinthians 7:1 ("It is well for a man not to touch a woman") was not Paul's view but a slogan Paul cited from an increasingly celibate and religiously enthusiastic Corinthian church. In this view, Paul's celibacy revealed no disdain for women but a response to the impending apocalyptic emergency. (It was common in Jewish circles to suspend normal activities in times of great crisis [e.g., during holy war men went celibate for the duration], and also during a priestly celebration at the altar.)

First Corinthians 11:2–16 posed more of a problem, however, for Scroggs. There Paul seems to locate woman in an inferior position in the hierarchy of creation. God is the head of Christ, Christ is the head of man, man is the head of woman, and woman is the head of the slave. Scroggs responded by noting that since Paul took Christ to be preexistent and therefore an active partner in the creation of the world, God comes first, then Christ, then (following the Genesis order), Adam is created from the dust, and then Eve, she who makes alive, from Adam. By taking the Greek for "head" (*kephalē*) to mean "source," Scroggs proposed a novel reading: God is the source of Christ, Christ the source of Adam, and Adam the source of Eve or woman (via the rib). If one follows Scroggs then this hierarchy is no recipe for subordination of woman, or to establish superiority and inferiority, but a midrash on the creation story of Genesis 2. Scroggs held that Paul here stressed different origins in order to maintain a distinction between men and women in a congregation tending to erode them. In other words, Paul here responded to what he judged to be a scandalous view that in Christ all distinctions disappear as spirit possession puts believers in the company of angels.[38]

Scroggs concluded that there is no substance to the charge that Paul was an "eternal enemy" of women. On the contrary, he found support in the letters for an enlightened or even liberationist view. Scroggs continued that Paul "proclaimed the complete equality within the community of all people and groups. Distinctions between groups remain. Values and roles built upon such distinctions are destroyed. Every human being is equal before God in Christ and thus before each other." Scroggs also noted that Paul lists women among his coworkers and alludes to a number of women who were active (presumably as leaders) in the church.[39]

Many scholars were delighted that Professor Scroggs was willing to step forward and challenge the historical accuracy of the popular and persistent notion of Paul's view of women. Few would quarrel with either the spirit or substance of his argument, for Paul is nowhere overtly hostile to women. Nevertheless, Scroggs's argument has met resistance not from the Christian right but from other Pauline scholars.

Professor Elaine Pagels expressed reservations about Scroggs's argument.[40] Although Paul can say that slaves are free in Christ, he quite obviously does not challenge the institution of slavery. In a similar way, Paul's affirmation that women are equal does not mean he is challenging "the social structures that perpetuate their subordination."[41] Pagels challenged Scroggs's interpretation of 1 Corinthians 11:2–16, an admittedly difficult passage. In his statement that Christ is the source of man and man the source of woman, Paul does seem to fall back on the natural order to argue for the subordination of women. Especially troublesome is Paul's statement in 11:7 that man is the glory of God while woman is the glory of man. Pagels believes Paul viewed "certain incidents or practices in the Corinthian community—provoked by the presence of unveiled women believers—to be disorderly or even scandalous," and that by appealing to the primeval (i.e., divine) order, he hoped to restrict women's activity and thus restore order.[42] Pagels does not mention Paul's corrections of male conduct; these would seem to make men also responsible for the restoration of order.

As the scholarly debate over Paul's view of women continues, much remains unresolved. But the discussion has borne good fruit. The conventional picture of Paul as a culture-bound male chauvinist has collapsed under scholarly investigation. In many ways Paul's views were in tension with dominant cultural patterns—Jewish and non-Jewish. He clearly expected that women would take an active role in the worship and witness of the church. Moreover, the evenhanded way he addressed both men and women in 1 Corinthians 7 is instructive. The equal share of responsibility apportioned to each suggests that he envisioned at least approximate equality in the partnership. That in itself was somewhat revolutionary. Professor David Daube, of Orthodox Jewish heritage himself, once pointed out that Paul's expectation that a woman (in Christ) could consecrate her marriage with an unbelieving husband had no Jewish precedent in Paul's day (see 1 Cor. 7:14).[43] According to Jewish tradition, it was the male and only the male who consecrated the marriage after conversion. That consecration meant that only the male could reconsecrate the marriage contract, which was temporarily abrogated when the person became a new person with a new name at conversion and could reconsecrate the marriage contract through sexual intercourse. However murky 1 Corinthians 11:2–16 may appear, it seems clear that Paul laid a heavy burden on male and female to preserve the order of the church. Some degree of subordination of woman, however, may be taken for granted (especially in 11:7), but it is often overlooked that Paul's main point was the distinction between the sexes, not the subordination of one to the other. With their claim of membership in an angelic company, did the Corinthian converts claim an existence above sexual distinction? We can hardly be certain.

In any case Scroggs and Pagels agreed that it is unfair to criticize Paul for not challenging the structures of discrimination against women from an enlightened modern, liberal viewpoint. While it is true that Paul's gospel did relativize social and political structures and may seem to make some look unjust, he did not overtly call for their abolition (e.g., slavery). We cannot conclude from this that Paul either did or did not approve of such social discrimination. Paul may simply have found it unnecessary to challenge social structures that were discriminatory because he thought they would soon be gone anyway. In 1 Corinthians 7:31 he expressly encouraged his readers to "deal with the world as though they had no dealings with it. For the present form of this world is passing away."

Even though the Scroggs-Pagels debate was groundbreaking, it occurred a generation ago, and now sounds dated. Since that time other scholars such as Elisabeth Schüssler Fiorenza, Daniel Boyarin, Elizabeth Castelli, Antoinette Clark Wire, Janice Capel Anderson, and others have offered a more developed and nuanced reading of the issues of power, gender, and metaphor. Certain texts from Galatians, 1 Corinthians, and Romans have taken center stage in this ongoing interpretive exercise. Of crucial importance in this discussion has been Galatians 3:28, where Paul says that in Christ, "There is no longer Jew or Greek, there is no longer slave or free, there is no longer male and female." Most agree that in this fragment of a baptismal confession that Paul used there was at least an implicit critique of the subordination of women, or for attempts to qualify and supplement his Gentile gospel.

To make being a Jew the primary referent, Paul argued, devalued the adequacy of his gospel. What scholars disagree about is the meaning of the phrase "there is no longer male and female" and the influence it had on Paul's thinking. Originally, Schüssler Fiorenza argued, the phrase echoed Jesus' critique of "patriarchal marriage," which by definition constructed and promoted a structure of dominance.[44] Paul, however, compromised this radical imperative when he condemned Christian wives to silence in the worshiping church (1 Cor. 14:34–36). Unmarried women, Schüssler Fiorenza argued, were allowed to speak by default if they had no husband to ask or to speak for them. Thus Schüssler Fiorenza sees a contradiction between the baptismal confession in Galatians 3:28, in which all gender distinctions and hierarchies were swept aside, and 1 Corinthians 11:2–16 and 14:34–36, in which discriminatory gender distinctions were reaffirmed and hierarchical structures reinforced. Moreover, even within 1 Corinthians there is a contradiction. Resisting cultural pressures, Paul allowed women to remain unmarried (1 Cor. 7:34, 38) and thus to enjoy a new level of equality and freedom, but at the same time he subordinated Christian married women to their husbands (11:3) and forbade them to speak in the assembly of "saints" (14:34–36). Thus Schüssler Fiorenza suggests that even in the equality in Christ promised in baptism there was an inequality implied. In citing with approval a student's creation of an apocryphal letter from Phoebe, Schüssler Fiorenza seems to endorse the suggestion that Paul's attempt to put women "in their place" was a vestige of Paul's "rabbinic prejudice."[45]

One of the sharpest critics of Schüssler Fiorenza has been a distinguished Jewish Pauline scholar, Daniel Boyarin. Boyarin criticizes Schüssler Fiorenza for her tacit approval of a view that traces Paul's chauvinism to "an incompletely exorcised demonized Jewish past."[46] While it is easy to agree that such historically "false and prejudicial depictions of Judaism" should have no place in Pauline interpretation, it may be more difficult to find a resolution to the apparent contradiction between the liberation promised in Galatians 3:28 from all hierarchies and structures of inequality and the reimposition of the hierarchies in 1 Corinthians 11.[47] It may be that Boyarin is correct, namely, that Paul was simply inconsistent.

While they disagree on much, Boyarin and Schüssler Fiorenza agree on one thing—the importance of Galatians 3:28 as a key text for understanding Paul. Appearing in bright green letters on the dust jacket of his hugely important book on Paul, this text, Boyarin argues, reveals Paul's "Hellenistic desire for the One, which among other things produced an ideal of a universal human essence, beyond difference and hierarchy. This universal humanity, however, was predicated on the dualism of the flesh and the spirit."[48] In Boyarin's view, Paul did not reject the body (i.e., its particularity as Jew or Greek, male or female), but he did subordinate it to the spirit, which he saw as universal.[49] In other words, Galatians contains a "theology of the spirit," and 1 Corinthians "a theology of the body." Boyarin argues that these two theologies are complementary, not contradictory. Whereas in the spirit there is no hierarchy, in the body there is a hierarchy.[50] These two opposed readings represent two realities—the "new creation" experienced in the ecstasy of baptism that negates all hierarchies, and the real world in which there are indeed hierarchies. Thus, Boyarin claims, there is "no contradiction between Galatians and Corinthians."[51] Paul's solution was a compromise. His gospel broke down all social hierarchies on one level, but was willing to accept them on another. At one level there is "a permanent change in the status of gender at baptism, but insofar as people still live in unredeemed bodies, gender transcendence is not yet fully realized on a social level."[52]

While Boyarin's work is provocative, it raises almost as many questions as it answers. Can we legitimately make such a neat distinction between a theology of the spirit in Galatia and a theology of the body in Corinth? For example, there is considerable evidence against his view that Paul unambiguously reinstitutes hierarchy in 1 Corinthians. Is Paul really instituting a social hierarchy in 11:3, or is he projecting his preexistent Christ (Phil. 2:6) back on to Genesis 2 and thus creating the lineage God, Christ, Adam, Eve? Moreover, in 1 Corinthians 12:7–13:1 Paul appears to be subverting all hierarchies, even charismatic hierarchies; realizing their silliness and self-contradiction, he suggests in a flash of insight: "I will show you a still more excellent way," and then offers his powerful ode to love (agapē) (13:1–13), the ultimate charismatic gift that relativizes all others.

Other questions also push forward. Can we isolate the experience of the transcendence of categories of gender to baptism's ecstatic moment? What role did Paul's eschatology play in his thinking that the age now breaking in was the age of the spirit, which could be experienced at many levels? Do the categories universal and particular adequately frame the whole of Paul's thought? Does the presentation of Paul as an agile practitioner of Realpolitik do justice to his deep conviction that he stood at history's decisive moment when compromise was impermissible? Boyarin, however, is correct to note the tension in Paul's thinking and the apostle's steadfast effort to keep one foot firmly planted in this world even as he moved the other toward the world to come. Such an awareness is surely useful in deciphering Paul's understanding of gender.

Of the feminist critics who have sensitized Pauline scholars to issues of power in the relationship between men and women in the ancient world, few have been more adept than Elizabeth Castelli and Antoinette Wire. Castelli argues that Paul emphasizes mimesis (imitation) as an artifice of power to control disruptive elements in the churches.[53] For example, in 1 Corinthians 11:1 Paul commands, "Be imitators of me, as I am of Christ." By identifying with Christ, Castelli notes, Paul secured his own superior position and used that advantage to suppress dissident voices such as the women prophets of 11:5.[54] By using a mimetic emphasis Paul sought to discredit other gospels: there was either his gospel or no gospel at all. In the interest of conformity and unity in the church, rival versions of the truth were suppressed. Although Castelli cautions that Paul did not actively coerce his converts against their will, she notes that his repression of difference later became a license for especially brutal reprisals against dissidents in the church and Western institutions.[55]

Antoinette Wire holds instead that Paul engaged Corinthian women prophets in conversation throughout 1 Corinthians and not merely in the isolated passages that explicitly name them (1 Cor. 11:5).[56] Partners in the conversation throughout the letter, these female prophets played an important leadership role in the church, and, Wire argues, Paul sought to limit their activity by urging them to surrender their status as holy prophets and to marry, thereby preserving the reputation of the community. (Unmarried ecstatic women were frequently suspected of loose sexual behavior.) Paul, so Wire notes, was disturbed by their wisdom theology, their spirit possession, their charismatic speech (glossolalia), their claim to a freedom allowing them to eat idol meat, to participate in free table fellowship with men, and to reject marriage for a celibate lifestyle. While all of 1 Corinthians includes these women prophets in conversation, two passages in particular play key roles in her investigation: 11:2–16 and 14:34–35. While Paul penned 11:2–16 to control women prophets, he wrote 14:34–35, Wire holds, to deny them a voice altogether. Wire takes the command "women should be silent" to be authentically Pauline, and to address female prophets specifically. Of course if 14:34–35 was part of the original letter, Wire has a point.

If, however, as I claimed earlier, this passage was most likely a non-Pauline interpolation written to bring 1 Corinthians and the role it gives to women into conformity with the more culturally conformist viewpoint of 1 Timothy 2:11–12, then Wire's argument is seriously weakened.[57] Given the second-century redaction of Pauline texts evident elsewhere, and evidence of tinkering with Gospel texts in the same period (notably the multiple endings of Mark), it is hardly useful to appeal to a later manuscript tradition (e.g., P46) to adjudicate this case. Finally, how could Paul have possibly cited the example of "all the churches of the saints" in which women are silent when that was patently false? Carolyn Osiek has shown that Euodia and Syntyche, mentioned in Philippians 4:2–3, were influential women leaders collaborating with Paul, Clement, and other coworkers, and obviously speaking in church.[58] Their disagreements, therefore, according to Osiek, were probably theologically substantive and not just the "petty quarrels of women." Moreover, the women in the Roman churches were hardly expected to be silent. Phoebe served as a deacon (Rom. 16:1); Prisca (or Priscilla) was probably a member of a female-male missionary team and had risked her life for Paul (Rom. 16:3; Acts 18:2); Junia (Rom. 16:7) was an apostle, the only female apostle named in the entire New Testament; Tryphaena and Tryphosa were "workers in the Lord," as was Persis (Rom. 16:12); the mother of Rufus served as a mother to Paul (16:13); Julia and the sister of Nereus were worthy of mention also, though we have no reference to their activity in the church. Of the twenty-six names noted in Romans 16, ten were women, and all were assigned important roles and obviously had a voice in the shaping of the mission of the early church. Although Paul may have sought to suppress a female voice at times, to deny the category of women a voice is historically in error. Clearly, Paul had a history of collaborating with women as well as men in the spread of the gospel. If 1 Corinthians 14:34–35 was from Paul's pen, then the passages above flatly contradict its assertion that the silencing of married women was Paul's practice in "all the churches." Gordon Fee is probably correct; these verses were not from Paul, but were added later to try to make Paul conform to the deutero-Pauline 1 Timothy.

Where does this discussion leave us? It is likely that Paul was neither a chauvinist nor a liberationist but something in between. The evidence is contradictory. One cannot dismiss Paul's evenhanded treatment of men and women in 1 Corinthians 7, his references to women as his coworkers (Rom. 16), or his assumption that women would actively prophesy in a service of worship or serve as deacons and apostles. Nor can one convincingly argue that Paul's statement in Galatians 3:28, that in Christ there "is no longer male and female," had little social relevance. There are glimpses of an exciting new order in parts of Paul's letters, and the second century opens a window onto the importance of the role women played in the church (see the *Acts of Paul and Thecla*, where Thecla appears as an apostle; see women performing priestly functions among the Marcionites and Montanists, and the powerful presence of women in early martyrologies).

At the same time, however, some degree of subordination seems to be taken for granted in Paul's statement that man is made in "the image and glory of God; but woman is the reflection of man" (1 Cor. 11:7). And even though Paul applied feminine metaphors such as "nurse" and "mother" to his own apostolic work (1 Thess. 2:7; Gal. 4:19; 1 Cor. 3:2), they were inversions of his status as a dominant male. That dominant status comes through in his use of masculine metaphors to persuade and threaten. In 1 Corinthians 4:14–21, for example, he claims the authority of a father and threatens to thrash his children when he comes if they do not renounce their arrogant ways. Castelli correctly notes this power factor in Paul's relationship with the churches, and Boyarin also correctly sees tension in Paul between his acceptance and rejection of hierarchies of domination.

So in Paul we find a mixture of the subversion and reinforcement of traditional hierarchical patterns. It would be remarkable indeed if Paul did not reflect some of the prejudice, superstition, and bias of his own time. The question is, how much should we worry about Paul's cultural views? Does his unconsidered prejudice against women vitiate his views on Jesus and on other important questions of life? Theologians have long argued that the gospel is greater than any particular witness to it. (Perhaps that is why we retain the versions of Matthew, Mark, Luke, and John rather than one work entitled "The Gospel.") Moreover, Paul's letters address a rather limited set of circumstances. It seems unfair to denounce him for not anticipating and addressing concerns that have only recently been rightly raised to a high level of consciousness. This is not to say, however, that we can appeal to Paul's apparent acceptance of discrimination in his day to justify discrimination in our own. It was the gospel Paul preached rather than his limited application of and witness to it that became definitive for the centuries following.

We have sketched only very broad contours in the history of interpretation of Paul. Hundreds of variations could be written on the five positions outlined here and others could be added. Someone is bound to ask, is Paul worth all of this attention? Millions of hours of devoted labor have gone into the copying, translation, study, and interpretation of his letters. Vast material resources have gone into great church buildings that bear his name, and even cities rest under the rubric he bequeathed.

Moreover, the influence he has exerted on key individuals such as Augustine, Luther, Wesley, Knox, and others has had enormous historical consequences. One can easily imagine that Paul would be embarrassed by all this attention and surprised if not horrified that his personal occasional letters were canonized as scripture. Yet the labors on his letters and the place they have assumed seem wholly justified, for he raised hard questions that the church had to face. And he dealt with real issues, most of which still lie near the heart of humankind. Does history have a purpose? Can a broken and alienated world be reconciled? What is the nature of the human? Of divine justice? Can the whole human and nonhuman world be saved from its futility and grief? How can one live with partialities—partial sight, partial knowing, partial being, and an unfinished narrative? What does it mean to be alive "in Christ" and have "Christ alive" in oneself in an age of disbelief? What did the redemption of the human and nonhuman world mean to Paul? And what are its implications still?

Notes

Introduction: Contrary Impressions

1. Richard L. Rubenstein, *My Brother Paul* (New York: Harper & Row, 1972), 6ff.

Chapter 1: Paul and His World

1. This has been proven by J. A. L. Lee in his *A Lexical Study of the Septuagint Version of the Pentateuch* (Chico, Calif.: Scholars Press, 1983). Also the work of Dietrich-Alexander Koch, *Die Schrift als Zeuge des Evangeliums: Untersuchung zur Verwendung und zum Verständnis der Schrift bei Paulus* (Tübingen: Mohr [Siebeck], 1986), who leaves no doubt that the Septuagint was the Bible of Paul.

2. Adolf Deissmann, *Paulus*, 2nd ed. (Tübingen: Mohr [Siebeck], 1925), 69. Eng. trans.: *Paul: A Study in Social and Religious History*, trans. William E. Wilson, 2nd ed. (New York: Harper & Brothers, 1927), 90.

3. See R. J. H. Shutt, "The Letter of Aristeas," in *The Old Testament Pseudepigrapha*, ed. James H. Charlesworth (Garden City, N.Y.: Doubleday, 1985), 2:7–34.

4. C. Burchard, "Joseph and Aseneth," in *Old Testament Pseudepigrapha*, ed. Charlesworth, 2:177–201.

5. A. Yarbro Collins, "Aristobulus." In *Old Testament Pseudepigrapha*, ed. Charlesworth, 2:831–42.

6. See C. H. Dodd, *The Bible and the Greeks* (London: Hodder & Stoughton, 1935), 65–69.

7. For a survey of the literature, see Hans Dieter Betz, *Galatians: A Commentary on Paul's Letter to the Churches in Galatia*, Hermeneia (Philadelphia: Fortress Press, 1979), 281–83.

8. A. J. Malherbe, "'Gentle as a Nurse': The Cynic Background to 1 Thess. ii," *Novum Testamentum* 12 (1970): 203–17.

9. Victor C. Pfitzner, *Paul and the Agon Motif: Traditional Athletic Imagery in the Pauline Literature* (New York: Humanities Press, 1967); and Roetzel, *Paul: The Man and the Myth* (Minneapolis: Fortress Press, 1999), 129–31.

10. Not "*true* circumcision" as in RSV. My emphasis.

11. Rudolf Bultmann, *Der Stil der paulinischen Predigt und die kynisch-stoische Diatribe* (Göttingen: Vandenhoeck & Ruprecht, 1910).

12. See Stanley Stowers, *The Diatribe and Paul's Letter to the Romans* (Chico, Calif.: Scholars Press, 1981), for an excellent treatment chaps. 1 and 2.

13. Betz, *Galatians*.

14. Hans Hübner's review, "Der Galaterbrief und das Verhältnis von antiker Rhetorik und Epistolographie," *Theologische Literaturzeitung* 109 (1984): 241–50.

15. Wilhelm Wuellner, "Where Is Rhetorical Criticism Taking Us?" *Catholic Biblical Quarterly* 49 (1987): 448–63, offers a positive assessment of this approach and a helpful bibliography.

16. Here I follow Johannes Munck, *Paul and the Salvation of Mankind*, trans. Frank Clarke (Richmond: John Knox Press, 1959).

17. The word "pagan" used here hardly refers to a religionless people, but instead to a people outside the orbit of the Abrahamic religion.

18. I recognize the falsity of the phrase "older religions" but I use it nevertheless for the sake of convenience.

19. Helmut Koester, *Introduction to the New Testament: History, Culture, and Religion in the Hellenistic Age* (Garden City, N.Y.: Doubleday, 1982), 1:170.

20. Martin P. Nilsson, *Greek Piety* (Oxford: Clarendon, 1948), 188.

21. Gilbert Murray, *Five Stages of Greek Religion* (Garden City, N.Y.: Doubleday, 1955), 4.

22. The term "mystery religion," though problematic, is used here for the sake of convenience. No definition of the mysteries is without objection. For example, if one defines the mysteries as religions of secret rites, one can place Christianity in this category, while excluding the cult of Dionysus, with its public rites and festivals. If one uses the term to refer to religions whose rites brought its devotees into a mystical union with the god, one may note the Christian union with Jesus. If one thinks of the mysteries as those promising to their initiates eso-

teric wisdom that sets them apart from the masses, and offering a new life or conversion that transcends human limit, mortality, or culpability, then the definition is so broad that it fits almost all religious movements and is therefore useless. Here I accept the self-description of the movements themselves—that is, as those that are privy to the divine mysteries, and as such can offer deliverance from this mortal web of fate, matter, and mortality.

23. See Frederick C. Grant, ed., *Ancient Roman Religion* (New York: Bobbs-Merrill, 1957), xxiv. For materials ascribed to the mystery religions see Charles K. Barrett, ed., *The New Testament Background: Selected Documents* (New York: Macmillan, 1957), 92–104.

24. Rudolf Bultmann, *Primitive Christianity in Its Contemporary Setting*, trans. R. H. Fuller (New York: World, 1947), 159.

25. Cicero, *De legibus* 2.38.

26. An old but still highly instructive work on Egyptian religion is Henri Frankfort's *Ancient Egyptian Religion* (New York: Columbia University Press, 1948). On Isis and Osiris see especially 104–23.

27. Ibid., 106.

28. Koester, *Introduction*, 191.

29. Apuleius, *Metamorphoses* 11.5.1.

30. Martin P. Nilsson, *The Dionysiac Mysteries of the Hellenistic Roman Age* (Lund: Gleerup, 1957), followed by Koester, traces Dionysus's origins back to Thrace and Phrygia. Walter Friedrich Otto, *Dionysus, Myth and Cult* (Bloomington, Ind.: Indiana University Press, 1965), 58, disputes Nilsson's claim, arguing that Dionysus was always thought to be of Greek origin.

31. Albert Henrichs, "Greek and Roman Glimpses of Dionysus," in *Dionysos and His Circle: Ancient Through Modern*, ed. Caroline Houser (Cambridge, Mass.: Fogg Art Museum, Harvard University, 1979), 6.

32. Nilsson, *Dionysiac Mysteries*, 143–47, usefully summarized the Dionysiac mystery religion; however, he overemphasized its elitist appeal to the rich and cultured conservatives. Caroline Houser's estimation is more convincing.

33. Caroline Houser, "Changing Views of Dionysos," in *Dionysos and His Circle*, ed. Houser, 24.

34. *Inscriptiones Graece* (Berlin, 1902), vol. 4, no. 951, 11:36, cited in Frederick C. Grant, ed., *Hellenistic Religions: The Age of Syncretism* (New York: Liberal Arts Press, 1953), 57; see also 49–59. See also Howard C. Kee, *Medicine, Miracle and Magic in New Testament Times* (Cambridge, Mass.: Harvard University Press, 1986), and E. J. and L. Edelstein,

Asclepius: A Collection and Interpretation of the Testimonies, 2 vols. (Baltimore: Johns Hopkins University Press, 1945).

35. Edwyn Bevan, *Stoics and Skeptics* (Oxford: Clarendon, 1913), 41.

36. As cited by Edward Vernon Arnold, *Roman Stoicism* (Freeport, N.Y.: Books for Libraries, 1971), 86.

37. Bultmann, *Primitive Christianity*, 159.

38. Diogenes Laertius, "Diogenes," in *Lives of Eminent Philosophers*, trans. R. D. Hicks (London: William Heinemann, 1925), 4.39.

39. Ibid., 6:41.

40. Bultmann, *Primitive Christianity*, 159.

41. Seneca, *Ad Lucilium Epistulae Morales*, trans. Richard M. Gummere, Loeb Classical Library (Cambridge, Mass.: Harvard University Press, 1979), 5:21.

42. For still the best treatment see Walter Burkert, *Lore and Science in Ancient Pythagoreanism*, trans. Edwin L. Minar Jr. (Cambridge: Harvard University Press, 1972), 482.

43. Hans Jonas, *The Gnostic Religion: The Message of the Alien God and the Beginnings of Christianity*, 2nd ed. (Boston: Beacon, 1973), 328. Although meant to describe an existential dimension in Gnosticism, it applies equally well to a developing mood shared by Neo-Pythagoreans.

44. Pliny, *Natural History*, trans. Harris Rackham, Loeb Classical Library (Cambridge, Mass.: Harvard University Press, 1938), 2.5.22.

45. Philostratus, *The Life of Apollonius of Tyana*, trans. F. C. Conybeare, Loeb Classical Library (Cambridge: Harvard University Press, 1960), vol. 1, vii–xvii, vol. 2, 273–317; E. R. Dodds, *The Greeks and the Irrational* (Boston: Beacon, 1951), 135–46, shows how interest grew in philosophical miracle workers; David L. Tiede, *The Charismatic Figure as Miracle Worker* (Missoula, Mont.: Society of Biblical Literature, 1972), 16ff., sees the tension between those traditions that view Pythagoras as a divine philosopher, and those that remember him as a miracle worker.

46. Philostratus, *Apollonius of Tyana* 8.7.

47. Holger Thesleff, *An Introduction to the Pythagorean Writings of the Hellenistic Period* (Abo: [Turku] Finland: Abo Akademi, 1961).

48. Most of these documents are included in *The Nag Hammadi Library*, ed. James M. Robinson (San Francisco: Harper & Row, 1977). For an older account needing correction see Jonas, *Gnostic Religion*.

49. A fuller development of these ties may be seen in Elaine Pagels, *The Gnostic Paul: Gnostic Exegesis of the Pauline Letters* (Philadelphia: Fortress Press, 1975).

50. *Sympatheia* stands behind the English word *sympathy*, meaning to suffer with someone. Here, however, the word is taken to mean feel with or acknowledge kinship or relationship to all things so that what affects one affects the whole.

51. John Knox, *Chapters in a Life of Paul* (Nashville: Abingdon, 1950), chap. 2.

52. In the Gospel of Matthew, for instance, the Pharisees are scorned as "viper[s]" (3:7; 12:34; 23:33), "hypocrites" (23:27), "blind guides" (23:16), keepers of the minutiae of the law who neglect "justice and mercy and faith" (23:23), murderers of the prophets (23:30), and "whitewashed tombs" (23:27); but when this description is read as one side of a vicious quarrel between church and synagogue, it sounds less like an objective historical description than a bitter competition.

53. Jacob Neusner, *From Politics to Piety: The Emergence of Pharisaic Judaism* (Englewood Cliffs, N.J.: Prentice-Hall, 1973), 89. Neusner's writings have totally altered an earlier approach of scholars to first-century Pharisaism.

54. Josephus, *The Jewish War*, trans. H. St. J. Thackeray, Loeb Classical Library (Cambridge: Harvard University Press, 1976), 2.162–63.

55. Josephus, *Antiquities*, trans. R. Marcus, Loeb Classical Library (Cambridge: Harvard University Press, 1957), 13.171–73.

56. Ellis Rivkin, *A Hidden Revolution: The Pharisees Search for the Kingdom Within* (Nashville: Abingdon, 1978), 72–75, 242.

57. Joachim Jeremias, "Paulus als Hillelit," in *Neotestamentica et Semitica: Studies in Honour of Principal Matthew Black*, ed. E. E. Ellis and Max Wilcox (Edinburgh: T&T Clark, 1969), 88–94.

58. For a list of these passages, see my *Judgement in the Community: A Study of the Relationship between Eschatology and Ecclesiology in Paul* (Leiden: Brill, 1972), 153–54.

59. See Jeremias, "Paulus als Hillelit," as well as Otto Michel, *Paulus und Seine Bibel* (Gütersloh: Bertelsmann, 1929).

60. The word "eschatology," signifying thinking or reasoning about the end, has come to refer to God's decisive conclusion to the "end time." Apocalyptic literature is normally the literature of an oppressed people dealing literally with God's revelation. Usually apocalyptic ideology is eschatological in character, but not all eschatological writings are apocalyptic in character. More highly imaginative, and more volatile, apocalypticism allows for anything the imagination can conjure— for example, seven-headed beasts, astral pyrotechnics, depictions of brutal and bloody vengeance, and victory for those who persevere.

Jesus' proclamation, "The rule of God is at hand," is eschatological; the depiction of the antichrist as Nero redivivus with the number 666 is apocalyptic. For an excellent discussion of apocalypticism, see the treatment by M. Rist, "Apocalypticism," *Interpreter's Dictionary of the Bible*, ed. G. A. Buttrick (Nashville: Abingdon, 1962), 1:157–61; now treated afresh by Christopher Rowland, "Apocalypticism," *New Interpreter's Dictionary of the Bible*, ed. Katharine Doob Sakenfeld (Nashville: Abingdon, 2006), 1:190–95. A vast literature on the nature and development of apocalyptic literature is now available. See John J. Collins, *The Apocalyptic Imagination: An Introduction to the Jewish Matrix of Christianity* (New York: Crossroad, 1984). For an outline of issues facing the interpreter of apocalyptic literature and a useful guide for further consideration, see Klaus Koch, *The Rediscovery of Apocalyptic*, trans. Margaret Kohl (Naperville, Ill.: Allenson, 1972).

61. Hans Joachim Schoeps, *Paul: The Theology of the Apostle in the Light of Jewish Religious History*, trans. Harold Knight (Philadelphia: Westminster, 1961), 38.

62. Edwin R. Goodenough. *Jewish Symbols in the Greco-Roman Period* (New York: Pantheon, 1953), 1:61ff.

63. W. D. Davies, "Paul and the Dead Sea Scrolls: Flesh and Spirit," in *The Scrolls and the New Testament*, ed. Krister Stendahl (New York: Harper & Brothers, 1957), 157.

64. Martin Hengel, *Judentum und Hellenismus* (Tübingen: Mohr [Siebeck], 1969), 453–68. English translation: *Judaism and Hellenism*, trans. John Bowden, 2 vols. (Philadelphia: Fortress Press, 1974), 1:247–54.

65. See Ralph Philip Martin, *Carmen Christi: Philippians ii.5–11 in Recent Interpretation and in the Setting of Early Christian Worship* (Cambridge: Cambridge University Press, 1967), for a dated but still excellent survey of the problems associated with this passage and the scholarly opinion regarding it.

66. Salo W. Baron, *A Social and Religious History of the Jews* (New York: Columbia University Press, 1952), 1:171.

67. See ibid.

68. See Munck, *Paul and Salvation*, 11–35.

69. See my "Paul as Mother: A Metaphor for Jewish-Christian Conversion?" in *Paul—A Jew on the Margins* (Louisville: Westminster John Knox, 2003), 9–18.

Chapter 2: The Anatomy of the Letters

1. Summarizing this topic is William Doty, *Letters in Primitive Christianity* (Philadelphia: Fortress Press, 1973). An excellent survey of recent

scholarship and the emerging consensus is available in John L. White, *Light from Ancient Letters* (Philadelphia: Fortress Press, 1986). Stanley K. Stowers, "Greek and Latin Letters," *Anchor Bible Dictionary*, ed. David Noel Freedman, 6 vols. (New York: Doubleday, 1992), 4:290–93; and idem, *Letter Writing in Greco-Roman Antiquity* (Philadelphia: Fortress Press, 1986), thinks Paul was influenced by the philosophical letter-writing tradition.

2. B.G.U. 27 (H.E. 113), as cited by C. K. Barrett, *New Testament Background and Selected Documents* (New York: Macmillan, 1957), 29.

3. I realize that to use the term "orthodoxy" in this period is anachronistic, I use it, nevertheless, for the sake of convenience in recognition that soon after Paul's day fierce debates would be under way to define the shape and outlook of the Jesus movement and the veracity of Paul's apostolic claims and his gospel.

4. Paul Schubert, *The Form and Function of the Pauline Thanksgiving* (Berlin: Töpelmann, 1939).

5. Erich Fascher, "Briefliteratur, urchristliche, formgeschichtlich," *Die Religion in Geschichte und Gegenwart*, ed. Hans von Campenhausen et al., 3rd ed. (Tübingen: Mohr [Siebeck], 1957), 1:1412–16.

6. The situation in 2 Corinthians is complicated by the likelihood that it is an anthology of letter fragments. For a plausible hypothesis regarding the number of letter fragments included in 2 Corinthians and their arrangement, see my *2 Corinthians*, Abingdon New Testament Commentaries (Nashville: Abingdon, 2007).

7. James M. Robinson, "The Historicality of Biblical Language," in *The Old Testament and Christian Faith*, ed. Bernhard W. Anderson (New York: Harper & Row, 1966), 270. He thinks Galatians and Romans were exceptions to this rule for good and sufficient reasons.

8. Robert W. Funk, *Language, Hermeneutic, and Word of God* (New York: Harper & Row, 1966), 270.

9. Ibid., 268. Funk also believed that the location of the announcement of his travel plans at the end of the letter is explicable in terms of Paul's imminent visit to Rome and the purpose the letter serves in preparing for that visit.

10. Ibid., 249.

11. Martin Dibelius, *Der Brief des Jakobus*, 11th ed. (Göttingen: Vandenhoeck & Ruprecht, 1964), 15ff. English translation: *James*, rev. Heinrich Greeven, trans. Michael A. Williams, Hermeneia (Philadelphia: Fortress Press, 1976), 3ff.

12. For relevant Hellenistic traditions see Francis W. Beare, "The Epistle to the Colossians, Introduction," in *The Interpreter's Bible*, ed. George

A. Buttrick (Nashville: Abingdon, 1955), 11:133ff. For Jewish and Hellenistic background, see Siegfried Wibbing, *Die Tugend- und Lasterkataloge in Neuen Testament* (Berlin: Töpelmann, 1959).

13. David G. Bradley, "The *Topos* as a Form in the Pauline Paraenesis," *Journal of Biblical Literature* 72 (1953): 238–46.

14. Gordon Wiles, *Paul's Intercessory Prayers* (Cambridge: Cambridge University Press, 1973); see my "1 Thessalonians 5:12–28: A Case Study," *Proceedings of the Society of Biblical Literature 108* (1972), 2:367–83. See also Harry Y. Gamble, *The Textual History of the Letter to the Romans* (Grand Rapids: Eerdmans, 1977).

15. *The Oxyrhynchus Papyri*, ed. Bernard Grenfell and Arthur Hunt (London: Oxford University Press, 1910), 3:261–62.

16. Heikki Koskenniemi, *Studien zur Idee und Phraseologie des griechischen Briefes bis 400 nach Christus* (Helsinki: Akateeminen Kirjakauppa, 1956), 169–80.

17. See my *Judgement in the Community* (Leiden: Brill, 1972), 145, 161.

18. Victor Paul Furnish, *Theology and Ethics in Paul* (Louisville: Westminster John Knox, 2009), 55.

19. Klaus Berger, "Hellenistische Gattungen im neuen Testament," in *Aufstieg und Niedergang der römischen Welt*, ed. Hildegard Temporini and Wolfgang Haase (Berlin: de Gruyter, 1984), part 2, vol. 25/2:1326–63.

20. For the data informing this article, Berger relies heavily on Abraham J. Malherbe, *The Cynic Epistles: A Study Edition* (Missoula, Mont.: Scholars Press, 1977), 38–39, 64–65, 178–79, etc.

21. See Stowers, *Letter Writing in Greco-Roman Antiquity*.

22. Ostracon III in *Ancient Near Eastern Texts Relating to the Old Testament*, ed. James B. Pritchard, 2nd ed. (Princeton: Princeton University Press, 1955), 322.

23. Paul sometimes dictated his letters to a secretary (amanuensis), appending a conclusion in his own hand (e.g., Gal. 6:11–18). First Corinthians 16:21–24 likewise displays an autograph. Although the secretary self-identifies in Rom. 16:22, whether chap. 16 was part of the original letter is disputed. On the strength of these two or three references it is arbitrary to conclude that Paul dictated all of his letters.

Chapter 3: Traditions behind the Letters

1. C. H. Dodd, *The Apostolic Preaching and Its Developments* (London: Hodder & Stoughton, 1936), 21–23.

2. "Even death on a cross" was most likely inserted here by Paul.

3. My translation follows Ernst Lohmeyer's arrangement in his *Der Brief an die Philipper*, 19th ed. (Göttingen: Vandenhoeck & Ruprecht, 1954), 96–97.

4. The Greek may suggest an unreal past condition, "even if I had known him (which of course I didn't). . . ." Since we cannot be sure that such was Paul's intention, the following discussion is necessary.

5. Victor Paul Furnish, *Theology and Ethics in Paul* (Louisville: Westminster John Knox, 2009), 55.

6. Joseph A. Fitzmyer, *Pauline Theology—A Brief Sketch* (Englewood Cliffs, N.J.: Prentice-Hall, 1967), 13.

7. Lloyd Gaston, *No Stone on Another* (Leiden: Brill, 1970), 407–8, makes a good case for the authenticity of this saying.

8. Martin Dibelius, *A Fresh Approach to the New Testament and Early Christian Literature* (New York: Charles Scribner's Sons, 1936), 143.

9. Dibelius correctly noted this in ibid., 143ff. Davies, *Paul*, 136, and Hunter, *Paul and His Predecessors* (London: SCM, 1961), 52–55, share this view.

10. Funk, *Language*, 270, and Furnish, *Theology and Ethics in Paul*, decisively qualify Dibelius's view.

11. Funk, *Language*, 33–34.

12. Furnish, *Theology and Ethics in Paul*, 84–85.

13. David G. Bradley, "The *Topos* as a Form in the Pauline Paraenesis," *Journal of Biblical Literature* 72 (1953): 246.

14. Calvin J. Roetzel, "I Thessalonians 5:12–28: A Case Study," *Proceedings of the Society of Biblical Literature*, 108.

15. See Bradley, "*Topos*," 246.

16. Of course, those who argue for the authenticity of Colossians and Ephesians would add another category—rules for the domestic life (*Haustafeln*). For example, see Col. 3:18–22: "Wives, be subject to your husbands, as is fitting in the Lord. Husbands, love your wives. . . . Children, obey your parents. . . . Slaves, obey your earthly masters in everything" (cf. Eph. 5:21–6:9). Such instruction is unparalleled in the undisputed Pauline letters.

Chapter 4: The Letters as Conversations

1. Joseph A. Fitzmyer, *Paul and His Theology: A Brief Sketch*, 2nd ed. (Englewood Cliffs, N.J.: Prentice-Hall, 1988), is excellent. Rudolf Bultmann, *Theology of the New Testament*, trans. Kendrick Grobel, 2 vols. (New York: Charles Scribner's Sons, 1951), is now almost a classic. Victor Paul Furnish, *Theology and Ethics in Paul* (Louisville:

Westminster John Knox, 2009), offers an excellent treatment of the major currents in Pauline interpretation. The Pauline Theology Group of the Society of Biblical Literature has produced four volumes of collected essays by the most outstanding scholars in the field. See *Pauline Theology*, vols. 2 and 3; ed. E. Elizabeth Johnson and David M. Hay (Minneapolis: Fortress Press, 1993, 1995); vol. 4, ed. E. Elizabeth Johnson and David M. Hay (Minneapolis: Fortress Press, 1997).

2. See my "Chronology of Paul's Life and Letters," in "Paul the Apostle," in *The New Interpreter's Dictionary of the Bible*, ed. Katharine Doob Sakenfeld, vol. 4 (Nashville: Abingdon, 2009). Older works available also: Robert Jewett, *A Chronology of Paul's Life* (Philadelphia: Fortress Press, 1979); and Gerd Lüdemann, *Paulus, Der Heidenapostel*, vol. 1, *Studien zur Chronologie* (Göttingen: Vandenhoeck & Ruprecht, 1980). For the relevance of this discussion for our understanding of Paul's theology, see John C. Hurd Jr. "Pauline Chronology and Pauline Theology," in *Christian History and Interpretation*, ed. William R. Farmer (Cambridge: Cambridge University Press, 1967), 225–48.

3. Richard B. Hays, *The Faith of Jesus Christ* (Chico, Calif.: Scholars Press, 1983), offers an excellent treatment of the narrative structure of Paul's gospel.

4. If the Thessalonian converts did indeed send a letter, it may have solicited guidance on three items: (1) Paul exhorted the converts to love one another, but what form should love take toward the eschatological enthusiasts who in expectation of the imminent end of the world had quit work and were sponging off the diligent? (2) Some believers had died. Does their death imply that God deemed them unworthy of the kingdom of God? (3) Converts had tried to be in readiness for an end that Paul predicted was at hand. Does its delay mean that Paul's prediction was false? When will it come? In 1 Corinthians the phrase *peri de*, "now concerning," was a marker of topics on which the Corinthians had written for guidance. A similar phrase appears in 1 Thess. 4:9 and 4:13, and a variation of the phrase appears in 5:1, but that hardly proves that the Thessalonians wrote a letter to Paul. Obviously, more letters were exchanged than have survived, and presumably some were from these little house churches.

5. The Greek *ataktoi* refers not just to the idle, as is often assumed, but also to the apostles of disorder (see 1 Cor. 14:40 also).

6. A useful summary of recent secondary literature and of issues is available in Gordon D. Fee, *The First Epistle to the Corinthians* (Grand Rapids: Eerdmans, 1987).

7. Some see 2 Cor. 6:14–7:1 as a fragment of this missing letter since it clearly was an insertion and since it also deals with immorality, which Paul wrote was the theme of the first letter (1 Cor. 5:9). Joseph A. Fitzmyer, however, has argued convincingly that the language of 6:14–7:1 is more characteristic of Qumran texts than of Paul. See his "Qumran and the Interpolated Paragraph in 2 Corinthians 6:14–7:1," *Catholic Biblical Quarterly* 23 (1961): 271ff.

8. Here I follow the outline offered by John C. Hurd Jr. *The Origin of I Corinthians* (New York: Seabury, 1965).

9. Note especially Luke 20:34–36, which suggests the same view: "And Jesus said to them, 'Those who belong to this age marry and are given in marriage; but those who are considered worthy of a place in that age and in the resurrection from the dead neither marry nor are given in marriage. Indeed, they cannot die anymore, because they are like angels and are children of God, being children of the resurrection'" (AT).

10. Dieter Georgi's *Die Gegner des Paulus im 2. Korintherbrief: Studien zur religiösen Propaganda in der Spätantike* (Neukirchen-Vluyn: Neukirchener Verlag, 1964) (Eng. trans.: *The Opponents of Paul in Second Corinthians* [Philadelphia: Fortress Press, 1986]) has profoundly influenced the scholarly understanding of the scope of Paul's opposition especially in 2 Corinthians.

11. The most influential commentary on 2 Corinthians to date is that of Victor Paul Furnish, *2 Corinthians*, Anchor Bible (Garden City, N.Y.: Doubleday, 1984). More accessible to the nonspecialist is Calvin J. Roetzel, *2 Corinthians*, Abingdon New Testament Commentaries (Nashville: Abingdon, 2007).

12. See Roetzel, "The Language of War (2 Cor. 10:1–6) and the Language of Weakness (2 Cor. 11:21b–13:10)," *Biblical Interpretation* 17 (2009): 77–99; and B. D. Shaw, "Body/Power/Identity: Passions of the Martyrs," *Journal of Early Christian Studies* 4 (1996): 305–11.

13. See Roetzel, *2 Corinthians*.

14. For this arrangement I owe much to Margaret M. Mitchell, "Paul's Letters to Corinth: The Interpretive Intertwining of Literary and Historical Reconstruction," in *Urban Religion in Roman Corinth, Interdisciplinary Approaches*, ed. Daniel Showalter and Steven J. Friesen (Cambridge: Harvard University Press, 2005), 307–38.

15. See Roetzel, *2 Corinthians*, and especially the careful and well-argued work of Mitchell, "Paul's Letters to Corinth."

16. See Roetzel, *2 Corinthians*, 34–35.

17. The best available discussion in English of the history of interpretation of Galatians and the major issues facing the interpreter is offered

by Hans Dieter Betz, *Galatians: A Commentary on Paul's Letter to the Churches in Galatia*, Hermeneia (Philadelphia: Fortress Press, 1979). Scholars disagree on the location of these churches. According to the Southern Galatian theory, they were in the region through which Paul traveled on his "first missionary journey" (Acts 13–14). This theory has the advantage of harmonizing Paul's letters with the Acts account. Those holding the Northern Galatian theory point to discrepancies between the Acts account and Paul's letters and further argue that Paul uses the ethnic name "Galatians" (3:1) to refer to his readers that would better fit the inhabitants of the north where the Galatians had settled than residents in the southern part of the Roman province. Those opting for the southern theory tend to date Galatians among the earliest of Paul's letters since it is assumed that he founded the church on the "first missionary journey." Those supporting the northern hypothesis tend to date Galatians somewhat later since it is assumed that it was on a later visit that Paul ventured to the heart of the old Celtic kingdom of Keltai near modern Ankara, Turkey. This later theory is also of some significance if one is interested in tracing the emergence of Paul's theology made evident in a comparison of the later Romans with Galatians. The dating of Galatians has been notoriously difficult for these reasons, and this uncertainty informs the broadest possible dating range assigned above.

18. Johannes Munck, *Paul and the Salvation of Mankind*, trans. Frank Clarke (Richmond: John Knox Press, 1959), 87–134.

19. Lloyd Gaston, "Paul and the Law in Galatians 2 and 3," in *Paul and the Torah* (Vancouver: University of British Columbia Press, 1987), 64–79.

20. Ignatius, "Epistle to the Philadelphians," in *Apostolic Fathers*, trans. Kirsopp Lake, 2 vols. Loeb Classical Library (Cambridge: Harvard University Press, 1912), 1:245.

21. See my, "*Ioudaioi* and Paul," in *The New Testament an Early Christian Literature in Greco-Roman Context: Studies in Honor of David E. Aune*, ed. John Fotopoulos (Leiden: Brill, 2006), 3–16.

22. Gaston, "Paul and the Law in Galatians 2 and 3," 73–76.

23. I am indebted to the late and revered Nils A. Dahl for this insight, which he advanced in a paper given to the Paul Seminar of the Society of Biblical Literature at the 1973 meeting. The paper was entitled "Paul's Letter to the Galatians: Epistolary Genre, Content, and Structure."

24. The use of the term "heretic" to apply to the early period is anachronistic, for it was only later, some would say much later, that the church

gained the power to define and enforce orthodox positions. In the time of Paul, multiple versions of the gospel were disputed, and acceptance came through persuasion rather than force. As late as the 4th century Augustine was one of the first to justify physical coercion as a valuable instrument to enforce doctrinal correctness.

25. See Harry Y. Gamble, *The Textual History of the Letter to the Romans* (Grand Rapids: Eerdmans, 1977).

26. Among an entire shelf of excellent commentaries on Romans, those by Leander Keck and Joseph Fitzmyer stand out. See Joseph A. Fitzmyer, *Romans: A New Translation and Introduction and Commentary*, Anchor Bible (New York: Doubleday, 1992). More recent and more accessible is that of Leander E. Keck, *Romans*, Abingdon New Testament Commentaries (Nashville: Abingdon, 2005).

27. See W. H. Auden, *Collected Poems*, ed. Edward Mendelson (New York: Random House, 1976), 303.

28. See my *Paul: The Man and the Myth* (Minneapolis: Fortress Press, 1999), 129–31.

29. Furnish, *Theology and Ethics in Paul*, has correctly shown that the ethical instruction in Paul's letters is hardly restricted to the closing "paraenetic" sections of the letters.

30. Parts of Luke's account give rise to considerable skepticism, however. Most especially the emphasis in Acts on Paul's Roman citizenship cannot be taken without question. See my *Paul: The Man and the Myth*, 19–22.

31. See Edgar Hennecke, *New Testament Apocrypha*, ed. Wilhelm Schneemelcher, trans. R. McL. Wilson, 2 vols. (Philadelphia: Westminster, 1964), 2:253–57.

32. The mention of the "imperial guard" and "those of the emperor's household" has led some to place the writing of Philippians in Rome during Paul's imprisonment there, but we now know the "imperial guard" was present in other cities on the shores of the Mediterranean. Moreover, Philippians notes five communications between Paul and the church, and given that it would have taken approximately eight weeks to traverse the distance between Rome and Philippi (some 730 miles by land), Ephesus at less than one hundred miles distant, is a more likely candidate for Paul's imprisonment than Rome when Philippians was written. The major objection to Ephesus as Paul's prison location is that neither he nor Acts mentions it. That silence, however, is hardly decisive, for Paul himself reports that he was imprisoned many times (2 Cor. 11:23) and suffered great affliction in Asia (2 Cor. 1:8). Moreover, Clement of Rome reports a generation later

that Paul "wore chains seven times," and the later *Acts of Paul and The-cla* speaks of an Ephesian imprisonment (see Hennecke, *New Testament Apocrypha*, 2:338). Although these late traditions cannot be invoked as primary evidence, they do offer important secondary support for Ephesus as Paul's imprisonment site. The decision on the provenance of the letter affects our dating of it and is relevant for the discussion of the emergence of Paul's theology. See my discussion of "Philippians, Letter to the," *Dictionary of Biblical Interpretation*, ed. John H. Hayes, 2 vols. (Nashville: Abingdon, 1999), 2:280–83.

33. Philippians is so loosely structured that many have suggested that it is a patchwork of at least three letter fragments. Helmut Koester, "The Purpose of the Polemic of a Pauline Fragment (Philippians iii)," *New Testament Studies* 8 (1962): 317 n. 1. For guidance here I have followed the excellent essay by Philip Sellew, "*Laodiceans* and the Philippians Fragments Hypothesis," *Harvard Theological Review* 87 (1994): 17–28. Sellew argues that Polycarp's reference to "Paul's letters to you" in his letter to the Philippians is factually correct and that "the bishop means what he says and he knows what he is saying" (p. 24). In the deutero-Pauline letter to the Laodiceans Sellew finds additional support that Philippians is a collection of letter fragments, and that the author has before him a copy of Philippians without 3:2–4:1. For a summary of this history see my "Philippians, Letter to the," *Dictionary of Biblical Interpretation*, ed. Hayes, 2:280–83.

34. See Walter Schmithals, "Die Irrelehrer des Philipperbriefs," *Zeitschrift für Theologie und Kirche* 54 (1957): 279ff.

Chapter 5: Paul and His Myths

1. Before the great German martyr theologian Dietrich Bonhoeffer appropriated this term, it was on the lips of Søren Kierkegaard, *Philosophical Fragments*, trans. David F. Swenson (Princeton: Princeton University Press, 1962), 68.

2. Henri Frankfort, *Before Philosophy* (Baltimore: Penguin, 1963), 16.

3. Gerardus van der Leeuw, *Religion in Essence and Manifestation*, trans. J. E. Turner (New York: Macmillan, 1938), 413.

4. *The Haggadah of Passover*, trans. Cecil Roth (London: Soncino, 1934), 11–12.

5. Jacob Neusner, *The Way of Torah: An Introduction to Judaism* (Belmont, Calif.: Dickenson, 1970), 17. Neusner develops these ideas at some length; see especially chap. 1.

6. Mircea Eliade, *The Myth of the Eternal Return*, trans. Willard R. Trask (New York: Pantheon, 1954), 21.

7. Ernst Käsemann, "The Pauline Doctrine of the Lord's Supper," in *Essays in New Testament Themes* (London: SCM, 1964), 124.

8. Richard L. Rubenstein, *My Brother Paul* (New York: Harper & Row, 1972), 173.

9. Robin Scroggs, *The Last Adam* (Philadelphia: Fortress Press, 1966), 84.

10. H. Richard Niebuhr, *The Meaning of Revelation* (New York: Macmillan, 1941), 71–72.

Chapter 6: Interpreters of Paul in the New Testament

1. R. H. Charles, ed., *The Apocrypha and Pseudepigrapha of the Old Testament*, vol. 2: *Pseudepigrapha* (Oxford: Clarendon, 1913).

2. Werner Georg Kümmel, *Introduction to the New Testament*, trans. A. J. Matlill Jr. (Nashville: Abingdon, 1966), 241.

3. Eduard Lohse, *Colossians and Philemon: A Commentary on the Epistles to the Colossians and to Philemon*, trans. William R. Poehlmann and Robert J. Karris, Hermeneia (Philadelphia: Fortress Press, 1971), 81. Lohse has pointed out how the author of Colossians integrates major motifs from the genuine letters. Especially noteworthy are the similarities of epistolary style, their view of Paul as the apostle to the Gentiles, the use of traditional ethical materials, the understanding of wisdom materials, and the significance of the suffering of the apostle.

4. Gunther Bornkamm, "The Heresy of Colossians," in *Conflict at Colossae: A Problem in the Interpretation of Early Christianity Illustrated by Selected Modern Studies*, ed. and trans. Fred O. Francis and Wayne A. Meeks (Missoula, Mont.: Scholars Press, 1973), 130.

5. Fred O. Francis, "Humility and Angel Worship in Col. 2:18," in *Conflict at Colossae*, 163–95; and Eduard Schweizer, *Der Brief an die Kolosser* (Zürich: Benziger, 1976), 104.

6. Wayne A. Meeks and Fred O. Francis, "Epilogue," in *Conflict at Colossae*, 209–18.

7. Ernst Käsemann, "Das Interpretationsproblem des Epheserbriefes," *Theologische Literaturzeitung* 86 (1961): 3.

8. See my "Jewish Christian–Gentile Christian Relations: A Discussion of Ephesians 2:15a," *Zeitschrift für die neutestamentliche Wissenschaft* 74 (1983): 81–89.

9. See J. Paul Sampley, "The Letter to the Ephesians," in Sampley et al., *Ephesians, Colossians, 2 Thessalonians, the Pastoral Epistles* (Philadelphia: Fortress Press, 1978), 10.

10. Edgar Johnson Goodspeed, *The Key to Ephesians* (Chicago: University of Chicago Press, 1956).

11. Nils A. Dahl, "Adresse und Prooemium des Epheserbrief," *Theologische Zeitschrift* 7 (1951): 261–64.

12. H. Chadwick, "Die Absicht des Epheserbrief," *Zeitschrift für die neutestamentliche Wissenschaft* 51 (1960): 145–53.

13. See Daniel Boyarin, "The Ioudaio in John and the Prehistory of 'Judaism,'" in *Pauline Conversation in Context: Essays in Honour of Calvin J. Roetzel*, ed. Janice Capel Anderson et al. (London: Sheffield Academic Press, 2002), 216–39.

14. Birger A. Pearson, "1 Thessalonians 2:13–16: A Deutero-Pauline Interpolation," *Harvard Theological Review* 64 (1971): 79–94.

15. See Gerhard Krodel, "2 Thessalonians," in Sampley et al., *Ephesians, Colossians, 2 Thessalonians, the Pastoral Epistles*, 80.

16. For one of the better commentaries and introductions see Martin Dibelius and Hans Conzelmann, *The Pastoral Epistles*, trans. Philip Buttolph and Adela Yarbro, Hermeneia (Philadelphia: Fortress Press, 1972), 22–25, 39–41. For an excellent, accessible, more recent treatment see Jouette M. Bassler, *1 Timothy, 2 Timothy, Titus*, Abingdon New Testament Commentaries (Nashville: Abingdon, 1996).

17. See my "Paul in the Second Century," in *The Cambridge Companion to St. Paul*, ed. James D. G. Dunn (Cambridge: Cambridge University Press, 2003), 227–41.

18. Ibid.

19. It is interesting that those who oppose the ordination of women or who seek to assign women a subordinate role most often appeal to the Pastorals rather than the undisputed Pauline letters.

20. See Jerome D. Quinn, *The Letter to Titus*, Anchor Bible (New York: Doubleday, 1990); and John Knox, *Marcion and the New Testament: An Essay in Early Christian History* (Chicago: University of Chicago Press, 1942). Both held Marcion to be the object of the mild polemic in the Pastorals.

21. From Luke's extended treatment of Paul's mission in Acts, the collection of Paul's letters noted in 2 Pet. 3:16, and the imitation of his epistolary style in Colossians and Ephesians, it is clear that Paul, who was unwelcome in many quarters during his lifetime, was widely hailed in Asia Minor and Greece after his death.

Chapter 7: Currents and Crosscurrents

1. Edgar Hennecke, *New Testament Apocrypha*, ed. Wilhelm Schneemelcher, trans. R. McL. Wilson, 2 vols. (Philadelphia: Westminster Press, 1964), 2:122.

2. This unfortunate juxtaposition of Paul and Jesus is discussed below.

3. As noted above, the term "heretics" in this early period hardly referred to a person who was doctrinally perverse and, therefore, to be damned, but rather to one of a different religious opinion.

4. See Elaine Pagels, *The Gnostic Paul: Gnostic Exegesis of the Pauline Letters* (Philadelphia: Trinity Press International, 1992).

5. James M. Robinson, ed., *The Nag Hammadi Library* (New York: Harper & Row, 1977), 134. See also a "Life of Rabbula," composd by a colleague of the bishop and cited in Walter Bauer, *Orthodoxy and Heresy in Earliest Christianity*, ed. Robert A Kraft and Gerhard Krodel, 2nd ed. (Philadelphia: Fortress Press, 1971), 26–27; and my "Paul in the Second Century," 227–41.

6. Birger A. Pearson, "Did the Gnostics Curse Jesus?" *Journal of Biblical Literature* 86 (1967): 301–5.

7. Ibid.

8. Church leaders of both East and West whose writings were the chief sources of emergent doctrine and church observance.

9. Origen, *Contra Celsum*, trans. Henry Chadwick (Cambridge: Cambridge University Press, 1965), 3.42; 4.66.

10. Maurice F. Wiles, *The Divine Apostle* (Cambridge: Cambridge University Press, 1967), 39.

11. Alexander Souter, *Pelagius's Expositions of Thirteen Epistles of St. Paul* (Cambridge: Cambridge University Press, 1926), vol. 2, gives 120 pages of Latin text for the Romans commentary and 177 pages of commentary on the Corinthian letters.

12. J. N. D. Kelly, *Early Christian Doctrines* (London: Adam & Charles Black, 1958), 357.

13. Souter, *Pelagius's Expositions*, 2:45.

14. See Jaroslav Pelikan, *The Christian Tradition: A History of the Development of Doctrine*, vol. 1: *The Emergence of the Catholic Tradition (100–600)* (Chicago: University of Chicago Press, 1971), 315, for his citation of and further treatment of this passage.

15. Augustine, *Confessions* 10.29.

16. Heiko A. Oberman, *Forerunners of the Reformation* (New York: Holt, Reinhart & Winston, 1966), 126.

17. Ibid., 127.

18. See my *Paul: The Man and the Myth* (Minneapolis: Fortress Press, 1999), 93–134, for a discussion of election in Paul.

19. See discussion in Wayne A. Meeks, ed., *The Writings of St. Paul* (New York: Norton, 1972), 303. Wellhausen quotation from *Einleitung in die drei ersten Evangelien* (Berlin: Georg Reiner, 1905), rev. ed., 113.

20. See John Locke, *The Reasonableness of Christianity* (London: Awnsham and John Churchil at the Black Swan in Pater-Noster Row, 1696), 308–15.

21. Wilhelm Wrede, "Paulus," in *Das Paulusbild in der neueren deutschen Forschung*, ed. Karl Heinrich Rengstorf (Darmstad: Wissenschaftliche Buchgesellschaft, 1964), 94. More recently see the excellent treatment by William Baird, *History of New Testament Research*, vol. 2: *From Jonathan Edwards to Rudolf Bultmann* (Minneapolis: Fortress Press, 2003), 144–51. Also useful is Meeks, *The Writings of St. Paul*, 363–64.

22. Geza Vermes, *Jesus the Jew* (London: Collins, 1973).

23. Please note the anachronism of using late talmudic materials, post–third century CE, to decipher first-century practice.

24. See Rudolf Bultmann, *History of the Synoptic Tradition*, trans. John Marsh, rev. ed. (repr. Peabody, Mass.: Hendrickson, 1993). First edition in German, 1921.

25. See also Schweitzer's *Quest of the Historical Jesus* (1906) in which he claims to have found the key for understanding the roots of Jesus' preaching and teaching in Jewish apocalyptic thought. For an excellent critical assessment of Schweitzer's work on Jesus, see James M. Robinson's introduction to the 1968 edition of Albert Schweitzer, *The Quest of the Historical Jesus* (New York: Macmillan, 1968), xi–xxxiii. See W. D. Davies, *Paul and Rabbinic Judaism* (London: S.P.C.K., 1955), vii–xv, for an incisive treatment on Schweitzer's estimation of Paul.

26. Augustine, *Confessions* 8.12.29.

27. See my *Paul: The Man and the Myth*, 44. For a fuller discussion, see my "Paul as Mother: A Metaphor for Jewish-Christian Conversion?" in *Paul—A Jew on the Margins* (Louisville: Westminster John Knox, 2003), 9–18.

28. See Geza Vermes, *An Introduction to the Complete Dead Sea Scrolls* (Minneapolis: Fortress Press, 1999), and his *Complete Dead Sea Scrolls in English* (New York: Penguin, 1997).

29. Rudolf Bultmann, *Theology of the New Testament*, trans. Kendrick Grobel, 2 vols. (New York: Charles Scribner's Sons, 1951–55), 1:190–252.

30. Ibid., 1:285.

31. This has been best shown in the approach to Paul by one of his students, Ernst Käsemann, who emphatically and correctly underscored the importance of the cosmic sweep of Paul's vision and emphasis.

32. Johannes Munck, *Paul and the Salvation of Mankind* (Richmond: John Knox Press, 1959).

33. See the stunning review essay of Munck's book by William David Davies in *New Testament Studies* 2 (1959): 60–72.

34. George Bernard Shaw, "The Monstrous Imposition upon Jesus," in *The Writings of St. Paul*, ed. Wayne A. Meeks (New York: Norton, 1972), 299.

35. Ibid.

36. See Robin Scroggs, "Paul: Chauvinist or Liberationist?" *Christian Century* 89 (1972): 307–9; "Paul and the Eschatological Woman," *Journal of the American Academy of Religion* 40 (1972): 283–303; and responding to critics, "Paul and the Eschatological Woman: Revisited," *Journal of the American Academy of Religion* 42 (1974): 532–37. Various authors have commented on one of the more problematic passages in Paul's letters, 1 Cor. 11:2–16: William O. Walker, "The Non-Pauline Character of 1 Corinthians 11:2–16?" *Journal of Biblical Literature* 95 (1976): 615–21; also Lamar Cope, "1 Cor. 11:2–16: One Step Further," *JBL* 97 (1978): 435–36; and G. W. Trompf, "On Attitudes toward Women in Paul and Paulinist Literature: 1 Cor. 11:3–6 and Its Context," *Catholic Biblical Quarterly* 42 (1980): 196–215. However, the removal of this passage would hardly alter the basic point of Scroggs, given the exhortation elsewhere on the important role women played in the early church (especially Rom. 16). J. Murphy-O'Connor has argued that 1 Cor. 11:2–16 makes sense in its present setting, "Sex and Logic in 1 Cor. 11:2–16," *CBQ* 42 (1980): 482–500.

37. See John C. Hurd Jr., *The Origin of I Corinthians* (New York: Seabury, 1965), in relevant sections noted above.

38. See Scroggs's "Paul and the Eschatological Woman," 283–303.

39. Scroggs, "Paul and the Eschatological Woman: Revisited," 533. See the relevant discussion above in chap. 4, and Phil. 4:2–3 and Paul's reference to Euodia and Syntyche, who he noted "struggled beside me in the work of the gospel," and Rom. 16 if genuine. Also note 1 Cor. 16:19, which speaks of Aquila and Prisca hosting the church in their house.

40. Elaine Pagels, "Paul and Women: A Response to Recent Discussion," *Journal of the American Academy of Religion* 42 (1974): 538–49.

41. Ibid., 545. S. Scott Bartchy makes a strong case for this view in *First-Century Slavery and 1 Corinthians 7:21* (Missoula, Mont.: Scholars Press, 1973), 161–72. More recently Jennifer A. Glancy, *Slavery in Early Christianity* (Minneapolis: Fortress Press, 2006), has offered a much acclaimed, wide-ranging investigation of slavery in early Christianity.

42. Pagels, "Paul and Women," 544.

43. David Daube, "Pauline Contributions to a Pluralistic Culture: Re-creation and Beyond," in *Jesus and Man's Hope*, ed. Donald H. Miller and Dikran Y. Hadidian, 2 vols. (Pittsburgh: Pittsburgh Theological Seminary, 1971), 2:223–45.

44. Elisabeth Schüssler Fiorenza, *In Memory of Her: A Feminist Theological Reconstruction of Christian Origins* (New York: Crossroad, 1983), 211.

45. Ibid., 182.

46. Daniel Boyarin, *Paul and the Politics of Identity: A Radical Jew* (Berkeley: University of California Press, 1994), 182.

47. Ibid., 182–83.

48. Ibid., 7.

49. Ibid.

50. Ibid., 184, 185.

51. Ibid., 190.

52. Ibid., 195.

53. Elizabeth A. Castelli, *Imitating Paul: A Discourse of Power* (Louisville: Westminster/John Knox, 1991).

54. Ibid., 112.

55. Ibid., 119–36.

56. Antoinette Clark Wire, *The Corinthian Women Prophet: A Reconstruction through Paul's Rhetoric* (Minneapolis: Fortress Press, 1990).

57. Gordon D. Fee, *The First Epistle to the Corinthians* (Grand Rapids: Eerdmans, 1987), 699–708, makes a compelling case for this being a later insertion. While Wire is aware of Fee's evidence, she does not respond to its substance.

58. See Carolyn Osiek's commentary on Philippians in *Searching the Scriptures*, vol. 2: *A Feminist Commentary*, ed. Elisabeth Schüssler Fiorenza (New York: Crossroad, 1994), 246–47.

Suggested Additional Reading

Chapter 1: Paul and His World

1. Hellenistic World (Introductory)

Boring, M. Eugene, Klaus Berger, and Carsten Colpe, eds. *Hellenistic Commentary to the New Testament*. Nashville: Abingdon, 1995.

Bultmann, Rudolf. *Primitive Christianity in Its Contemporary Setting*. Translated by R. H. Fuller. New York: World, 1957.

Dodds, E. R. *The Greeks and the Irrational*. Berkeley: University of California Press, 1966.

Hengel, Martin. *Judaism and Hellenism*. Translated by John Bowden. 2 vols. Philadelphia: Fortress Press, 1974.

Meeks, Wayne A. *The First Urban Christians: The Social World of the Apostle Paul*. New Haven: Yale University Press, 1983.

Schürer, Emil. *The History of the Jewish People in the Age of Jesus Christ*. Revised and edited by Geza Vermes, Fergus Millar, and Martin Goodman. 4 vols. Edinburgh: T&T Clark, 1973–87.

Tcherikover, Victor. *Hellenistic Civilization and the Jews*. Translated by S. Applebaum. New York: Atheneum, 1970.

Walbank, F. W., et al., eds. *The Cambridge Ancient History*. Vol. 7, part 1, *The Hellenistic World*. 2nd ed. Cambridge: Cambridge University Press, 1984.

2. The Greek Translation of the Bible (The Septuagint, LXX)

Bickerman, Elias. *Studies in Jewish and Christian History*. 2 vols. Leiden: Brill, 1976–80.

Dodd, C. H. *The Bible and the Greeks*. London: Hodder & Stoughton, 1935.

Jellicoe, Sidney. *Studies in the Septuagint: Origins, Recensions, and Interpretation.* New York: KTAV, 1974.

Peters, Melvin K. H. "Septuagint." In *Anchor Bible Dictionary.* Edited by David Noel Freedman, 5:1093–1104. New York: Doubleday, 1992.

3. Argumentation

a. Diatribe

Stowers, Stanley K. *The Diatribe and Paul's Letters to the Romans.* Chico, Calif.: Scholars Press, 1981.

b. Rhetoric

Marrou, H. I. "Education and Rhetoric." In *The Legacy of Greece: A New Appraisal.* Edited by M. I. Finley, 185–201. Oxford: Clarendon, 1956.

———. *A History of Education in Antiquity.* London: Sheed & Ward, 1956.

c. Allegory

Barr, James. "Typology and Allegory." In *Old and New in Interpretation: A Study of the Two Testaments*, 103–48. London: SCM, 1966.

4. Hellenistic Religion and Philosophy

a. General

Burkert, Walter. *Greek Religion.* Translated by John Raffan. Cambridge: Harvard University Press, 1977.

Nilsson, Martin. *Greek Piety.* Oxford: Clarendon, 1948.

Teixidor, Javier. *The Pagan God: Popular Religion in the Greco-Roman Near East.* Princeton: Princeton University Press, 1977.

b. Mystery Religions

Metzger, Bruce M. "A Classified Bibliography of the Graeco-Roman Religions 1924–1973 with a Supplement 1974–1979." In *Aufstieg und Niedergang der römischen Welt.* Edited by Hildegard Temporini and Wolfgang Haase. Berlin: de Gruyter, 1984. Part 2, vol. 17/3:1259–1423.

Reitzenstein, Richard. *Hellenistic Mystery Religions: Their Basic Ideas and Significance.* Translated by J. E. Steely. Pittsburgh: Pickwick, 1978.

(1) The Eleusinian Mystery

Burkert, Walter. *Ancient Mystery Cults.* Cambridge: Harvard University Press, 1987.

Mylonas, George E. *Eleusis and the Eleusinian Mysteries.* Princeton: Princeton University Press, 2000.

(2) Isis and Osiris Mystery (or Serapis Cult)

Frankfort, Henri. *Ancient Egyptian Religion.* New York: Columbia University Press, 1948.

Heyob, Sharon Kelley. *The Cult of Isis Among Women in the Greco-Roman World.* Leiden: Brill, 1975.

Solmsen, Friedrich. *Isis among the Greeks and Romans.* Cambridge: Harvard University Press, 1979.

Witt, R. E. *Isis in the Graeco-Roman World.* Ithaca, N.Y.: Cornell University Press, 1971.

(3) The Dionysiac Mystery

Houser, Caroline. *Dionysus and His Circle: Ancient Through Modern.* Cambridge: Fogg Art Museum, Harvard University, 1979.

Nilsson, Martin. *The Dionysiac Mysteries of the Hellenistic and Roman Age.* Lund: Gleerup, 1957.

Walter, Friedrich Otto. *Dionysus, Myth and Cult.* Bloomington, Ind.: Indiana University Press, 1965.

c. The Healing Cult of Asclepius

Edelstein, E. J., and L. Edelstein. *Asclepius: A Collection and Interpretation of the Testimonies.* 2 vols. Baltimore: Johns Hopkins University Press, 1945.

Kee, Howard C. *Medicine, Miracle, and Magic in New Testament Times.* Cambridge: Cambridge University Press, 1986.

Kerenyi, C. *Asclepios: Archetypal Image of the Physician's Existence.* Translated by Ralph Manheim. Princeton: Princeton University Press, 1959.

d. Stoicism

Colish, Marcia L. *The Stoic Tradition from Antiquity to the Middle Ages.* Leiden: Brill, 1985.

Engberg-Pedersen, Troels. *Paul and the Stoics.* Edinburgh: T&T Clark, 2000.

Rist, John M. *Stoic Philosophy.* London: Cambridge University Press, 1969.

e. Cynicism

Attridge, Harold W. "The Philosophical Critique of Religion under the Early Empire." In *Aufstieg und Niedergang der römischen Welt.* Edited by Hildegard Temporini and Wolfgang Haase. Berlin: de Gruyter, 1984. Part 2, vol. 16/1:45–78.

Mahlerbe, A. J. *The Cynic Epistles: A Study Edition.* Missoula, Mont.: Scholars Press, 1977.

Sloterdijk, Peter. *Critique of Cynical Reason.* Translated by Michael Eldred. Minneapolis: University of Minnesota Press, 1987. See especially, pp. 101–6 and 155–68.

f. Neo-Pythagoreanism

Burkert, Walter. *Lore and Science in Ancient Pythagoreanism.* Translated by Michael Edwin L. Minar Jr. Cambridge: Harvard University Press, 1972.

Philostratus. *The Life of Apollonius of Tyana.* Translated by F. C. Conybeare. Loeb Classical Library. Cambridge: Harvard University Press, 1960.

Thesleff, Holger. *An Introduction to the Pythagorean Writings of the Hellenistic Period.* Abo [Turku], Finland: Abo Akademi, 1961.

g. Gnosticism

Pagels, Elaine H. *The Gnostic Paul: Gnostic Exegesis of the Pauline Letters.* Philadelphia: Fortress Press, 1976.

Robinson, James M., ed. *The Nag Hammadi Library in English.* Leiden: Brill: 1988.

Rudolph, Kurt. *Gnosis: The Nature and History of Gnosticism.* Translated by R. McL. Wilson. San Francisco: Harper & Row, 1983.

5. Jewish Context

Baron, Salo W. A. *Social and Religious History of the Jews.* 2nd ed. 2 vols. New York: Columbia University Press, 1952–1980.

Green, William Scott, ed. *Approaches to Ancient Judaism.* Vols. 2–4. Chico, Calif.: Scholars Press, 1980–83.

———, ed. *Approaches to Ancient Judaism.* Vol. 5. Decatur, Ga.: Scholars Press, 1985.

Hengel, Martin. *Judaism and Hellenism.* Translated by John Bowden. 2 vols. Philadelphia: Fortress Press, 1974.

Safrai, Shemuel, and M. Stern, eds. *The Jewish People in the First Century: Historical Geography, Political History, Social, Cultural and Religious Life and Institutions.* Philadelphia: Fortress Press, 1974.

Schürer, Emil. *The History of the Jewish People in the Age of Jesus Christ.* Revised and edited by Geza Vermes, Fergus Millar, and Martin Goodman. 4 vols. Edinburgh: T&T Clark, 1973–87.

Smallwood, E. Mary. *The Jews under Roman Rule: From Pompey to Diocletian.* Leiden: Brill, 1976.

Talmon, Shemaryahu. "The Emergence of Jewish Sectarianism in the Early Second Temple Period." In *Ancient Israelite Religion: Essays in Honor of Frank Moore Cross.* Edited by Patrick D. Miller Jr., Paul Hanson, and S. Dean McBride, 587–616. Philadelphia: Fortress Press, 1987.

Tcherikover, Victor. *Hellenistic Civilization and the Jews.* Translated by S. Applebaum. New York: Atheneum Press, 1970.

a. Pharisaism

Baeck, Leo. *The Pharisees, and Other Essays.* New York: Schocken, 1966.
Saldarini, Anthony J. "Pharisees." In *Anchor Bible Dictionary.* Edited by D. N. Freedman, 5:289–303. New York: Doubleday, 1992.
Schwartz, Seth. *Imperialism and Jewish Society from 200 BCE to 640 CE.* Princeton: Princeton University Press, 2001.

b. Scripture Interpretation

Carson, D. A., and H. G. M. Williamson, eds. *It Is Written: Scripture Citing Scripture.* Cambridge: Cambridge University Press, 1988.
Hays, Richard B. *Echoes of Scriptures in the Letters of Paul.* New Haven: Yale University Press, 1989.

c. Apocalypticism

Charlesworth, James H., ed. *Old Testament Pseudepigrapha.* Vol. 1, *Apocalyptic Literature and Testaments.* Garden City, N.Y.: Doubleday, 1983.
Collins, John J. *The Apocalyptic Imagination: An Introduction to the Jewish Matrix of Christianity.* 2nd ed. New York: Crossroad, 1998.
———, ed. *The Encyclopedia of Apocalypticism.* Vol. 1: *The Origins of Apocalypticism in Judaism and Early Christianity.* New York: Continuum, 1998.
Hellholm, David, ed. *Apocalypticism in the Mediterranean World and the Near East.* Tübingen: Mohr (Siebeck), 1983.
Rowland, Christopher. "Apocalypticism," In *The New Interpreter's Dictionary of the Bible.* Edited by Katharine Doob Sakenfeld, 1:190–95. Nashville: Abingdon, 2006.
———. *The Open Heaven: A Study of Apocalyptic in Judaism and Early Christianity.* New York: Crossroad, 1982.
VanderKam, James C., and Peter W. Flint. *The Meaning of the Dead Sea Scrolls: Their Significance for Understanding the Bible, Judaism, Jesus, and Christianity.* San Francisco: Harper SanFrancisco, 2002.
Vermes, Geza. *The Complete Dead Sea Scrolls in English.* New York: Penguin, 1998.

Chapter 2: The Anatomy of the Letters

Aune, David E. *The New Testament in Its Literary Environment.* Philadelphia: Westminster, 1987.
Dahl, Nils A. "Letter." In *Interpreter's Dictionary of the Bible, Supplementary Volume.* Edited by Keith Crim, 538–41. Nashville: Abingdon, 1976.

Richard, E. Randolph. "Letter." In *The New Interpreter's Dictionary of the Bible*. Edited by Katharine Doob Sakenfeld, 3:638–41. Nashville: Abingdon, 2008.

Stowers, Stanley K. *Letter Writing in Greco-Roman Antiquity*. Philadelphia: Westminster, 1986.

White, John L. "New Testament Epistolary Literature in the Framework of Ancient Epistolography." In *Aufstieg und Niedergang der römischen Welt*. Edited by Hildegard Temporini and Wolfgang Haase. Berlin: de Gruyter, 1984. Part 3, vol. 25/2:1730–56.

Chapter 3: Traditions behind the Letters

Betz, Hans Dieter. "A Catalogue of Vices and Virtues." In *Galatians: A Commentary on Paul's Letter to the Churches in Galatia*, 281–83. Philadelphia: Fortress Press, 1979.

Davies, W. D. "Ethics in the New Testament." In *Interpreter's Dictionary of the Bible*. Edited by G. A. Buttrick, 2:167–76. Nashville: Abingdon, 1962.

Furnish, Victor Paul. *The Moral Teaching of Paul*. 3rd ed. Nashville: Abingdon, 2009.

Matera, Frank. "Ethics in the New Testament." In *The New Interpreter's Dictionary of the Bible*. Edited by Katharine Doob Sakenfeld, 2:328–38. Nashville: Abingdon, 2007.

Sampley, J. Paul. *Walking between the Times: Paul's Moral Reasoning*. Minneapolis: Augsburg Fortress, 1991.

Sanders, Jack T. *New Testament Christological Hymns: Their Historical Religious Background*. Cambridge: Cambridge University Press, 1971.

Schnackenburg, Rudolf. *Baptism in the Thought of St. Paul: A Study in Pauline Theology*. Translated by G. R. Beasley-Murray. New York: Herder & Herder, 1964.

Schweizer, Eduard. *The Lord's Supper according to the New Testament*. Translated by James M. Davis. Philadelphia: Fortress Press, 1967.

Chapter 4: The Letters as Conversations

1 Thessalonians

Donfried, Karl P. "The Cults of Thessalonica and the Thessalonian Correspondence." In *Paul, Thessalonica, and Early Christianity*, 21–48. Grand Rapids: Eerdmans, 2002.

Furnish, Victor Paul. *1 Thessalonians, 2 Thessalonians*. Abingdon New Testament Commentaries. Nashville: Abingdon, 2007.

Koester, Helmut. "1 Thessalonians—Experiment in Christian Writing." In *Continuity and Discontinuity in Church History: Essays Presented to George*

Huntston Williams. Edited by F. F. Church and T. George, 33–44. Leiden: Brill, 1979.

Krentz, Edgar M. "Thessalonians, First and Second Epistles to the." In *Anchor Bible Dictionary.* Edited by David Noel Freedman, 6:515–23. New York: Doubleday, 1992.

1 Corinthians

Barrett, C. K. *A Commentary on the First Epistle to the Corinthians.* New York: Harper & Row, 1968.

Betz, Hans Dieter, and Margaret M. Mitchell. "Corinthians, First Epistle to the." In *Anchor Bible Dictionary.* Edited by David Noel Freedman, 1:1139–54. New York: Doubleday, 1992.

Castelli, Elizabeth A. *Imitating Paul: A Discourse of Power.* Louisville: Westminster/John Knox, 1991.

Horsley, Richard A. *1 Corinthians.* Abingdon New Testament Commentaries. Nashville: Abingdon, 1998.

Hurd, John C., Jr. *The Origin of I Corinthians.* New York: Seabury, 1965.

Mitchell, Margaret M. *Paul and the Rhetoric of Reconciliation: An Exegetical Investigation of the Language and Composition of 1 Corinthians.* Tübingen: Mohr, 1991.

Pagels, Elaine H. "Paul and Women: A Response to Recent Discussion." *Journal of the American Academy of Religion* 40 (1972): 538–49.

Scroggs, Robin. "Paul and the Eschatological Woman." *Journal of the American Academy of Religion* 40 (1972): 283–303.

———. "Paul and the Eschatological Woman Revisited." *Journal of the American Academy of Religion* 42 (1974): 532–37.

Wire, Antoinette Clark. *The Corinthian Women Prophets: A Reconstruction through Paul's Rhetoric.* Minneapolis: Fortress Press, 1990.

2 Corinthians

Furnish, Victor Paul. *II Corinthians.* Anchor Bible. Garden City, N.Y.: Doubleday, 1984.

Mitchell, Margaret M. "Paul's Letters to Corinth: The Interpretative Intertwining of Literary and Historical Reconstruction." In *Urban Religion in Roman Corinth.* Edited by Daniel N. Schowalter and Steven J. Friesen, 307–38. Cambridge: Harvard Theological Studies, 2005.

Roetzel, Calvin J. *2 Corinthians.* Abingdon New Testament Commentaries. Nashville: Abingdon, 2007.

Galatians

Betz, Hans Dieter. *Galatians.* Hermeneia. Philadelphia: Fortress Press, 1979.

————. "The Literary Composition and Function of Paul's Letters to the Galatians." *New Testament Studies* 21 (1974–75): 353–73.

Hays, Richard B. *The Faith of Jesus Christ.* Chico, Calif.: Scholars Press, 1983.

Williams, Sam K. *Galatians.* Abingdon New Testament Commentaries. Nashville: Abingdon, 1997.

Romans

Badenas, Robert. *Christ the End of the Law: Romans 10:4 in Pauline Perspective.* Sheffield: JSOT Press, 1985.

Bassler, Jouette. *Divine Impartiality: Paul and a Theological Axiom.* Chico, Calif.: Scholars Press, 1982.

Beker, J. Christiaan. *Paul the Apostle: The Triumph of God in Life and Thought.* Philadelphia: Fortress Press, 1980.

Fitzmyer, Joseph A. *Romans: A New Translation with Introduction and Commentary.* Anchor Bible. New York: Doubleday, 1992.

Jewett, Robert. *Romans.* Hermeneia. Minneapolis: Fortress Press, 2007.

Käsemann, Ernst. *Commentary on Romans.* Translated by Geoffrey W. Bromiley. Grand Rapids: Eerdmans, 1980.

Keck, Leander E. *Romans.* Abingdon New Testament Commentaries. Nashville: Abingdon, 2005.

Stendahl, Krister. "The Apostle Paul and the Introspective Conscience of the West." In *Paul among Jews and Gentiles and Other Essays,* 78–96. Philadelphia: Fortress Press, 1976.

Stowers, Stanley K. *A Rereading of Romans: Justice, Jews, and Gentiles.* New Haven: Yale University Press, 1994.

Philippians

Furnish, Victor P. "The Place and Purpose of Philippians III." *New Testament Studies* 10 (1963–64): 80–98.

Roetzel, Calvin J. "Philippians, Letter to the." In *Dictionary of Biblical Interpretation.* Edited by John H. Hayes, 2:280–83. Nashville: Abingdon, 1999.

Sellew, Philip. "*Laodiceans* and the Philippians Fragments Hypothesis." *Harvard Theological Review* 87 (1994): 17–28.

Philemon

Petersen, Norman R. *Rediscovering Paul: Philemon and the Sociology of Paul's Narrative World.* Philadelphia: Fortress Press, 1985.

White, J. L. "The Structural Analysis of Philemon: A Point of Departure in the Formal Analysis of the Pauline Letters." *Society of Biblical Literature Seminar Papers* 1 (1971), 1–45.

Winter, S. C. "Paul's Letter to Philemon." *New Testament Studies* 33 (1987): 1–35.

Chapter 5: Paul and His Myths

Bultmann, Rudolf. *Jesus Christ and Mythology.* New York: Charles Scribner's Sons, 1958.

———, et al. *Kerygma and Myth: A Theological Debate.* Edited by Hans Werner Bartsch. Translated by Reginald H. Fuller. New York: Harper & Brothers, 1961.

Cassirer, Ernst. *Language and Myth.* Translated by Susanne K. Langer. New York: Harper & Brothers, 1946.

———. *The Philosophy of Symbolic Forms.* Vol. 2, *Mythical Thought.* Translated by Ralph Manheim. New Haven: Yale University Press, 1955.

Douglas, Mary. "Deciphering a Meal." In *Myth, Symbol, and Culture.* Edited by Clifford Geertz, 61–81. New York: Norton, 1971.

Eliade, Mircea. *The Myth of the Eternal Return.* Translated by Willard R. Trask. New York: Harcourt, Brace, 1959.

———. *Rites and Symbols of Initiation.* New York: Harper & Row, 1965.

Forsyth, Neil. *The Old Enemy: Satan and the Combat Myth.* Princeton: Princeton University Press, 1987.

Frye, Northrop. *The Great Code: The Bible and Literature.* San Diego: Harcourt Brace Jovanovich, 1983.

———, et al. *Myth and Symbol: Critical Approaches and Applications.* Lincoln: University of Nebraska Press, 1963.

Geertz, Clifford. *The Interpretation of Cultures.* New York: Basic Books, 1973.

Harrison, Jane E. *Mythology.* 1924. Reprint, New York: Harcourt, Brace & World, 1963.

Kluckhohn, Clyde. "Myths and Rituals: A General Theory." *Harvard Theological Review* 35 (1942): 45–79.

Leach, Edmund. *Claude Lévi Strauss.* New York: Viking, 1970.

———. *Genesis as Myth, and Other Essays.* New York: Grossman, 1970.

———, ed. *The Structural Study of Myth and Totemism.* London: Tavistock, 1967.

Ricoeur, Paul. "The Adamic Myth and the Eschatological Vision of History." In *The Symbolism of Evil,* 232–78. Boston: Beacon, 1982.

Turner, Victor. *The Ritual Process: Structure and Anti-Structure.* Hawthorne, N.Y.: Aldine, 1982.

Wilder, Amos N. *Jesus' Parables and the War of Myths: Essays on Imagination in Scripture.* Philadelphia: Fortress Press, 1982.

Chapter 6: Interpreters of Paul in the New Testament

Colossians

Dahl, Nils A. "Christ, Creation, and the Church." In *Jesus in the Memory of the Early Church*, 120–40. Minneapolis: Augsburg, 1976.

Dunn, James D. G. "Colossians, Letter to." In *New Interpreter's Dictionary of the Bible*. Edited by Katharine Doob Sakenfeld, 1:702–6. Nashville: Abingdon, 2006.

Francis, Fred O., and Wayne A. Meeks, eds. and translators. *Conflict at Colossae*. Missoula, Mont.: Scholars Press, 1973.

Käsemann, Ernst. "A Primitive Christian Baptismal Liturgy." In *Essays on New Testament Themes*. Translated by W. J. Montagne, 149–68. Philadelphia: Fortress Press, 1964.

Wilson, R. McL. *Colossians and Philemon: A Critical and Exegetical Commentary*. Edinburgh: T&T Clark, 2005.

Ephesians

Caird, G. B. *Principalities and Powers: A Study of Pauline Theology*. Oxford: Clarendon, 1956.

Perkins, Pheme. *Ephesians*. Abingdon New Testament Commentaries. Nashville: Abingdon, 1997.

Roetzel, Calvin J. "Jewish Christian–Gentile Christian Relations: A Discussion of Ephesians 2:15a." *Zeitschrift für die neutestamentliche Wissenschaft* 74 (1983): 81–89.

Sampley, J. Paul et al. *Ephesians, Colossians, 2 Thessalonians, the Pastoral Epistles*. Philadelphia: Fortress Press, 1978.

Schlier, Heinrich. *Principalities and Powers in the New Testament*. New York: Herder & Herder, 1961.

Turner, Max. "Ephesians, Letter to the." In *The New Interpreter's Dictionary of the Bible*. Edited by Katharine Doob Sakenfeld, 2:269–76. Nashville: Abingdon, 2007.

Wink, Walter. *Naming the Powers: The Language of Power in the New Testament*. Philadelphia: Fortress Press, 1984.

2 Thessalonians

Furnish, Victor P. *1 Thessalonians, 2 Thessalonians*. Abingdon New Testament Commentaries. Nashville: Abingdon, 2007.

Krentz, Edgar M. "Through a Prism: The Theology of 2 Thessalonians as a Deutero-Pauline Letter." Paper read at the annual meeting of the Society of Biblical Literature, 1986.

———. "Thessalonians, First and Second Epistles to the." In *Anchor Bible Dictionary*. Edited by David Noel Freedman, 6:515–23. New York: Doubleday, 1992.

1 and 2 Timothy and Titus (The Pastorals)

Barrett, C. K. "Pauline Controversies in the Post-Pauline Period." *New Testament Studies* 20 (1973–74): 229–45.

Bassler, Jouette M. *1 Timothy, 2 Timothy, Titus*. Abingdon New Testament Commentaries. Nashville: Abingdon, 1996.

Dibelius, Martin, and Hans Conzelmann. *The Pastoral Epistles*. Translated by Philip Buttolph and Adela Yarbro. Hermeneia. Philadelphia: Fortress Press, 1972.

Gealy, Fred D. "The First and Second Epistles to Timothy and the Epistle to Titus, Introduction and Exegesis." In *The Interpreter's Bible*. Edited by G. A. Buttrick, 6:343–551. Nashville: Abingdon, 1955.

Käsemann, Ernst. "Paul and Early Catholicism." In *New Testament Questions of Today*, 236–51. Philadelphia: Fortress Press, 1969.

Quinn, Jerome D. "The Letter to Titus." *Anchor Bible*. New York: Doubleday, 1990.

Chapter 7: Currents and Crosscurrents

Bauer, Walter. *Orthodoxy and Heresy in Earliest Christianity*. Edited Robert A. Kraft and Gerhard Krodel. Philadelphia: Fortress Press, 1971.

Boyarin, Daniel. *Paul and the Politics of Identity: A Radical Jew*. Berkeley: University of California Press, 1994.

Brooten, Bernadette J. "Jewish Women's History in the Roman Period: A Task for Christian Theology." In *Christians among Jews and Gentiles*. Edited by George W. E. Nickelsburg, 22–30. Philadelphia: Fortress Press, 1986.

Brown, Peter. *The Making of Late Antiquity*. Cambridge: Harvard University Press, 1978.

Castelli, Elizabeth A. *Imitating Paul: A Discourse of Power*. Louisville: Westminster/John Knox Press, 1991.

Lerner, Gerda. *The Creation of Feminist Consciousness: From the Middle Ages to 1870*. Oxford: Oxford University Press, 1993.

Schüssler Fiorenza, Elisabeth. *In Memory of Her: A Feminist Theological Reconstruction of Christian Origins*. New York: Crossroad, 1988. See especially 205–41.

Wiles, Maurice F. *The Divine Apostle*. Cambridge: Cambridge University Press, 1967.

Index